D1097972

Basic Issues in the

Philosophy of Religion

Basic Issues in the Philosophy of Religion

Keith E. Yandell
University of Wisconsin

∽

Allyn and Bacon, Inc.
Boston

BL
51
Y27

© Copyright 1971
by Allyn and Bacon, Inc.
470 Atlantic Avenue, Boston.

All rights reserved. No part of this book
may be reproduced in any form, or by any means,
without permission in writing from
the publisher.

Library of Congress
catalog card number: 72-107427.

Printed in the United States of America.

Dedicated to

Mr. and Mrs. P. R. Yandell

33855

Table of Contents

Preface

I wish to express my thanks to my colleague, Professor Julius Weinberg, and my teacher and former colleague, Professor Marvin Fox, both of whom, in reading the complete manuscript, were so generous with their critical faculties and vast knowledge of the history of philosophy. This book is much the better for their constructive criticism and friendly encouragement. I wish also to express my thanks to Professor Alvin Plantinga, from whom I took my first courses in the philosophy of religion. My treatment of the strong formulation of the problem of evil is much indebted to his work in this area.

A word about the selection of topics and the particular treatments of topics discussed in this book: I have chosen the problems discussed on the basis that, conceptually and traditionally, they are core issues in the philosophy of religion. The particular treatments or attempted solutions which have been appraised have been selected as follows: the solutions discussed have been influential and viewed with respect by intelligent critics. They possess some inherent plausibility and are currently of interest. Either they are "classic" positions, stamped with the status of their originator, or "current" positions, reflecting the atmosphere of a significant portion of the intellectual community (or both). At least, the solutions discussed seem to fit these criteria.

The topics are treated in the context of the Judeo-Christian tradition. This seems eminently reasonable, since the philosophy of religion arose in good part due to the interaction of that tradition with Greek philosophy. Further, this is the tradition (if any) with which most undergraduates at present are likely to be acquainted. Finally, the apparent absence of any very significant essence of religion, plus the similarity of problems which various religious traditions face, combine to make treatment in terms of some one tradition simultaneously essential and representative.

The topics treated cluster around six questions: is religious discourse meaningful? does evil refute theism? can God's existence be proved? does religious experience provide evidence for religious belief? how are religion and morality, and faith and reason related?

Keith E. Yandell

Basic Issues in the

Philosophy of Religion

I

RELIGION AND LANGUAGE

It is the height of philosophic fashion these days to say that while the question about religion used to be, "are its claims true?" it now is, "are its claims meaningful?" Certain philosophers concern themselves with translating as much as possible of traditional Judeo-Christian thought into statements which are either empirically testable or which express decisions but make no assertions, with any remainder granted at best the status of expressing or evoking emotion. Some theologians happily follow this example, sometimes seeming to attempt to outdo their philosophic colleagues in the endeavor to strip the battleship of traditional theism down to the proportions of an outrigger canoe. One reason offered for the conceptual dismantling of traditional theism is that people need to have the same thing said in a new way, or, more radically, that now people find it hard to believe that much; so the church should ask them to believe a lot less. We can safely leave these issues of communication and church policy to one side, as there is a much more fundamental reason offered. It is that religious language is, in fact, "cognitively" meaningless—that it is neither true nor false. It has meaning, the suggestion goes, only in that people respond emotively to it; religious language belongs to the realm of nerve ending excitation, and is not the proper object of careful analysis and thought. Nonetheless, men operating on this assumption have offered some rather remarkable analyses of traditional religious claims. It has been suggested, for example, that to assert that God exists is really to declare that one is going to endeavor to live agapeistically,[1] or to say that

3

some men and women have had experiences of a certain sort. More charming still is the claim that "God created the world from nothing" really means "everything we call material can be used in such a way that it contributes to the well-being of men." While we could multiply such examples, it is more profitable to ask why in the world anyone should offer them. Their proponents are serious; in spite of appearances, they are not pulling our leg. Why, then, would anyone suggest these translations or analyses, which seem about as plausible as saying, "every event has a cause" really means "sometimes we profit from our mistakes, but sometimes we don't."

We should note, if only in passing, that the problem of meaning, or of religious language, is by no means a new one. Plato wrote that ". . . the Maker and Father of All . . . it is a hard task to find, and having found him, it would be impossible to declare him to all men."[2] There is a long tradition of discussion and debate which we will not attempt to summarize or appraise on the question of whether God can be even partially described in human language.[3] Problems concerning the existence and nature of universals and of the simplicity of the divine being are intertwined with traditional philosophical discussions of the possibility of talking intelligibly about God. We will do better to begin more modestly by considering crucial contemporary discussions of the issue, although following the traditional example of taking sentences concerning God as our paradigm of religious language.[4]

THE VERIFICATION PRINCIPLE

The verification principle codified the suspicions about metaphysics, ethics, and religion felt by a group of philosophers, scientists and mathematicians who met in Vienna in the late 1920's.[5] Classically expressed in A. J. Ayer's youthful polemic, *Language, Truth and Logic*,[6] the point of the verification principle was to sort out discourse that was cognitively meaningful from discourse that was not. Possessing cognitive meaning seemed simply to amount to having what logicians call truth value—i.e., being *either* true *or* false. If we agree to say that an assertion is any sentence possessing truth value or cognitive meaning, the verification principle was intended to sort out assertions from other kinds of sentences. There are other ways of being meaningful besides possessing cognitive meaning; "Hurrah" emits an emotion and "Duck" evokes a reaction if its utterance is successful, but neither makes any assertion. Under slight pressure, the proponents of verificationism granted that the putative assertions of religion were meaningful in some of these other ways. Most defenders of the cognitive significance of religious claims were understandably not appeased.

The verification principle was stated and restated in various manners by its proponents. The changes were elicited by the telling force of certain criticisms and the reformulations that were required have been superbly recorded by Carl Hempel; we need only note the highlights of this piece of philosophic history.[7]

Tautologies, roughly, are statements whose truth value can be determined simply on the basis of the meanings of the words they contain. They were not in dispute; essentially, verificationists held them to be indubitably meaningful but absolutely uninformative.[8] Leaving tautologies to one side, then, one formulation of the verification principle stated that: sentence S is cognitively meaningful just in case S follows from some finite set C of observation statements. (An observation statement is any statement whose truth or falsity can be determined by sensory observation.)[9] Thus, "Some elephants are grey" should plainly turn out to be meaningful on this criterion, since witnessing one grey elephant should verify it conclusively. The difficulty of providing appropriate examples will become evident shortly. Three objections, each fatal, have been made to this formulation. First, consider the statement "All elephants are grey"; this claim does not follow deductively from the relevant observation statement "All observed elephants are grey" for its scope concerns all elephants and we cannot assume that no elephant has escaped observation. Further, "All elephants have been observed" is not itself an observation statement. So our original statement is not meaningful on the present criterion. Since it plainly is meaningful, the criterion must be abandoned. Second, consider the observation statement "This elephant is grey." This statement, by itself, entails (by an elementary rule of the propositional calculus held in high esteem by the verificationists) "This elephant is grey or the Hegelian Absolute unfolds in history."[10] Since the statement is entailed by a meaningful statement, it is meaningful. So each of its parts is meaningful. But "The Hegelian Absolute unfolds in history" is just the sort of statement which, among others, the criterion under discussion was intended to rule out, but does not. One might object that this argument is not really sufficient to show that our sentence concerning the Absolute is meaningful, since by the same argument it could be shown that "Egregious sausages ploy truffles tenderly" turns out also to be cognitively meaningful. But this would entirely miss the point of the objection. The argument is not meant to show that "The Hegelian Absolute unfolds in history" is meaningful. Its more modest intent is to point out that this formulation of verificationism does not, contrary to its intent, show that it is meaningless. For this purpose, the argument is patently adequate and the criticism stands. The criterion does not live up to its pretensions. Third, "This elephant is grey" entails "Some elephant is grey," which is the contradictory of "No elephant is grey." If a sentence is meaningful, so (and in the same manner) is its contradictory. Hence "No elephant is grey" is meaningful; and, on the assumption that there is at least one elephant, it entails in turn that its contrary "All elephants are grey" is false and so not meaningless after all. Hence the same proposition is both meaningful and not meaningful given this criterion. To use the same argument in reverse, if "All elephants are grey" is meaningless, so is "No elephants are grey" and hence "Some elephant is grey" is meaningless too. Thus all, or at least most, observation statements themselves become meaningless on this criterion. Once this was seen, revision was obviously in order.

A second version went as follows: a sentence S is cognitively meaningful just in case not-S, the contradictory of S, follows from some finite set C of observation statements. Thus, "All elephants are grey" should be meaningful since observing a white elephant would prove it false. Once again, three criticisms are relevant. Consider the sentence, "Somewhere there is a troll." No finite set of observation statements entails the denial of this sentence.[11] So it is, on the present criterion, meaningless; but it is plainly meaningful. One could substitute more ordinary nouns for "troll" and the same results follow. Second, "All animals are unicorns" is presumably conclusively falsifiable on this criterion, since "This is a cow" is an observation statement which falsifies it. Thus the complex statement, "All animals are unicorns and the Absolute wears green trousers" is falsifiable, for if one member of a conjunct is false, the conjunct as a whole is false. So the second sentence of the conjunct is not shown to be meaningless by this version of the criterion. Hempel retracts this criticism and its analogue concerning the first version on the ground that the rules of inference appealed to apply only to assertions and neither "The Absolute unfolds in history" nor "The Absolute wears green trousers" are assertions. But if they are not assertions, this is not shown by either version of verificationism, and this seems to be the only relevant consideration. Hence I see no reason why these objections should be retracted, though I agree with Hempel when he writes that

> . . . the remaining arguments mentioned in section 2 of my article seem . . . fully sufficient . . . to disqualify both complete verifiability and complete falsifiability as criteria of cognitive significance.[12]

Finally, "All animals are unicorns" is meaningless on this version since its denial, "Some animal is not a unicorn," is meaningless; thus it is not conclusively falsifiable after all. This version of verificationism fails for reasons parallel to those which defeated the previous version.

Another version of the verification principle reads as follows: A sentence S is meaningful just in case it entails some observation statement O, alone or in conjunction with some hypothesis or set of hypotheses H, where O is not entailed by H alone. Thus "If anything is an elephant, it is grey" is meaningful, since it plus "This is an elephant" entails "This is grey." But a man who believes S, "The Absolute is happy every day," can accept this criterion of meaning with equanimity, for S together with H, "The Absolute is happy every day, thus the sun rises every day," entails O "The sun rises every day." Or, if difficulties arise about "every day," let each occurrence of that phrase be replaced by the word "today."

One could attempt to repair this difficulty[13] by allowing only hypotheses which in turn passed the same test for meaning as that expressed in the previous version. This will not do either. Let S be "It is raining" and H be "If it is raining, the sidewalks are wet." Together, they entail O, "The sidewalks are wet," and O is not entailed by H alone. Now suppose we substitute S' for S where S' reads "The Absolute is happy and it is raining." S' entails, when conjoined with H, an observation statement—namely, O—not entailed by H alone. So S' is meaningful. It is worth noting in passing that Hempel ought to reject this criticism too, for no proof has been offered that the first conjunct in S' is meaningful and the rule that if P entails Q, then P and R together entail Q—to which implicit appeal is made in the criticism—applies only to cognitively meaningful sentences. But, once again, the point is that the criterion in question does not rule out the first conjunct in S', though it was intended to do so.

Another objection to the verification principle is worth mention because, although it was offered as a criticism of the version just discussed, it applies quite generally to all the versions of the verification principle which we have discussed. Alonzo Church pointed out that from any three observation statements, A, B and C, one can derive any statement one pleases.[14] His argument can be stated with minimum appeal to technicalities in the following manner. Suppose that A, B, C are observation statements each of which is logically independent of (has no entailment relation to) any of the others. Take as original premises the statements, expressed in standard notation, (1) A and (2) $(-A.B) \vee (C.S)$. We can see that (1) and (2) entail (3) S. Thus, since (1) alone does not entail S, (2) is meaningful. The deduction requires only elementary techniques,[15] and a consequence of its validity is, as noted, that (2) is meaningful given the present version of verificationism. But then, of course, so is each of the elements of (2), among which are the observation statements or their denials, plus S. Since S can be any statement we please, any statement we please can be shown to be meaningful on the present version of verificationism.[16]

Rather than attempt still further reformulations of verificationism conceived along the original lines, let us briefly notice Hempel's own refurbished attempt. His criterion for cognitive meaning was translatability into an empiricist language. The vocabulary of such a language would include the customary terms of some familiar system of logic (terms such as *some, all, if-then, and, or, class, element,* etc.) and terms which designate observable qualities (*red, sour,* etc.), plus any terms definable by means of logical and/or observable quality terms. The rules for sentence formation will be those adopted in some standard system of formal logic. Then a sentence is cognitively meaningful just in case it is translatable into such a language.

This proposal also met with severe difficulties which need not occupy us here.[17] Even this refurbished and much more elaborate version has been abandoned by its author. Hempel has since altered at least the emphasis of his views on the topic of meaning; he writes in a quite different vein as follows.

> But no matter how one might reasonably delimit the class of sentences qualified to introduce empirically significant terms, this new approach seems to me to lead to the realization that cognitive significance cannot well be construed as a characteristic of individual sentences but only of more or less comprehensive systems of the sentences (corresponding roughly to scientific theories).[18]

So long as we do not limit ourselves to scientific theories, and why should we?, Hempel's remarks seem unexceptionable. Patently, they are a far cry from original verificationism.

This raises a final question concerning verificationism. Suppose some version of verificationism were formulated which successfully segregated sentences in the intended manner. Why should anyone accept it as the criterion for possessing truth value? So far as I know, no cogent reason has ever been offered.[19] Nonetheless, verificationism raises a significant issue with peculiar urgency. How could one, even in principle, discover the truth or falsity of, say, "God exists"? This difficult question will occupy us in various contexts in the pages that follow. But of course the fact that verificationism raises this issue with peculiar urgency is no justification of verificationism. Nor, so far as we have discovered, is any such justification to be found elsewhere.

THE UNIVERSITY DISCUSSION

The contemporary *locus classicus* for the problem of meaning is the much-anthologized discussion between Anthony Flew, R. M. Hare, and Basil Mitchell, published in the now defunct journal, *University*.[20] Flew's initial challenge, with Hare's and Mitchell's quite different responses, offer a study in miniature of most of the issues involved, for many later, more detailed discussions of the same issues can be seen as more elaborate elucidations of suggestions offered in the original debate.

The thrust of Flew's challenge to the theist is simple and straight-forward, though not quite so simple as Flew seems to have imagined. He begins with the claim that a meaningful assertion must be incompatible with some conceivable state of affairs, and hence be in principle falsifiable. If a putative assertion is compatible with anything that happens, it is not a genuine assertion after all. Flew, in a footnote, even makes it out that this claim is no more than a restatement of the elementary logical principle that a statement P and its denial, not—P, cannot simultaneously be true. But, he continues, the theist will not allow anything to count against the putative claim that God exists. So, as the theist uses it, the putative claim is not a genuine assertion after all, since it is not even in principle falsifiable.

There are three things to be noted about Flew's challenge. First, the claim he makes about what constitutes, or is at least a necessary condition of, a statement being meaningful is not at all an obvious truth, and the sleight-of-hand by which he makes it appear to be obvious is sheer mystification. Of course if a statement is false its denial is true, and conversely. But Flew is saying far more than this. If he were not, his part of the discussion could be excised without irreparable loss. He is saying that a statement has truth value, is either true or false, only if some state of affairs would count against its being true. And, by implication, not just any old state of affairs would do. There is a possible state of affairs that would, if it existed, count overwhelmingly against the truth of "God exists," namely, His not existing. But this is not what Flew has in mind, nor would he admit this as a defense of the claim that "God exists" has truth value. The state of affairs must be observable. But that a statement has truth value or is cognitively meaningful, just in case some observable state of affairs would count against it, is nothing like as obvious as the claim that if a sentence is false, its contradictory is true. Indeed, the statement that "every event necessarily has a cause" is not falsifiable by any possible observable state of affairs. A putatively uncaused event could always be viewed as an event which had an undiscovered cause. Still, it is by no means obvious that it has no truth value. Secondly, there is another reason for denying that Flew's claim is true: there are other sorts of counter-examples to it. He assumes that any statement that has truth value is falsifiable. But if a statement is verifiable, it plainly has truth value, and there are some statements that are verifiable but are not falsifiable. So there are some statements that have truth value but are not falsifiable. The following provide relevant examples: "Someone living today will be alive tomorrow," "Someone now alive will be alive ten minutes hence," and perhaps "I will be able to remember my own physical death." (We will discuss this example in another context.) "Someone living today will be alive tomorrow" cannot be falsified, for if it is not or will not be true then no human will be around to record this fact, and so falsify it. There are also statements which are falsifiable but not verifiable: "No one living today will be alive tomorrow," "No one now alive will be alive ten minutes hence."[21] If these sentences are or will be true, once again no one will be able to record this fact and so verify them. Finally, even if we granted Flew his claim, it is not at all obvious that a theist could not admit that, had our universe been quite different than it is, he would have to abandon his claim. A universe in which every sentient creature was always wracked with gruesome pain for every moment of its existence would not be one for which theism was a plausible interpretation. So if that state of affairs had held, theism would be falsified. Flew might respond that no theist would admit this; but of course some at least do admit it, and even if none did, this would show only that theists were obdurately obstinate beings, not that their belief had not been falsified.[22]

In the light of these considerations, it is somewhat surprising to be told by Hare that Flew has entirely succeeded on the grounds he has marked out, and that we must find a different starting place if we are to escape his conclusions. Nonetheless, Hare's own starting point has been influential and is intrinsically interesting. He introduces the now famous concept of a "blik," which is, roughly, a way of interpreting a set of experiences or data which is (a) not demonstrably right (i.e., does not follow from self-evident premises), (b) not defensible by appeal to probability arguments, (c) serves to orient the conduct of those who adopt it, (d) interprets the data in question in a way both self-consistent and not contradicted by the data, (e) is opposable by other, competing bliks, (f) is either right or wrong, (g) is not an explanation in the sense that Boyle's law explains the behavior of gases under pressure (i.e., is not intended to provide for prediction and control of events in our physical environment).[23] He adds that explanations assume bliks; ". . . for it is by our *bliks* that we decide what is and what is not an explanation."[24] Hare's suggestion is tantalizing, and we will return to it, though not by name, in another context.[25] For now, it suffices to notice how many questions it leaves unanswered. What makes one blik right and others wrong? How do we choose between bliks? Is a blik really necessary if we are to offer explanations of anything? Is a blik composed of one sentence, or many? E.g., is it a blik that God exists, or is the whole gamut of Judeo-Christian thought a blik, or both? Are there nonreligious bliks? One would have thought that "Everything that happened, happened by sheer chance" was, if a blik at all, a nonreligious one, but Hare leaves us wondering.[26] Until these questions, and perhaps others, are answered we are not likely to be helped much by Hare's hints.

Mitchell's reply is, apparently at least, more straightforward. He grants without hesitation that the fact of evil counts against theism, although not conclusively. There is also evidence, he suggests, on the other side—perhaps religious experience or the fact that good things occur as well as evil.[27] How much evidence against theism can be amassed without making it unreasonable for anyone aware of that evidence to be a theist is difficult to say, but the fact that a man recognizes some evidence as being contrary to a thesis he continues to maintain does not show he is irrational in maintaining that thesis. Indeed, a necessary condition of his being rational is his recognizing the force of evidence which is clearly against his thesis when it is presented to him. Still, Mitchell suggests, no theist can ever admit that the evidence is or can ever be conclusive against his view.[28] One wonders exactly what this means. Of course, if a man admits that a view he has deeply held is false, he no longer holds that view; surely Mitchell means more than this. Again, a man can hold a view even though there is good evidence that the view is false; if he does so, he is in that instance irrational, as Mitchell presumably admits. Mitchell may only be saying that to be a theist one must not only believe that God exists, but must also believe that no evidence as yet undiscovered will prove him wrong. Perhaps so, but this is true of any belief if it is true of the belief in question. If I believe that my friend will return the book he has borrowed, perhaps I also believe that my belief will not be refuted by any as yet undiscovered evidence; but it may be refuted for all that. What Mitchell seems in fact to be saying is that a theist must believe not only that God exists, but that any evidence to the contrary is inconceivable. Surely, this is patently false; I can believe that God exists but admit that if the world were like the one described a short while ago—with torture for all and respite for none—then my belief would be false. Mitchell comes close to saying that all theists must claim that "God does not exist" is self-contradictory, a claim perhaps stronger than even Anselm would wish. That "God exists" is not, even in principle, falsifiable is no essential part of a theistic creed, though of course a theist must claim that it is not false. To put the same point in different words, the theist holds that "God exists" is not in fact falsifiable for the same reason that "Lincoln was the sixteenth president of the U.S." is not in fact falsifiable—because it is true. But this is not at all tantamount to saying that "God does not exist" is literally inconceivable, as Mitchell seems to suggest. Thus it seems rather clear that neither Hare nor Mitchell give adequate reply to Flew, but equally clear that Flew's challenge is not nearly so formidable as, for some reason, is often supposed.

In his response to Mitchell, Flew as much as abandons his claim that theological assertions are only putative assertions. He grants that Mitchell is right in saying that the theologian will usually claim that there is some explanation of evil which is compatible with God's existence. He adds that the theologian ". . . has given God attributes which rule out all saving explanations."[29] But if this is so, then it follows that the theologian's claims are false, not meaningless.[30] It is only if the theologian so alters his claim that the facts, as Flew sees them, cannot in principle count against it, that his claim becomes meaningless. Nonetheless, Flew admits that the theologians claim that God exists is incompatible with evidence we purportedly possess.[31]

To Hare's comments, Flew makes a dual reply. On Hare's analysis, religious or theological sentences are never assertions. Flew is quite correct in responding that in offering his analysis Hare does not capture, in this respect, orthodox or normative Judeo-Christian thought. He is again right in insisting that by offering theological statements as reasons for courses of action (One ought to favor civil rights, for all men are made in the image of God), types of behavior (e.g., worship), or beliefs about the future (After death, comes the judgment) the religious traditions presuppose that the reasons offered are true claims, and hence that they are indeed claims. This means that Hare's remarks, as they stand, do not at all suffice as a response to Flew, whom Hare admits to be victorious on the ground he has marked out. Nonetheless, we have also seen reason to believe that Flew's challenge is hardly overwhelming.

This becomes even clearer when other aspects of Flew's remarks receive careful consideration. Flew argues that if an

> . . . utterance is indeed an assertion it will necessarily be equivalent to a denial of the negation of the assertion. Anything which would count against the assertion . . . must be part of (or the whole of) the meaning of the negation of the assertion.[32]

Alvin Plantinga argues that this doctrine has disastrous consequences.[33] Let us take for a sample utterance the sentence, "Flew does not exist." It will count against the claim if Flew weighs 180 pounds for, of course, anything having that weight exists. It will count equally against this claim if Flew weighs only 170 pounds. So "Flew weighs 180 pounds" and "Flew weighs 170 pounds" are part of the meaning of "Flew exists," since they count against its denial. But nothing can weigh both 180 and 170 pounds simultaneously; that is logically impossible. But that Flew weighs 180 pounds and that he weighs 170 pounds are both part of the meaning of "Flew exists," given Flew's analysis just quoted. Thus "Flew exists" is contradictory and "Flew does not exist" expresses a necessary truth.[34] Any mention of simultaneity would be actually superfluous; a concept containing p and also not-p, where neither p nor not-p are temporally qualified at all, is contradictory.

Flew can respond by saying that the two sentences about his weight should be disjoined, not conjoined. Thus to say that Flew exists is to say that he weighs either 180 pounds or 170 pounds or has some other weight. The same comments apply, *mutatis mutandis*, to Plantinga's own examples. This response is, I think, well taken. But the discussion from which it arises points out an interesting feature of Flew's criterion of meaning. This criterion entails that the meaning of "Flew exists" includes the meanings of such diverse statements as "Flew was never devoured by a dinosaur," "Flew was not just exploded by the detonation of a small bomb which he unknowingly swallowed," "Flew was not recently at the center of an atomic explosion," etc. Further, we could never complete the list of all the things which are incompatible with his present existence, and so of course could not provide an exhaustive list of the denials that those events had occurred, each denial being part of the negation of the negation, and so of the meaning of the original claim. So one can never know fully what "Flew exists" means. Normally, when not under the madness of Flew's anti-metaphysics, one would suppose he knew what the sentence meant, but not everything that might count against it. Indeed, unless one knew what it meant, one wouldn't know what would count against it. Further, when we say that Flew exists, we surely don't simply mean, if we mean this at all, that all sorts of things have failed to happen to him.

An important point lurks behind Flew's comments. It is the point that statements do not stand in splendid isolation from one another. To accept one assertion is to accept others as well, and of course to deny still others; at the very least, this is very often the case. Statements come, so to speak, in sets. To accept "Jones is in Chicago" as true is to agree to a good deal of geographic classification as a means of locating him as well as assenting to the thesis that Jones is located where he is said to be.

Empirical data are not likely to be absolutely coercive for the acceptance of one statement as opposed to another. As W. V. O. Quine has aptly commented,

> It is misleading to speak of the empirical content of an individual statement—especially if it is a statement at all remote from the experiential periphery of the field. Any statement can be held true, come what may, if we make dramatic enough changes elsewhere in the system. Even a statement very close to the periphery can be held true in the face of recalcitrant experience by pleading hallucination or by amending certain statements of the kind called logical laws. Conversely, by the same token, no statement is immune to revision.[35]

It follows from Quine's remarks that the empirical verification or falsification of a statement is not as simple as Flew's comments suggest. Although Flew's challenge is starkly stated, without qualifications he might have supplied if writing in other contexts, it is the case that verificationists generally talked as if the model of empirical verification were simple and straightforward.[36] They were, as one of their *ex officio* members was later to suggest of others of his predecessors, captured by a picture; in another manner of speech, they fixated on an oversimplified model. Although defective as a theory of meaning, Flew's comments are at least suggestive of the covert complexity of verifying or falsifying a statement. This complexity, and its relationship to statements occurring in systematic contexts, will concern us elsewhere.[37]

THEORIES OF RELIGIOUS LANGUAGE

Even though it seems quite clear that verificationist reservations about ethical, metaphysical and theological statements are difficult to formulate with precision, and at least equally difficult to justify, these suspicions are widely shared.[38] It is worthwhile to investigate some of the analyses of religious discourse which various verificationists and others influenced by them have presented as alleviating their suspicions and still retaining the essence of that discourse. Such analyses have been provided in abundance, and we can take only a representative sampling. Still, we can insure a fair sampling by picking quite varied perspectives for examination. Should none of the analyses offer much promise, it will not be unreasonable to abandon any lingering verificationist leanings to investigate other lines of approach to the problems of the philosophy of religion. We propose to consider four rather different analyses of religious discourse, each of which is to some degree motivated by fear of Flew's challenge. David Cox's "The Significance of Christianity" was a pioneering attempt at translating theological statements into claims which satisfy the verification principle.[39] It will serve as an example of relatively pure verificationist endeavors in the area, and concludes that religious discourse is emotive in character. Professor R. B. Braithwaite's *Eddington Memorial Lecture* 1953, represents an attempt to reformulate religious claims in the light of a modified principle of meaning and emphasizes the conative function of religious discourse.[40] Professor John Wisdom's elusive essays on the present topic can perhaps be viewed as a subtle elucidation of Hare's "blik" approach to religious discourse. Finally, Professor Ian Ramsey, in several small books, provides a distinctive theory of religious language which endeavors to compromise between the traditional approach in which theological statements make straightforward claims and the verificationist approach in which they make no claims at all.

AN EMOTIVE THEORY: DAVID COX

David Cox has suggested that the point of Christian theological statements and presumably of the statements of other theological systems as well—e.g. those of Judaism and Islam—is to "safeguard Christian experience."[41] Insofar as this is their purpose, and so long as we count any human experience, not merely sensory experience, as relevant data for verification, Christian doctrinal statements can be verified. Thus Cox states as his version of verificationism that ". . . an ostensible statement of fact is significant if, and only if, it can, in principle, be verified by human experience."[42] In order to show that a statement is significant, we must, if we accept this principle,

> . . . show that there are experiences (actual or possible) which would take place in one way if the statement were true, and in another way if it were false.[43]

The result, Cox admits, will be that every significant theological statement will be either a formal rule indicating how theological terms are to be used or an empirical hypothesis testable by reference to human experience.

With this as his background, Cox offers three restatements of theological statements.

(1) 'God is loving' means 'No experience of meeting a person who is not someone who loves you can rightly be called an experience of meeting God' or (to make it an empirical hypothesis) 'Some experiences called "meeting God" will probably be experiences of meeting a person who loves you.'[44]

(2) 'God exists' means 'Some men and women have had, and all may have, experiences called "meeting God." ' (Cox admits that some account of "meeting God" will have to be given.)[45]

(3) 'God created the world from nothing' means 'Everything which we call "material" can be used in such a way that it contributes to the well-being of men.'[46]

What, if any, are the virtues of these translations?[47] Several points are worth making. First, they do not seem to capture anything like the force of the original assertions. Given (2), God could not predate the first men, since God's existence is made to have a connection of meaning, a necessary connection with the existence of human beings. "God created men" could have no meaning, since it entails "God could exist without men existing," and on the analysis Cox provides this latter statement (and so the former also) would be meaningless. But there is no need to belabor the obvious. Only given the most coercive reasons would anyone who began by taking the original statements in the way they are taken by orthodox Jews and Christians agree to translate them in anything like a Coxian manner. Indeed, were such radical revision of the original statements necessary, surely the clearest tack would be to abandon their use altogether. But we have seen that verificationism provides no such coercive reasons.

Second, Cox treats the phrase "meeting God" as if it were unproblematic while the sentence "God exists" is, without translation, unintelligible. It is at least equally plausible to reverse the evaluation, but in any case the phrase "meeting God" itself requires considerable analysis. What is to count as "meeting God"? When can we rightly say that a man has met God as opposed to only thinking he has? Are there tests for this—and if so are they empirical tests? And if the claim that God exists has no meaning apart from the possibility of experiences of meeting Him, what can the phrase mean? Normally, a sentence of the form "X meets Y" will allow us also to utter a sentence of the form "Y exists independently of Y's being met by X." To deny that such independence is possible radically alters any sense in which X can meet Y. Thus saying that God cannot be said to exist in any way in which this is not translatable into His being met, or possibly being met, leaves the sense of the phrase "meeting God" altogether unclear. In sum, normally what can be met can be said to exist independently of its being met. To deny this about God is to also alter the sense of the word "meeting" when used in the phrase "meeting

God." Further, when can one, even without Coxian translation of "God exists," properly be said to have met God? Are there empirical tests for having done so? If not, then the *analysans* is unverifiable, quite contrary to Cox's intent.[48] I am taking into account Cox's stress on human, not simply sensuous experience; I cannot see that it helps here. Thus the *analysans* for (2) is doubly problematic: problematic because of the difficulty of providing a clear analysis of "meeting God," and problematic because of the difficulty in meeting anything that cannot be said to exist other than by saying it is, or might be, met.

Perhaps all that Cox is saying is that we have certain experiences and that we talk about them as "experiences of God" when they are only experiences of bliss or the like. An experience of bliss, however, is simply a blissful experience, but an experience of God is not simply a godly experience. If this is what Cox is suggesting, the result surely should be the abandonment of theological discourse as useless redundancy, and Cox could have put his case so much more simply. Cox's claim would then be overwhelmingly implausible. It is simply false that we use the word "God" to describe any of our experiences. Sometimes it is claimed that God is the cause of certain of some men's experiences. Whether this is true or not requires careful argument, and Cox provides none on this topic.[49] So while this last reading of Cox's claims is easy to comprehend, it is equally easily discredited.

Very likely, Cox's claims are those we at first ascribed to him. If so, then they must, for the reasons offered, be rejected. If Cox provided the only alternative open to us short of taking the central sentences of the Judeo-Christian tradition as assertions, then we could confidently conclude that these sentences are in fact assertions. But other alternatives are available and must be considered.

A CONATIVE THEORY: R. B. BRAITHWAITE

R. B. Braithwaite offers a conative theory of religious language.[50] He begins with a theory of meaning.

> The meaning of any statement . . . will be taken as given by the way it is used. The kernel for an empiricist of the problem of the nature of religious belief is to explain, in empirical terms, how a religious statement is used by a man who asserts it in order to express his religious convictions.[51]

Given these remarks, one would expect that on Braithwaite's analysis there are assertions which express religious beliefs. We shall see that this turns out not to be the case. He rejects the view that religious statements simply express emotions, offering two reasons for doing so.

One is the obviously correct claim that few, if any, religious men would recognize this as an adequate account of their use of religious language.[52] The second is that "it is the intention to behave that constitutes what is known as religious conviction."[53] There are, he suggests, two kinds of religious sentences. One kind expresses an intention to follow a behavioral policy; the other expresses that policy.[54] He mentions both kinds when he writes about

> . . . the intentions to pursue the behaviour policies, which may be the same for different religions, are associated with thinking of different *stories* (or sets of stories). By a story I shall mean a set of propositions which are straightforward empirical propositions capable of empirical test and which are thought of by the religious man in connection with his resolution to follow the way of life advocated by his religion.[55]

Now if Braithwaite's analysis is correct, every religious sentence will either express an intention to behave, or will be a straightforward empirical proposition. With this in mind, let us consider some standard sentences patently central to the religious tradition in which they occur.

(1) In the beginning, God created the heavens and the earth. (Genesis 1:1)
(2) God is love. (I John 4:8)
(3) God so loved the world that he gave his only begotten Son. (John 3:16)

Now these sentences, quite obviously, express no intentions. Braithwaite denies this, at least with respect to our second example.

> Unless a Christian's assertion that God is love—which I take to epitomise the assertions of the Christian religion—be taken to declare his intention to follow an agapeistic way of life, he could be asked what is the connection between the assertion and the intention . . . Unless religious principles are moral principles, it makes no sense to speak of putting them into practice.[56]

One can easily agree with the last of Braithwaite's sentences, but why should anyone suppose that one can put "God is love" into practice, except to fit it into Braithwaite's mold? The sentence "God is love" is, in its original context, an assertion about God's nature and a reason for loving one's neighbor. To quote the passage in context,

> He that loveth not, knoweth not God, for God is love. In this was manifested the love of God toward us, because . . . God sent his only begotten Son into the world . . . if God so loved us, we ought to love one another. (I John 4:8–10)

Christians are thus exhorted to imitate God by practising self-giving love, or *agape*. This is how "God is love" is related to intentions to behave and to actual behaviour: as model and reason. Were one's use of "God is love" identical to his use of "I intend to live in a self-giving manner," the former sentence could not serve the function assigned to it in the passage under consideration. But if "God is love" is not analyzable in terms of expressing an intention, surely this is equally or even more clear in the case of our other examples which are but representative of hosts of others.

They must therefore be straightforward empirical statements, if we are to accept Braithwaite's account. But precisely how they are to be empirically tested is far from obvious, and Braithwaite offers no suggestions on this topic. Indeed, it is just the apparent impossibility of designing empirical tests for such sentences as these that led the Positivists to view them, with however little justification, as meaningless. Whether these sentences, in particular the second, could in principle be empirically falsified is a topic we will deal with separately.

The result of our brief discussion of Braithwaite is this: our examples of religious sentences, which are obviously central to the traditions in which they occur, neither express any intentions nor are straightforwardly empirically testable. One is thus faced with a choice: One must either reject these examples, and lots of others of which they are representative, as meaningless; or one must reject Braithwaite's analysis. For all the appearance of charity and of divergence from verificationism, nothing can be an assertion for Braithwaite unless it is empirically testable. If the verification principle, which Braithwaite continues to assume, at least as a test for assertionhood, were itself incorrigibly correct, one could opt against treating "God is love" as an assertion with optimum plausibility. If one continued to use the sentence, he would have to torture it into Braithwaite's mold. Given, however, the overwhelming difficulties of verificationism, opting in favor of Braithwaite's claims seems quite gratuitous. The analysis is inadequate to its *analysandum*, and no cogent reasons in its favor are available. Hence the reasonable move seems to be to reject the analysis.[57]

JOHN WISDOM: PATTERNS AND ATTITUDES

John Wisdom has written two subtle essays related to our topic. One, entitled "Gods," has been widely anthologized.[58] The other has not appeared so widely in print, but is in some ways a more profound piece of work.[59] We will follow and appraise the argument of these essays.

Turning to "Gods" first, Wisdom makes a series of points which are straightforward and relevant to the issue of the meaning of religious discourse. His paradigm is, once again, "God exists." This claim, he notes, is not a simply empirical one; one cannot decide the matter by, say, praying for rain and waiting to see what happens. Our realization of this is, in part, due to our greater scientific knowledge. Wisdom could have added that it is also due, in part, to a development of religious thought not related to science. Elijah's experiment on Mt. Carmel when he prayed for a fire that Molech could not send is not characteristic of either Testament.[60] But neither is the difference between theist and atheist merely one of what each expects concerning the existence and nature of an afterlife. The difference concerns "a world that now is, though beyond the senses."[61]

To become clearer about this difference between theism and atheism, which in turn is intended to elucidate the meaning of "God exists," Wisdom asks what would count in favor of the statement. Granting that our belief in other human minds is reasonable,

> . . . the question of the reasonableness of belief in divine minds then becomes a matter of whether there are facts in nature which support claims about divine minds in the way facts in nature support our claims about human minds.[62]

Thus we have the question:

> (1) "Is there *ever any* behavior which gives reason to believe in any sort of mind?"[63]

and assuming an affirmative answer to (1),

> (2) "Are there other mind-patterns in nature beside the human and animal patterns which we can all easily detect, and are these other mind-patterns super-human?"[64]

The questions are partly empirical; witness the host of data to which supporters of the argument from design appeal.[65] But they are not merely empirical, for the dispute is generally not over the data itself, but rather over the degree to which the data justifies the inference to a Designer. How similar must nonhuman patterns be to human mind-patterns to justify our regarding them as mind-patterns too? And no matter how similar they are, can they be rightly called manifestations of a Divine Mind?

Given the difficulties in answering these questions, one might suggest that what is at issue is only whether the word "God" should be used in talking about these patterns. Wisdom responds that

> . . . *the line between a question of fact and a question of decision as to the application of a name is not so simple as this way of putting things suggests* . . . . It is possible to have before one's eyes all the items of a pattern and still to miss the pattern.[66]

One could say that the question "Is he guilty or innocent?," "Was he negligent or not?," only concern the application of a word and "Is he the same John Jones who disappeared twenty-five years ago?" only concerns the application or not of a name. But they are, in context, serious questions and there are nonarbitrary means for answering them. Noticing this fact can lead to a further recognition—namely, that all reasoning is not explicitly deductive or inductive. This is part of the point Wisdom is making in his famous parable of the garden. Two people return to a garden they own but have neglected. They find a few plants, artistically arranged and vigorous, among the weeds. One regards this as evidence that a gardener has been at work; the other does not. No gardener has been seen; the weeds grow vigorously too and are not artistically arranged. The two people comb the garden for new evidence. They find other places with plants artistically arranged, but also other areas where weeds abound and are choking out the few remaining plants. They study other gardens, tended and untended, noting the similarities and differences of each to their own. Each knows the facts the other does. Each retains his original view. Do they really now disagree? Need one add that the garden is the world and the gardener is God?

Wisdom's contention is that they do disagree. Sometimes in court cases there is also factual agreement between opposing sides, with a remaining difference as to whether, for example, negligence was involved or reasonable care was exercised. Wisdom offers an analysis of such cases which he extends to the gardener case and its theological analogue.

> In such cases we notice that the process of argument is not a *chain* of demonstrative reasoning. It is a presenting and representing of those features of the case which *severally cooperate* in favor of the conclusion . . . . The reasons are like the legs of a chair, not the links of a chain. Consequently although the discussion is *a priori* and the steps are not a matter of experience, the procedure . . . is a matter of the cumulative effect of several independent premises, not of the repeated transformation of one or two. And because the premises are severally

inconclusive the process of deciding the issue becomes a matter of weighing the cumulative effect of one group of severally inconclusive items against the cumulative effect of another group of severally inconclusive items, and thus lends itself to description in terms of conflicting "probabilities." This encourages the feeling that the issue is one of fact—that it is a matter of guessing from the premises at a further fact, at what is to come. But this is a muddle. *The dispute does not cease to be a priori, because it is a matter of the cumulative effect of several inconclusive premises.*[67]

It should be noted that by fact Wisdom means empirical fact or observable state of affairs.

The comparison is completed when Wisdom concludes that

With the judges' choice of a name for the facts goes an attitude, and the declaration, the ruling, is an exclamation evincing that attitude. But *it is an exclamation which not only has a purpose but also has a logic,* a logic surprisingly like that of "futile," "deplorable," "graceful," "grand," "divine."[68]

The two people with the garden each emphasize certain of its features as evidence of the appropriateness of his attitude toward the garden, an attitude expressed in one case by the exclamation "There is a gardener" and in the other by the exclamation "There is none." The disagreement is not over what observable data is available, or merely one involving expectations. Nor is it merely an arbitrary dispute with no criteria for settlement. This, in sum, is Wisdom's analysis of the sort of dispute which arises between theism and atheism, and Wisdom's treatment of the nature of religious language.

He also offers a hint at least as to the resolution of this dispute, although here the interpretation of Wisdom's text, never very easy, becomes a risky endeavor. He notes that sometimes the source of a belief may be relevant to our appraisal of that belief. Suppose an eminent critic finds great artistic merit in a landscape painting in which we find only little worth. We will look again, ask for his reasons, try to see what he sees in it. But we will have less confidence in his judgment in this case, and so feel less diffident about disagreeing with him, if we learn that the landscape reminds him of his boyhood and the artist is a boyhood friend. Wisdom seems to take an analogous line in terms of discrediting theism when he compares it to Wordsworth's feeling that "something watches in the hills and manages the stars"[69] and refers to Freud's contention that belief in Providence is "so patently infantile, so incongruous with reality."[70] He mentions that there are indeed facts which make theological or religious systems less fantastic, namely, patterns in human reactions which are well described by saying that we are as if there were hidden within us powers, persons, not ourselves and stronger than ourselves. . . . Now the gods, good and evil, have always been mysterious powers outside us rather than within. But they have also been within.[71]

The implication seems to be that, for Wisdom, they are really *only* within; that talk about the gods and God once again must be translated into language ". . . not entirely new, but *practically* the same as the old"[72]—i.e., having the same function.

One gets a somewhat different impression, however, from Wisdom's later piece on "The Modes of Thought and the Logic of 'God.'" Wisdom constructs an imaginary dialogue in which one of the participants says

> . . . if the logic of God and of the Devil is more eccentric than it seems, so also is the logic of the Super Ego, and the Id, and the Unconscious. Indeed what makes us speak of the unconscious and the good and the evil in it, the wine of life and the poison of death so mixed, is closely connected with what makes us speak of a hidden power for good—God—and a hidden power for evil—the Devil.[73]

This is, in part at least, to say that there are other sentences besides religious ones which are not straightforwardly empirically testable and that they are not for that reason meaningless or without truth value. This aspect of Wisdom's view is reinforced when he notes that the claim that

> . . . the words, "In Nero God was incarnate" are not without any meaning; one who utters them makes a statement which is absurd and *against* all reason and therefore *not* beyond the scope of reason. Now if a statement is not beyond the scope of reason then any logically parallel statement is also not beyond the scope of reason. . . . The statement "In Jesus God was incarnate" is logically parallel to "In Nero God was incarnate." . . . Therefore the statement "In Jesus God was incarnate" is not beyond the scope of reason.[74]

Factual evidence—evidence about the birth, life, deeds, views, attitudes and death of Jesus—is relevant to the claim that in Jesus God was incarnate.

> The question calls for investigation, but it also calls like every other question for thought, reflection, reason.[75] . . . And to this question every incident in the history of the world is relevant—whether it is the fall of a sparrow or the coming of a harvest, the passing of an empire or the fading of a smile.[76]

Here, there is no attempt to translate "In Jesus God was incarnate" into a statement about powers within us. It is a claim within the scope of reason, and if the corresponding claim about Nero is against all reason it does not follow that the claim made with respect to Jesus is. Since Wisdom claims that "In Jesus God was incarnate" is not beyond the scope of reason, and since if it is true it follows that God exists, one would expect Wisdom to also assert that "God exists" is not beyond the scope of reason. This he does, but in a way which introduces the ambiguity we have already noticed in his treatment of religious language.

> The old questions "Does God exist?" and "Does the Devil exist?" aren't senseless, aren't beyond the scope of thought and reason. On the contrary, they call for new awareness of what has so long been about us, in case knowing nature so well we never know her.[77]

On the one hand, the claim that in Jesus God is incarnate is not a disguised way of speaking about powers within ourselves, nor it would seem does it entail any such way of speaking. On the other, answering the questions about God and the Devil call for a new awareness of nature; the claims and counter-claims concerning God's existence serve (only? primarily? derivatively?) to point up features of the natural world which we might otherwise have missed. These two emphases are not, so far as I can see, logically incompatible. Nonetheless, they are divergent, leading to quite different reflections concerning, and treatment of, such sentences as "God exists" or "God is Lord of Nature and of History." There is an ambivalence in Wisdom's approach which both fascinates and frustrates.[78]

Perhaps we can help remove the ambivalence. Insofar as it rests on an appeal to Freudian theory, it will be discussed below.[79] Our concern here is with a different question. To what extent are such sentences as "God exists" rightly viewed as "exclamations evincing an attitude"?[80]

To say that "God exists" serves to point up features of order and goodness in our world would be misleading. Such order and goodness are often offered as evidence for the claim that God exists. Evidence serves to prove, or at least make plausible, a claim based upon it. This is quite different from serving as a way of emphasizing the existence of that evidence, which would be at most a side effect. Of course, a defender of Wisdom might claim that offering evidence for "God exists" differs from offering evidence for other statements just in this way—in this case apparently arguing for the conclusion is really only a way of pointing up the facts adduced as apparent evidence. But why say this?

It would be plausible, perhaps, to make this exception in the case of the claim that God exists were this claim not at all related logically to any evidence. This, however, is not the case—as Wisdom admits. For one thing, theist and atheist have different expectations. Wisdom sometimes limits it to a future life, but this seems arbitrary. In the parable of the garden, the disappearance of order and beauty would considerably reduce the plausibility of the view that there is a gardener and correspondingly increases the plausibility of the opposite view. Were nothing good and everything evil, surely this would have a similar effect in the theism-atheism dispute. The disappearance of all weeds and the presence of only intricately arranged flowers of exquisite beauty throughout the garden would affect the plausibility of the views in question in a reverse manner. So also would there being all good and no evil alter the parallel case, though this is a rather complex matter.[81] And there are different expectations as to an after-life, or at least as to its character (another complex topic). So it is not true that "God exists" is not related logically to any evidence, and thus it is not at all clear why it should be made an exception in the manner proposed above.

If asserting that God exists, then, serves to point up those features of the world (e.g., order and goodness) taken to be evidence for that claim, this is a secondary function. How does this affect the claim that religious assertions evince an *attitude*? A good deal depends on what one packs into the word attitude. Taking an attitude toward x often at least involves making, explicitly or implicitly, certain assumptions about x as well as about other things. If one has, say, a negative attitude toward socialism, one claims or assumes that certain forms of government, socialism among them, have certain consequences and/or features, and that these consequences and/or features are undesirable. Very roughly, this involves both beliefs and feelings. That asserting that God exists also involves these seems perfectly clear. Further, the taking of an attitude can be appraised. Not every attitude toward a war, a politician, or a proposal can be equally reasonable with every competing attitude. Thus one way of taking Wisdom's thesis is that asserting that God exists is a way of expressing a set of beliefs and feelings, those beliefs and feelings associated with traditional theism, in the hope that others will come to share them. This way of reading Wisdom would emphasize the weighing of relevant considerations in evaluating religious claims, as opposed to deducing conclusions from self-certifying axioms or making inductive generalizations from observed data. Part of the value of Wisdom's essays is that they effectively challenge the infrequently stated but widely assumed thesis that all reasoning worthy of the name explicitly fits one or the other of these

models. One could speak of the asserting of "God exists" as expressing a conceptual scheme if one wished to emphasize its cognitive role,
or as evincing an attitude if one wished to stress its conative and
emotive function in discourse. To this account of the matter, I have
no objection. But if one takes Wisdom's discussion in this manner,
we are no longer limited to viewing the assertion that God exists as
serving only to point out features of our world or as a way of speaking of mysterious powers within us.

IAN RAMSEY:
MODELS AND DISCERNMENT

Ian Ramsey's prolific writings on the topic of religious language are
variations on a single plot.[82] The plot is complex; we will attempt
to trace its development, and to appraise it. He asserts that any analysis of religious language must begin by characterizing the settings in
which such discourse is actually used. Essential to all such settings are
discernment and commitment.[83] The analysis is completed by mapping
the relationships between the terms of discourse used in these settings.
Thus the analysis is conducted in the formal, not the material, mode;
it consists of discourse about linguistic terms, not about nonlinguistic
entities and their qualities. Ramsey's logical empiricism is constituted
by these claims.[84]

Ramsey consciously develops his analysis as an alternative to all traditional treatments of his topic. If we take "God is—" as a paradigm
of religious discourse and note that words or phrases filling the blank
must be predicate terms, we can concisely express his central thesis.
No use of a predicate term in any sentence which has the form of
our paradigm will be univocal, equivocal, or analogical with respect
to the use of that term as applied to persons or things. Thus no sentence of the form of our paradigm ascribes a quality to God. The relation between the word "God" and any predicate term will be that
between the key word of any disclosure model and the term qualifying that model. Thus the central notion in Ramsey's analysis is that
of a disclosure model.

Models[85] make theory construction possible. They provide a means
of expressing patterns discovered among phenomena and of focusing
attention on crucial explanatory concepts or key words in terms of
which the model is developed. Thus a model with "wave" as key word
provides a way of recording regularities in the behaviour of light-
phenomena in such a way as to explain observed regularities and make

predictions of further regularities possible. They organize otherwise isolated data. Models are adequate to the degree that they make such explanation and prediction possible. We have no need to canvass Ramsey's ambitious claim that models are essential to science and mathematics in the sense that theorizing in either discipline would be impossible without them.[86]

Not all models provide means for expressing patterns discovered among phenomena. This is the function of first-order models. Other models relate various first-order models into one conceptual scheme. They make possible general conceptual frameworks into which lower-level explanations of diverse phenomena are woven. General scientific theories, as well as traditional metaphysical systems, are thus models on Ramsey's view. In part, the discourse of any religion expresses such a model.

Any theory subsumable under a wider-ranging theory is less basic than that under which it is subsumed. A religious model is basic in that it endeavors to correlate the disclosure models of science, morality, and self-awareness, whereas it itself is not subsumable under any other model. Some experiences require interpretation in terms of only one model. For example, Ramsey claims that religious disclosures are not subsumable under the model entitled "psychological aberrations."

Picturing models share qualities with what they model. Any scale model is a picturing model. *Disclosure models*[87] share the structure of what they model, but share no qualities with it. They are isomorphic with what they model. If we follow Ramsey in assuming that a description can be given of an entity just in case a quality can be ascribed to that entity, disclosure models will not justify descriptions of what they model.[88] Hence some other term is needed for sentences purportedly expressing claims about structural similarity between model and modeled. Let us adopt the term "comparatives" for such sentences. Ramsey's thesis can now be rephrased as saying religious discourse is always, insofar as it makes assertions, comparative but not descriptive. All religious assertions arise from, and are justified by, disclosure models and no disclosure model is also a picturing model. That there are nonassertive uses of religious language is neither denied nor relevant.

Models, basic or otherwise, can be mutually incompatible.[89] Ramsey is thus obligated to provide some procedure for deciding between conflicting basic models if he is to claim superiority for a religious basic model. There is no need to emphasize the standard requirement that statements articulating a given model must be individually consistent as well as mutually compatible. Ramsey's criteria for decision between basic models are these. First, the model most adequate with respect to empirical fit is superior. Second, no nonpersonal model can be adequate.[90]

The empirical reference of a basic model is mediated through that of the less basic models it unifies. A logically necessary condition of formulating a basic model is that there be less basic ones for it to unify. Thus decision procedure with respect to two or more basic models presupposes a prior supply of less basic, but adequate, models. The degree of empirical fit possessed by a basic model is a function of the number of less basic models it can correlate, without *ad hoc* adjustment, into one conceptual scheme.

A nonpersonal basic model is one which cannot be basic to a personal model. A model whose key phrase is "atoms in motion" could not, perhaps, be basic to a model whose key word was "agent." That one model could not be basic to another would, of course, have to be argued. The history of philosophy is filled with such arguments. The dispute between proponents and opponents of any given program of reductionism will provide a case in point. This elucidation of nonpersonal model simply shifts the weight to the concept of a personal model. My attempt to explain Ramsey's doctrine on this point must wait.

We have seen that paradigmatically religious situations are those in which discernment is followed by commitment.[91] No definition of discernment is offered, nor perhaps is one possible. It can be characterized as "that which happens when . . . ," where we continue our characterization by specifying cases. One such case is that of a student who "sees what infinity means" upon being told that were one to spend his life expanding the series of whole numbers beginning with "1" he would still not have produced an infinite series. Another is that of the scientist who recognizes that Copernican theory relates the data we possess concerning celestial phenomena in such a way as to make calculation and prediction possible. A third instance is that of a man who finds the plight of a drowning child an occasion of obligation to attempt a rescue. Moses' numinous experience at the burning bush provides yet another example. Discernment, in Ramsey's phrase, is "empirical and more."[92] A necessary condition of discernment occurring is that there be an environment to which qualities can be ascribed. An equally necessary condition is that what is discerned not be describable.

Commitment is the appropriate response to what is discerned. Accepting claims about infinite series which follow from the concept of such a series, using the Copernican interpretive pattern for prediction and explanation,[93] acquiescing to one's feeling of duty by attempting to rescue the child, and worshipping the numinous object are ways of committing oneself to what is discerned in the cases characterized above. That there are obvious and important disanalogies between the discernments and commitments made in these cases Ramsey does not deny. His claim that there is an important similarity between them rests upon the possibility of viewing them all as disclosures.[94]

X is disclosed just in case X is an object of discernment. Since what is discerned cannot be described, what is disclosed cannot be described. Disclosures are expressed by means of disclosure models. Thus they can only be expressed in comparatives. The capacity to receive disclosures is the capacity to have experiences which can be expressed in comparative, but not in descriptive, sentences.

These indescribable disclosures, in Ramsey's view, provide both the occasion and the empirical referent of religious language. Were there no disclosures, there would be no context in which religious language could arise and hence none to which it could apply. Further, only insofar as a model is adequate to what is disclosed can it be correct or justified. Part of the test of the correctness of a model consists in a purported direct comparison of model to modeled. This is true even of religious discourse conceived as a basic model.

Our way of putting the matter has presupposed a *subject of disclosure—disclosure process—object of disclosure* pattern. Ramsey also uses language suggesting this pattern. Nonetheless, this is strictly incorrect. The distinction between the subject of experience and the object of experience is purportedly inapplicable to disclosures. Ramsey's rationale for this claim is that God is always the discloser in a disclosure situation, and God can never become an object. Two senses of "object" seem relevant here. In one, to be an object is to be describable. In the other, to be an object is to be experienced by a subject. The concept of an object of experience is less than lucid. Nonetheless, it is plausible to claim that whatever can be experienced can be described. Ramsey seems to accept this claim. While God can disclose Himself to us, we can never experience Him, since to experience is to be the subject of an experience which has an object. The formal mode way of putting this claim will be examined shortly. The difficulty of saying clearly what is meant by denying that the subject-object distinction applies to disclosures plagues Ramsey's analysis. His central attempt to clarify this matter is found in his discussions of self-awareness and awareness of God.

The "meeting place *par excellence* of models and mystery" occurs "in what to each of us is the disclosure of himself, the insight by which we know ourselves distinctively as ourselves."[95] In accord with the purported indescribability of any subject, we cannot claim an awareness of ourselves as mental substances. To be a substance is to possess qualities and thus to be describable. Thus we can express self-disclosure only by speaking of the role of "I" in ordinary discourse. We must articulate self-awareness by means of a disclosure model. What Ramsey says about the role of "I" as key word in such a model is phrased as much as an argument for the occurrence of the relevant disclosure as it is an expression of what is purportedly disclosed.

Self-awareness is, for Ramsey, awareness of an indescribable subject. No proof is offered that this analysis of self-awareness is correct. "Stories" are told until the insight that one is "empirical and more" is elicited. By describing contexts in which one feels obligated to take action, falls in love, or fears death, the disclosure may be effected. It may not. If no such story succeeds, argument can hardly avail, for such arguments as Descartes' "I think, therefore I am" are only instruments intended to effect insight.[96] This is Ramsey's official line: disclosures are primary and self-warranting; arguments at best elicit disclosures.

Argument is nonetheless required. Perhaps no proof can be offered that each man is aware of himself. Certainly proof is required that one analysis among many possible alternatives is the proper way to construe self-awareness. No repetition of stories until the "penny drops" will suffice to show that those who claim awareness of themselves as "more than an object" are other than deluded. Such stories neither prove, nor provide evidence, that men are other than simply physical objects, let alone that the essential man is indescribable.

Hume canvassed his experience without Ramseyian disclosure. He discerned only a pattern of experiences. Insofar as "mind" referred at all on Hume's view, it referred to this pattern. The pattern is "empirical and more" in that the pattern is not reducible to the experiences it relates. Hume suggested that we model our talk about minds on our talk about nations. There is, he in effect suggested, structural similarity or isomorphism between minds and nations. Criteria of identity applicable in the one case are also applicable in the other. Since minds are not entities, they have no qualities. The Humean model is not unlike a disclosure model; there is some sort of echo between the model and the phenomena it enables us to understand, while at the same time denying replica picturing.[97] This is Ramsey's characterization of a disclosure model.

In contrast, Descartes claimed awareness of himself as a mental substance. The model for talk about minds was, in his view, the substance-attribute model which was equally appropriate for speaking of physical objects. If Ramsey's model is superior, either to Hume's or Descartes', he must prove it. In the absence of argument, the best he can claim is that he has insight where Hume was blind and Descartes misled. Anyone espousing Hume's view, or Descartes', can make analogous claims about Ramsey. An impasse is reached and rational controversy ends.

A dilemma has developed. Ramsey can retreat to claiming to have insight where others have none, extending to his opposition the courtesy of making the same claim. Or he can appeal to something other than the purported disclosure to defend his claim that his model is superior. Ramsey chooses the latter horn of the dilemma. He appeals to certain putative facts about third person discourse. He also points to the formal properties of his model. The official line was that disclosure was sufficient. Argument at best elicits disclosure, at worst misleads one into thinking that proof is relevant and important. But the official line is inevitably abandoned.

The putative fact about third person discourse is its inescapable incompleteness.[98] Any sentence of the form "He said . . . ." is short for "I say that he said. . . ." And language presupposes a speaker, or a programmer. The speaker must be a subject who is indescribable in the language he speaks. This last claim is the crucial one for Ramsey. He offers two arguments for it.

One can be stated in some such terms as the following. No exhaustive description of Smith can be given by Jones since Jones cannot know Smith in the way that Smith does.[99] Nor can any exhaustive description of Smith be given by Smith, since the very giving of that description constitutes a further fact about Smith. Let "D" be a description of Smith including all his qualities, dispositions, actions, and the like. Let "S" be the sentence expressing D. The sentence "Smith says S" states a further fact about Smith not included in D or expressed by S. So S does not express an exhaustive description of Smith.[100] So neither Jones nor Smith can provide an exhaustive description of Smith. It does not, of course, follow that Jones and Smith cannot together provide an exhaustive description of Smith. Let us suppose, however, that we are also given a proof of that claim. The interesting fact is that nothing follows relevant to Ramsey's thesis. Even if it is impossible to produce an exhaustive description of Smith, the reason why this is impossible lies in the conditions for description, not in the nature of the described. Nothing in the argument shows that some fact about Smith is indescribable. It at best shows that some fact or other about Smith must escape any particular description. We are not even given grounds for distinguishing between types of descriptions, let alone for making a type-distinction between the properties mentioned in a given description and the subject of the description. For all that Ramsey has shown, the descriptions in question could all be descriptions of a Humean pattern or Cartesian substance.

We could add a premise which would generate something like Ramsey's conclusion. It would go something as follows: "For every level of description, there is a new type of entity described." A criterion for levels of description would have to be provided. Given some such criterion, there would be as many types of entities as there were levels of description. The additional premise is certainly dubious enough. Even if it were granted, it would prove that each of us is as many subjects as there are levels of description which can be provided of us, even though not all possible levels of descriptions can be given and thus an exhaustive enumeration of how many subjects we are could not be offered. This conclusion obviously will not serve Ramsey's purposes.

Ramsey also argues for his model of self-awareness by appealing to its formal properties. The relevant formal properties of Ramsey's model for "I" are its capacity to account for personal eccentricities and to correlate diverse areas of discourse. His competitors can forward the same claims. Personal eccentricities provide no problem for Hume. They can be regarded as peculiarities of pattern; no two patterns are identical. They give Descartes no difficulty. He can regard personal eccentricities as peculiarity of properties; no two substances have exactly the same set of properties.

Humean and Cartesian models for self-awareness may also succeed in correlating areas of discourse. Hume can offer a utilitarian account of responsibility; a man is responsible for doing action A only insofar as he can be prevented from doing A again by punishment. Descartes presents an account of responsibility; a man is responsible for doing A if he did A freely. An analysis of "doing A freely" can be readily provided. If Hume or Descartes cannot relate their analyses of a self to their accounts of responsibility, this must be shown by careful argument.

Articulate theories of personal identity and self-awareness are thus available which do not require the existence of an indescribable subject. (There are others besides those mentioned.) The theories can account for personal eccentricity. They may correlate discourse about action, choice, responsibility, freedom, and punishment. They are, it would seem, defensible without appeal to disclosures. By implicitly presenting the choice as one between a behavioristic model and a disclosure model, Ramsey creates spurious plausibility for his claims. This is not to say that he refutes behaviorism. Viewing the issue in proper perspective, whatever evidence he provides for the superiority of his own model is either irrelevant or can equally be accounted for by his opponents who make no appeal to disclosures.

Not much has been said about the details of Ramsey's model of self-awareness. The disclosure which gives rise to the model is indescribable, and can be expressed only in terms of comparatives justified by the model in question. The model is constituted by the use of "I" in ordinary discourse. One wonders how much of a model this really provides, even if we waive questions as to its justifiability. The same question arises concerning Ramsey's model for "God."

God is, *par excellence*, the disclosed.[101] "God" and "I" function analogously. Each expresses something disclosed in all disclosures. All disclosure is disclosure of both self and God. Discernment of order in science is disclosure of the activity of a person. Discernment in moral contexts is disclosure of the will of a person. Discernment in a numinous setting is disclosure of an indescribable and awe-inspiring Thou. Discernment and commitment are disclosure and response.

This exposition has been framed in the eschewed material mode. It thus requires restatement in the formal mode. The claim then reads as follows. A religious basic model is a disclosure model with "God" as key word or central concept. Only a religious basic model can, with maximal empirical fit, unify less basic scientific, moral, and personal models. Religious discourse is the unifying language for scientific, moral, and personal language. Ramsey's discussion of his model for "God" is of central importance. It is in this connection that he offers his most detailed account of how disclosure models are constructed. It is here that the crux of his account of religious language is offered.

The word "God" gets its use, on Ramsey's view, in such contexts as these. Impressed by the ceaseless panorama of changes in nature and human experience, a man is led to reflect on the opposite of change. A discernment occurs in that the changeless is disclosed. Thus the sentence "God is unchanging" arises. No mention is made of the distinction between something which does not change and something which cannot change, so no explanation is offered as to which is disclosed. Again, a man reflects on the fact that everything within his visual field has a cause, and that the cause of each thing in his visual field has its cause, and so on. He is thus led to reflect on the opposite of that which is caused, and something which does not need explanation is disclosed. Thus the sentence "Something is a first cause" arises. The distinction between something which is not caused and something which cannot be caused is not mentioned, so no explanation is provided as to which is disclosed. Also, Ramsey offers no account whatever of how the concepts of the uncaused or the unchanging are derivable from the contexts specified. Even if all our knowledge of God begins with disclosures, it does not follow that it all arises from disclosures.

"Change" and "cause" do not function as words ascribing qualities to objects. Each of these words is a key word in a model. These models can be qualified by qualifying the key words in question. "Unchanging" and "first cause" become key words in qualified models. These qualified models can be unified by a more basic model whose key word is "God." Thus "God" becomes the subject term for "is a first cause" and "is unchanging."

Ramsey's rationale for restricting himself to the formal mode in this context is primarily his contention that treating religious statements as material mode sentences leads to paradoxes, or, worse, contradictions. The prime advantage of the formal mode treatment of religious sentences is that it has no such consequences. The philosophical value of the formal versus material mode distinction has been questioned.[102] If one can translate from material mode to formal, surely a translation from formal to material is possible. Further, if "Christ is man" and "Christ is God" are incompatible, then " 'Christ' designates a man" and " 'Christ' designates what 'God' designates" are also incompatible. Ramsey offers no convincing argument that any given religious statement in the material mode is self-contradictory or that any particular set of religious statements in the material mode is incompatible. He offers no argument that if two sentences are incompatible in the material mode, their formal mode analogues will nonetheless be compatible. Without these arguments, the formal mode preference seems spurious. I know of no reason to be especially sanguine about this defect being remedied.

We have seen that the construction of models for God requires us to qualify predicates used in nonreligious contexts. A major point in so doing in traditional theology is to say something about God in the sense of providing a true, if partial, description of Him. Ramsey parodies this as attempting to give a "map of God." The function of all disclosure models is to "point to" God.[103] No one model is indispensible. Disclosure models serve to point out cosmic patterns of order and of obligation and to point to the Discloser.

If a disclosure model points to something, then it must be structurally similar to what it points to or models. There is, however, no place in Ramsey's account of religious language for a sentence reporting the similarity of model to modeled in any way that will justify the model in terms of which this sentence is framed. Any claim made about a disclosure must be comparative, not descriptive. It must hence be framed in terms of the discourse of some particular disclosure model.[104] To appeal to a claim made about a disclosure is hence to appeal to some disclosure model as adequate to expressing that disclosure. Hence no direct appeal to the disclosure itself can be expressed. Further, there would seem to be no way to judge between disclosure models save with respect to their formal properties. Suppose I have a disclosure D, and only two disclosure models M1 and M2. Any claim I make about D must be made in terms of a comparative framed in the language of M1 or M2. Any claim framed in the language of M1 will, if it is relevant to showing that M1 is the proper model for expressing the disclosure, beg the question against M2. The same will be true with respect to any analogous claim framed in the language of M2.

We remain puzzled as to how a model can successfully point to something. In addition, we are not told satisfactorily why all disclosure models must point to the same thing. This raises still graver difficulties. The crucial function of Ramsey's account of religious language is to offer an analysis of such discourse which makes clear how it is meaningful. It is altogether puzzling as to how structural similarities can be expressed by comparatives when no description can be given of at least one of the terms of the comparison. The point is not simply that one would find it hard to justify such comparatives. It is that it is hard to see what a comparative could mean. It would seem that comparatives are unintelligible if at least one term of the comparison is indescribable. But then religious language is possible only if some description of God can be meaningful and true. Worship, for example, can be said to be a more appropriate reaction than blasphemy to a being all-knowing, all-powerful, and all-good. If we cannot describe God in this manner, or in any manner at all, it is no longer clear that any reaction to God is still possible, let alone appropriate. What could count as a reaction to an absolutely indescribable subject? On Ramsey's analysis, religious language is reduced to a silence that cannot even be reverent as opposed to irreverent.

LANGUAGE AND MEANING: CONCLUSION

We have canvassed some representative treatments of religious language. Common to each was the denial that such sentences as "God exists" and "God is love" are assertions. In each case, at least a contributing factor to this denial was concern lest verificationism be directly challenged. This was patently the case for Cox, and only slightly less patently so for Braithwaite. Wisdom provided material evidence against verificationism, but seemed nonetheless to revert in the end to an account of religious discourse in which its putative claims required restatement in psychological or anthropological (in a wide sense) sentences in order to be intelligible. Ramsey, too, though furthest from orthodox verificationism, nonetheless as a logical empiricist took the ascription of observable predicates to spatio-temporal objects as the single instance of a clearly assertive sentence. Other sorts of discourse are viewed as odd in such a manner as calls their assertiveness into question. If the argument of the latter portion of the chapter is correct, none of these analyses of religious language will do as they stand. Their adherence to verificationism in various degrees restricts their adequacy as analyses of religious discourse. Therefore neither verificationism itself, nor those theories of religious language constructed in its shadows which we have discussed, provide any justification for the contemporary fashion of regarding the relevant issue in the philosophy of religion to be that of meaning, not of justification. Just as further versions of verificationism might be formulated, so further theories of religious discourse along one or another of the lines examined might be explored. By now, however, it looks as if allegiance to verificationism is, at least for the philosopher of religion and for the theologian, as stifling as it is gratuitous.

FOOTNOTES ∽ I

[1] I.e., in a manner manifesting self-giving love. Cf. Anders Nygren, *Agape and Eros* (London: SPCK Press, 1953).

[2] *Timaeus*, 28c.

[3] For a series of helpful elucidations of the issues involved, see the articles by Professor Harry Austryn Wolfson referred to in the bibliogaphy at the end of this chapter.

[4] There are, of course, religions which do not include belief in any deity— Theravada Buddhism for example. But problems essentially similar to those we will consider arise with respect to beliefs which they do include, and contemporary philosophers too have treated sentences concerning God as paradigmatic or representative of religious claims.

[5] Cf. Victor Kraft, *The Vienna Circle* (New York: Philosophical Library, 1953) and Julius Weinberg, *An Examination of Logical Positivism* (Paterson, N.J.: Littlefield, Adams and Co., 1960); see also J. O. Urmson, *Philosophical Analysis* (London: Oxford U. Press, 1967). The Weinberg volume was first published in London by Routledge and Kegan Paul, 1930 and the Urmson volume in London by the Clarendon Press, 1956. The Kraft volume was originally published under the title *Die Wiener Kreis* and was translated from the German by Arthur Pap.

[6] See also A. J. Ayer (ed.), *Logical Positivism* (New York: The Free Press, 1959). Ayer's *Language, Truth and Logic* was originally published in 1936 but is conveniently available in a paperback version published in New York by Dover Publications, Inc., n.d.

7 "An Empiricist Criterion of Meaning," included in Ayer, *Logical Positivism*. Ayer has, of course, considerably altered his views on the topic of meaning.

8 Exceptions to this generalization, and the more important question as to the connection between necessity, analyticity, and being tautologous can be ignored for the present purposes; i.e. we need not concern ourselves as to whether there are propositions which are necessary but not analytic or tautologous.

9 The claim that only "sense data statements" count as observation statements is not essential to the verificationist criterion. Further, we need only be able to conceive of such observation statements, not actually be successful in making confirming or disconfirming observations.

10 The rule is simply that if any statement p is true, then the complex statement *(p or q)* is also true. The present version of the verification principle, and the following version as well, also fail to allow for the meaningfulness of statements involving mixed (universal and existential) quantifiers, e.g. "some octopus has a coral rock in each of its tentacles."

11 Since "All places have been observed" is not an observation statement. If one wished to say that after all a perceiver might be able to view all spatial locations at once, and hence observe each to be empty of trolls, the response is that this makes the notion of an observation statement too loose for the polemic purposes of the verificationist. At this point, God could be the omnicompetent observer.

12 Ayer, *op. cit.*, p. 128. This passage is taken from remarks appended to his article by Hempel in 1958 as he commented on the article in terms of his current views.

13 This version is not circular, being stated recursively. See *Language, Truth and Logic*, Sec. Ed., p. 13.

14 Alonzo Church, "Review of *Language, Truth and Logic*, Sec. Ed.," *Journal of Symbolic Logic*, Vol. 14 (1949), p. 52, 53.

15 The argument, slightly altered, is:
(2a) $-(-A \cdot B)$ implies (C·S), by M. I. from (2).
(2b) (Av−B) implies (C·S), by DeM. from (2a).
(2c) (Av−B), addition to (1).
(2d) (C·S), M. P. from (2b) and (2c).
(2e) S, transp. and simp. from (2d).

16 For a criticism of Church, see Peter Nidditch, "A Defense of Ayer's Verifiability Principle Against Church's Criticism" *Mind*, Vol. LXX (1961), p. 88, 89. For a reply to Nidditch and further discussion of the verification principle, see Alvin Plantinga, *God and Other Minds* (Ithaca: Cornell U. Press, 1967), p. 165ff.

17 Cf. Hempel's references in Ayer, *op. cit.*, p. 128 and also p. 118.

18 *Ibid.*, p. 129.

19 See Plantinga, *op. cit.*, p. 167ff.

20 The University Discussion was reprinted in A. Flew and A. McIntyre, ed., *New Essays in Philosophical Theology* (London: SCM Press, 1955), p. 96–108.

21 The reply that these statements, being future-tense, have no truth value can be met by rephrasing them on the following model: "No one alive at time t_1 is also alive at time t_2," with the "is" tenseless. And of course it is obvious that Flew could not say that these claims are all both falsifiable and verifiable by some non-human sentient creature (we can include any such creature in "someone" or "no one"), or by God for obvious reasons. Of course we might have good evidence for a theory T where T entailed that at some specifiable future time all human life will, in its present form, have ceased.

22 The slogan "The meaning of a sentence is given by how it is used" seems here to mislead Flew into confusing the question of when someone is willing to give up a belief with the quite different question as to when he ought to give it up.

If a contemporary of ours believes he is Napoleon no matter what evidence we give him, does that mean his belief hasn't been falsified? It ought to mean that by parity of reasoning with Flew's treatment of the theist's claim; but plainly it does not.

23 This characterization of a blik results from a consideration of Hare's examples of bliks and what little he explicitly says about them. I take it to capture his intentions.

24 Flew and McIntyre, *op. cit.*, p. 101.

25 See below, Chapter Six.

26 See his comments in Flew and McIntyre, *op. cit.*, p. 101ff.

27 The point of his parable of the Stranger is that the evidence is not decisive —some points toward theism, some away from it. He does not say what he takes the positive evidence to be.

28 Flew and McIntyre, *op. cit.*, p. 103 and p. 105 (concluding paragraph).

29 *Ibid.*, p. 107.

30 Whether Flew is right about the force of the problem of evil as a case against the theist will be investigated in the following chapter.

31 This approach is also in line with Flew's "Divine Omnipotence and Human Freedom," included in Flew and McIntyre, *op. cit.*

32 *Ibid.*, p. 98.

33 Alvin Plantinga, *op. cit.*, p. 158ff.

34 If one is suspicious about "Flew exists," he can substitute "Flew is happy" or "Flew now sits at his desk," or the like; all the comments made above will, *mutatis mutandis*, still hold.

35 W. V. O. Quine, "Two Dogmas of Empiricism" in *From a Logical Point of View* (New York: Harper and Row, 1963). Cf. also Quine, "Semantic Ascent" in *Word and Object* (Cambridge: M. I. T. Press, 1960). I cannot, however, agree that, e.g., the law of contradiction is "amendable."

36 On this and related topics, see T. S. Kuhn, *The Structure of Scientific Revolutions* (Chicago: U. of Chicago Press, 1962).

37 Cf. below, Chapter Six.

38 Not only by philosophers. Cf. P. Van Buren, *The Secular Meaning of the Gospel* (New York: Macmillan, 1963).

39 *Mind*, Vol. LIX (1950), p. 209–218.

40 R. B. Braithwaite, *An Empiricist's View of the Nature of Religious Belief* (London: Cambridge U. Press, 1955).

41 David Cox, "The Significance of Christianity," *Mind*, Vol. LIX (1950). Reprinted in G. MacGregor and J. Robb, eds. *Readings in Religious Philosophy* (Boston: Houghton, Mifflin Co., 1962), p. 359. References to Cox will be to this reprint. The language of each tradition is of course intended to safeguard the experience of its own adherents.

42 *Ibid.*, p. 357.

43 *Ibid.*, p. 358.

44 *Ibid.*, p. 361.

45 *Ibid.*, p. 362.

46 *Loc. cit.*

47 For an interesting appraisal of Cox's views, cf. Thomas McPherson, "The Reply," *Mind*, Vol. LIX (1950) p. 545–550. Also reprinted in MacGregor and Robb, *op. cit.*, p. 363ff. References will be to this reprint.

48 *Ibid.*, p. 364. Cf. C. B. Martin, *Religious Belief* (Ithaca: Cornell U. Press, 1959), esp. Chapter Five.

49 See below, Chapter Three, for a discussion of these topics.

50 R. B. Braithwaite, *An Empiricist's View of the Nature of Religious Belief.* Most conveniently available in Ian Ramsey, ed., *Christian Faith and Moral Philosophy* (London: SCM Press, 1966). See Braithwaite's comments in this volume on his own view; they do not alter any criticisms made below.

51 Ramsey, *op. cit.*, p. 59.

52 *Ibid.*, p. 238.

53 *Ibid.*, p 62.

54 *Loc. cit.*

55 *Ibid.*, p. 66.

56 *Ibid.*, p. 63.

57 *Ibid.*, p. 235ff. Part of the defense Braithwaite provides for his view rests on an appeal to his account of moral discourse. The problem is that this analysis is also defective. See the present author's "Empiricism and Theism;" *Sophia*, October, 1968. For other critiques of Braithwaite's analysis of religious belief, see John Hick, *Philosophy of Religion* (Englewood Cliffs, N.J.: Prentice-Hall, 1963), p. 90ff.; "Professor Braithwaite and Billy Brown," *Australasian Journal of Philosophy*, 1958, by H. J. N. Horsburgh; John Passmore, "Christianity and Positivism," same journal, 1957. A defense of Braithwaite is provided by Kai Nielsen in the issue of *Sophia* mentioned above, and is responded to by the present author in "A Reply to Professor Nielsen," same issue. The criticisms by Hick, Horsburgh, and Passmore provide still further reasons for rejecting this analysis.

58 John Wisdom, "Gods," *Proceedings of the Aristotelian Society*, Vol. LIV, (1944).

59 John Wisdom, "The Modes of Thought and the Logic of 'God,'" originally a BBC address, printed for the first time in J. Hick, *The Existence of God*, p. 275ff. Further references will be made to this volume.

60 Cf. M. B. Foster, *Mystery and Philosophy* (London: SCM Press, 1957) for a discussion of the "Thou shalt not tempt (test) the Lord thy God" passage. Foster's remarks will be dealt with below in Chapter Four.

61 Wisdom, *op. cit.*, p. 150.

62 *Ibid.*, p. 151.

63 *Loc. cit.*

64 *Loc. cit.*

65 Cf. William Paley, *Natural Theology*, ed. F. Ferre (New York: Library of Liberal Arts, 1963) and Lecomte DeNuoy, *Human Destiny* (New York: Mentor Books, 1952).

66 Wisdom, *op. cit.*, p. 150.

67 *Ibid.*, p. 157. Cf. p. 159 where Wisdom says that the resolution of the dispute between theist and atheist would in one sense be the discovery of a new fact (or facts).

68 Cf. *ibid.*, p. 158 where Wisdom adds "excellent" and "beautiful" in the same context. See also Hick, *op. cit.*, p. 278, 282ff.

69 *Ibid.*, p. 164.

70 *Ibid.*, p. 166. Wisdom adds: "'So incongruous with reality'! It cannot be denied."

71 *Loc. cit.*

72 *Ibid.*, p. 167. Cf. Hick, *op. cit.*, p. 292ff.

73 Hick, *op. cit.*, p. 294.

74 *Ibid.*, p. 296.

75 *Loc. cit.*

76   *Ibid.*, p. 297.

77   *Ibid.*, p. 298.

78   One can profitably compare his other writings in the collection *Philosophy and Psychoanalysis* (New York: Philosophical Library, 1953) with the two discussed here, especially the papers on p. 36ff. and p. 169ff.

79   See Chapter Four below.

80   As Wisdom says. J. Wisdom, *Philosophy and Psychoanalysis*, p. 158.

81   See below, Chapter Two.

82   Ramsey's writings include *Miracles* (Oxford: Clarendon Press, 1952); *Religious Language* (New York: Macmillan, 1963): *Prospect for Metaphysics* (London: George Allen and Unwin, 1961); *Religion and Science* (London: SPCK Press, 1964); *Models and Mystery* (London: Oxford U. Press, 1964); *Christian Discourse* (London: Oxford U. Press, 1965). It will be convenient to refer to these volumes respectively as *M, RL, PM, RS, MM,* and *CD.* In lieu of copious quotation, I will give detailed references.

83   Cf. *M*, 3f; *RL*, p. 14–48; *CD*, p. 6–11.

84   *M*, p. 3; *RL*, p. 13.

85   Cf. *M*, p. 4; *MM*, Chapter 1; *RS*, p. 20, 34.

86   *MM*, p. 4, 19. Ramsey appeals at this point to Max Black, *Models and Metaphors* (Ithaca: Cornell U. Press, 1962).

87   *RS*, p. 68; *MM*, p. 7–15.

88   *MM*, p. 10. I will discuss "structural similarity" in connection with Ramsey's claims about self-awareness and awareness of God.

89   *M*, p. 13; *MM*, p. 38; *CD*, p. 82.

90   *RS*, p. 86.

91   Cf. *M*, p. 5ff; *RL*, Chapter 1. Ramsey's view seems to entail that a man can comprehend religious language only if he has had discernment and made commitment. Were this so, no unbeliever could comprehend religious language. Thus the obvious fact that unbelievers, who had never been believers, have made relevant criticisms of religious belief would be inexplicable.

92   *PM*, p. 168; *RL*, p. 20, 51, 70.

93   Cf. Ramsey's comments on induction, *M*, p. 5.

94   *RL*, Chapter 1; *RS*, p. 20; *CD*, p. 6, 7.

95   Cf. *RS*, p. 37ff; *RL*, Chapter 1; *M*, p. 14ff. See *M*, p. 6ff. for an analogous argument, subject to analogous criticism, about the language of science. Ramsey makes tantalizing claims with respect to self-awareness and the subject-object distinction. Examples: no language is possible unless there is an indescribable subject, so that one could infer the existence of such a subject from the existence of any language; no personal identity is possible without an indescribable subject. The problem is that, so far as I can see, they are unsubstantiated, though perhaps no worse off than the claims he is attacking. Cf. Ramsey, "The Systematic Elusiveness of 'I,' " *Philosophical Quarterly* (1955) for another version of the argument.

96   Cf. *RL*, Chapter 3.

97   *MM*, p. 10.

98   Cf. *RS*, p. 41ff. With respect to both "God" and "I" the question arises as to whether Ramsey has given any reason for taking them as any more than ways of referring to relations among empirically observable events.

99   *Loc. cit.* Cf. John Wisdom, *Other Minds* (New York: Philosophical Library, 1952).

100   The argument assumes that if D were self-referring, type problems would arise parallel to those in the case of "the class of all classes."

101   *M*, p. 18ff; *RS*, p. 72–89; *RL*, Chapter Two.

102 See Everett Hall, *Philosophical Systems* (Chicago: U. of Chicago Press, 1960) p. 7–12 and 55, 56.

103 *MM*, p. 67. Ramsey's phrase is "points to another dimension."

104 The general claim that to exist is to be a possible object of description, and thus of singular reference, is not at issue. For the dispute on that issue, see W. V. O. Quine, "On What There Is," *From a Logical Point of View* (New York: Harper Brothers, 1963); Gottlob Frege, "Concept and Object" in P. Geatch and M. Black, *Translations from the Philosophical Writings of Gottlob Frege* (London: Oxford U. Press, 1952); Everett Hall, *What Is Value?* (New York: Humanities Press, 1952).

BIBLIOGRAPHY ⁓ I

Blackstone, W., *The Problem of Religious Knowledge*. Englewood Cliffs, N.J.: Prentice-Hall, 1963.

Clark, G., *Religion, Reason and Revelation*. Philadelphia: Presbyterian & Reformed Press, 1961.

Ferre, F., *Language, Logic, and God*. New York: Harper & Bros., 1961.

Hepburn, R., *Christianity and Paradox*. London: Watts Press, 1958.

MacIntyre, A., *Difficulties in Christian Belief*. London: SCM Press, 1959.

————, *Metaphysical Beliefs*. London: SCM Press, 1957.

Mascall, E. L., *Existence and Analogy*. Hamden, Conn.: Archon Books, 1967.

Trap, W., *Divine Personality*. Ann Arbor: G. Wahr, 1927.

Wolfson, H. A., "Albinus and Plotinus on Divine Attributes," *Harvard Theological Review*, Vol. 45 (1952), p. 115–130.

————, "Avicenna, Algazali and Averroes on Divine Attributes" *Homeja a Millas-Vallicrosa*. Barcelona: Consejo Superior de Investigaciones Cientificas, 1954, p. 545–571.

————, "Crescas on the Problem of Divine Attributes," *Jewish Quarterly Review* (New Series) Vol. 7 (1916), p. 1–44 and p. 175–221.

————, "The Amphibolous Terms in Aristotle, Arabic Philosophy and Maimonides," *Harvard Theological Review*, Vol. 31 (1938), p. 151–171.

————, "Infinitive and Privative Judgments in Aristotle, Averroes and Kant," *Philosophy and Phenomenological Research*, Vol. 8 (1947), p. 173–187.

————, "Maimonides on Negative Attributes," in *Louis Ginsberg Jubilee Volume*. New York: The American Academy of Jewish Research, 1945, p. 411–446.

————, "Negative Attributes in the Church Fathers and the Gnostic Basilides," *Harvard Theological Review*, Vol. 50 (1957) p. 145–156.

————, "St. Thomas on Divine Attributes," in *Melanges Offerts a E. Gilson*, p. 673–700. Toronto: Pontifical Institute of Medieval Studies, 1959.

—————, "The Knowability and Describability of God in Plato and Aristotle," *Harvard Studies in Classical Philology,* 1947, p. 233–249.

—————, "The Muslim Attributes and the Christian Trinity," *Harvard Theological Review,* Vol. 49 (1956).

—————, "The Aristotelian Predicables and Maimonides Division of Attributes," *Essays and Studies in Memory of Linda Miller* New York (1938).

—————, "Maimonides and Gersonides on Divine Attributes as Ambiguous Terms," *Mordecai M. Kaplan Jubilee Volume* (1953).

II

THE PROBLEM
OF EVIL

THE STRONG AND WEAK FORMULATIONS

A forceful statement of the problem of evil runs as follows.

> Let us assume that God exists, is omnibenevolent (all-good), omnisci-
> ent (all-knowing) and omnipotent (all-powerful). If He is omnibenevo-
> lent, it is often suggested, then He is willing to always prevent evil.
> If He is omniscient, He knows how to do so. If He is omnipotent, then
> He can do so. Hence, if God exists then evil does not. But evil plainly
> does exist. So God does not exist.[1]

This is the strong formulation of the objection; in essence it is claimed
that (A) "God exists" and (B) "There is evil" are logically incompatible, and since the latter statement is true, it follows that the
former statement is false. The strong formulation is successful just in
case an explicit contradiction is derived from (A) and (B) alone, or
from (A) and (B) plus other statements which the theist must accept.
The difficulty of making the strong formulation of the objection into
a refutation of traditional theism is illustrated by the fact that the
above argument is in fact invalid: the conclusion can be false even
though all the premises are true.[2] We will discuss the strong formulation in some detail.

There is also a weak formulation of the objection. The logical structure of this formulation is simple: if there is evil, it is improbable
that God exists; But there is evil; So it is improbable that God exists.

The interest of this objection lies in the discussion of the conditional premise "if there is evil, it is improbable that God exists." Thus it is with this premise that our discussion of the weak formulation will be chiefly concerned.

The strong formulation asserts that an explicit contradiction arises when one conjoins the following claims:

(A)   God exists
(B)   God is omnipotent
(C)   God is omniscient
(D)   God is omnibenevolent
(E)   There is evil in the world.

We must first say something about the meaning of omnipotence.[3] For God to be omnipotent is not for God to be able to perform any action whose description is contradictory. Rather, to say that God is omnipotent is to say that, for any sentence S, if:

(a)   S is not contradictory
(b)   S is not absurd and
(c)   "God makes S true" is not contradictory

then God can make S true. An example of each sort of sentence ruled out by this definition may be helpful. "This object is round and square" is self-contradictory; thus God cannot make that sentence true of some object. "Sausages spell better than giraffes" is absurd in an easy to recognize but hard to define manner; so God cannot make this sentence true. "The world was not created" does not seem to be either self-contradictory or absurd, but God cannot create a world that is not created since it is contradictory to say that God made a world that was not made. This should be sufficient to indicate what is meant by omnipotence. It should be noted that any ambiguity in "absurd" has no especial connection with the problem of defining omnipotence; the problem of stating a criterion of intelligible (nonabsurd) discourse is a generally vexing one in philosophy with no peculiar relevance to the concept of omnipotence.

It will suffice for our purposes to briefly characterize what is meant by omniscience. To say that God is omniscient is to say that if sentence S is true, and if it is logically possible that S be known to be true, then God knows S.

The notion of omnibenevolence will be dealt with to some extent in the discussion that follows, but it will be helpful to suggest part of its meaning at the outset. It has been claimed that "good" and hence "all-good" or "omnibenevolent" cannot be applied to God in any sense analogous to that in which it is applied to human beings.

Sometimes this is defended on the general ground that no description of God can be given; if this is so, it is difficult to see how theism is even possible, but that issue is a complex one distinct from the one now under discussion.[4]

A different defense of this claim about goodness as applied to God is the argument that the Ten Commandments do not apply to God. He cannot steal, for "the cattle on a thousand hills" are His; i.e., the world is His creation so that all things belong to Him. He obviously cannot commit idolatry or adultery. It would make no sense to say that God had done any of these things. This is true, but is by no means sufficient to support the weight placed upon it. Consider, for example, the claim that God cannot lie. Here is a commandment that would seem to apply to God. It is useful to see in what sense it does and in what sense it does not.

First, it is obviously not the case that this commandment, or any other, applies to God in the sense that He is accountable to some superior authority for His conduct or subject to the decree of any other being. Nonetheless, that God cannot lie is relevant in the discussion of His omnibenevolence in a way that His not being able to commit idolatry is not. We can conceive of a being who was omnipotent and omniscient, but evil and thus not omnibenevolent. Such a being might, for example, promise heaven for all who trusted Him in certain specific ways and then send all who did trust him in those ways to hell just for spite. But we cannot, I suggest, conceive of such a being worshipping or committing idolatry, for were he omnipotent he would not depend on anything for his existence and worship is appropriate only for contingent, limited creatures.

It is not hard to see the model from which divine omnibenevolence is extrapolated. A good father does not lie to his children if he can help it; God will never lie to His children since being omnipotent He can always help it. A good father will not let his children suffer is he can prevent it; God will not let his children suffer if He can prevent it, and He always can, since He is omnipotent.[5] What a good father is, with his limitations of power and knowledge, the Heavenly Father is, with no limitations of power and knowledge. Of course no earthly father is completely good but we can let that pass. Enough should have been said by now to indicate what omnibenevolence means and to reveal how it is consideration of that divine attribute that leads us directly into the problem of evil.

I shall take it that the willful causing of human suffering for its own sake and the killing of a human being for the sake of some pleasure derived therefrom are evil actions in the sense that the man who freely and knowingly performs them is morally culpable. Hurri-

canes that take human life and cancers which cause suffering if not
death are evils in the sense that a being who created a world with
them when he could have created a world without them with no loss
of over-all balance of good over evil would be an evil or malevolent
being. If this is not so, then it is difficult to see what sort of problem
of evil there might be. Thus the meaning, and the truth, of "there is
evil" seems sufficiently clear.[6]

We have now discussed the original set of statements in terms of
which the problem of evil is most often initially formulated. The
theist is committed to the truth of (A) through (D), and (E) is patently
true. In fact, the theist is committed to (E) as well; witness the Old
Testament recognition of the fact that the wicked prosper and per-
secute the righteous or the New Testament doctrine of the Atonement. If a formal contradiction can be derived from (A-E), I take it
that theism is, in its orthodox formulation, refuted. One could at best
have a God who was very powerful but not omnipotent, or very knowledgeable but not omniscient, or very good but not perfectly so, or
some combination of these. Further, I take it as obvious that (A-E)
alone do not entail any formal contradiction. This is so even if we add:

(F)   God created the world.

The question now arises as to whether any further statements can
be added to (A-F) which will yield a formal contradiction. Any statements added to this list must fulfill one at least of these conditions:
(a) it must be a necessary truth, or (b) it must be an essential tenet
of orthodox theism, or (c) it must be an obvious truth. I know of no
way to specify this last condition precisely. Nonetheless, if we could
add "There are people who weigh over 100 pounds" to (A-F) and
produce a formal contradiction from the conjunction of this claim
with (A-F), then I am sure that we would have refuted theism. This
will be the case if the addition of any statement as obviously true as
"There are people weighing over 100 pounds" to (A-F) will enable us
to derive a contradiction from (A-F) plus that claim.

SHOULD EVILS ALWAYS BE PREVENTED?

In the absence of any formal contradiction with respect to (A-F), it
might be suggested, we need only add the following propositions to
our list.

(G)   An omnibenevolent being will always do what is good if he can.

(H)   An omnipotent, omnibenevolent being can always do what is
       good.

(I)   It is always good to prevent evil.

(J)   An omnipotent, omniscient being will always prevent evil.

(A-D) and (F-J) entail "There is no evil in the world" which is the denial of (E). So the set (A-J) is logically inconsistent. Hence, if (G-J) all satisfy one of the three criteria mentioned above, a refutation of traditional theism has been provided.

(G) and (H) would both seem to be necessary truths, (G) eliciting further what is involved in the notion of omnibenevolence and (H) following from (G) and (B). (J) follows from (G), (H), and (I). Thus the crucial premise is (I). Now (I) is neither a necessary truth nor an essential tenet of theism, nor is (I) an obvious truth. This follows from the fact that, as it stands, (I) is obviously false. That (I) is false can be shown quite simply.

In any one of cases W through Z, it will be false that it is good to prevent evil E:

W: the prevention of E will also prevent some good G which is of equal value to the nonexistence of E and for which E is a logically necessary condition.

X: the prevention of E will entail the existence of E' which is as evil as E.

Y: the prevention of E will also prevent some good G which is of greater value than the nonexistence of E and for which E is a logically necessary condition.

Z: the prevention of E will entail the existence of E' which is a greater evil than E and for which the nonexistence of E is a logically sufficient condition.

In cases W and X, it is permissible, but not obligatory, to prevent E. Thus in such cases the prevention of E is neither good nor evil. In cases Y and Z, the prevention of E is not permissible, and the permission of E is obligatory. The prevention of E in such cases is evil, not good. Thus (I) must be replaced by (I'): It is always good to prevent evil if the evil that one prevents can be prevented without causing any equivalent evil, without preventing any good which is of equal value with the nonexistence of the evil prevented, without prevent· ing a good whose value outweighs the evil that one prevents, and without precipitating any evil which is worse than the evil prevented.[7]

Now providing that cases W, X, Y and Z describe all the kinds of cases in which the permission of the existence of an evil is either morally permissible or morally obligatory, (I') replaces (I). What follows from this set is "Every evil there is exists in a context which satisfies the description of W, or of X, or of Y, or of Z." And this claim is plainly consistent with (E).

It is dubious that cases W, X, Y and Z exhaust the instances of evil which it would not be good to prevent. It is plausible that evils arising from the free choices of moral agents are evils it would not be good to prevent. This topic will be considered shortly. First an important feature of cases W, X, Y and Z must be mentioned and emphasized.

While the elaboration of possible cases of W, X, Y, Z, will be left as an exercise for the reader, there is one proviso to be made with respect to these cases. It is obvious that if a father can prevent his daughter from taking a penny from her mother's purse only by shooting her, the cost of preventing the evil of stealing is too great to justify his firing the shot. It is obvious that if the pain of drilling will be no greater than the pain of an injection of Novacaine, the dentist is under no obligation to administer the drug. But it is logically possible that the daughter not steal the penny or be prevented from doing so by less radical means than those suggested. It is also logically possible that the injection be painless, or that the drilling be painless. While the father and the dentist are limited by their resources and the causal laws which govern our world, God's resources are, by definition, unlimited and He is not limited to doing what accords with causal law. The connection between any evil that God permits and the good which justifies the existence of that evil must be a logical one; it must be logically impossible for the good to exist in the absence of the evil in question. The most frequently suggested instance of such an evil is that of the possibility of evil or wrong choices made by free agents;[8] insofar as it is a logically necessary condition of there being moral value that there be free agents, and insofar as it is logically necessary for there being free agents that they be fully capable of making evil choices, the existence of the possibility of evil choices is a logically necessary condition of there being any moral value. Whether such choices are made will be up to the free agent capable of making them, and to him alone. This particular example of at least the possibility of an evil often said to be a logically necessary condition of a far greater moral good, namely free and mature moral agents, provides a consideration relevant to the next stage of our argument.

THE NOTION OF A "BEST POSSIBLE WORLD"

Thus far, no proposition has been added to the set which both meets at least one of the requirements, and yields a contradiction within the new set which results when it is added. Let us try again. Consider:

(K) An omniscient, omnipotent, omnibenevolent being is one who would create a world with the highest logically possible amount of moral value.

(L) No world containing evil is a world containing the highest logically possible amount of moral value.

Now (A-J), with (I′) replacing (I), together with (K) and (L) entail that "There is no evil in the world," for the world was, according to this set of claims, created by God who is omnipotent and omniscient and omnibenevolent. But this sentence is the denial of (E) which is a member of the set. Hence the set contains (E) but entails not-(E); so the set is inconsistent. Thus, if (K) and (L) each meet at least one of the aforementioned conditions, the orthodox theist is refuted.

So far from being true, however, that (K) meets one of those conditions, it can be shown that (on an assumption perfectly open to the theist) (K) is self-contradictory. The argument that (K) is, on this assumption, self-contradictory is this one.

(1) It is a logically necessary condition of any world in which there is moral value that there be free agents in that world. This is the assumption.

(2) It is a logically necessary condition of the world with the greatest possible amount of moral value that there be free agents in that world. (from 1)

(3) It is logically impossible that God, in a world where there are free agents, prevent that any evil choices are made. (since then the agents would not be free)

(4) It is logically impossible that God, in the world containing the highest possible amount of moral value, prevent evil choices from being made. (from 2 and 3)

(5) In the world containing the highest possible amount of moral value there would be no evil choices made. (self-evident)

(6) It is logically impossible that God create the world containing the highest possible amount of moral value. (from 4 and 5)

Thus, while God could create the conditions in which free agents can become good men, he cannot guarantee that they do become good men without destroying their freedom and thus (cf. premise 1) the moral value of the world which contains them. Hence, if (1) is true, (K) is false.[9] (K) presupposes that God could create the world with the highest possible amount of moral value (for if He could not create such a world it is false that we can infer from the notion of an omnipotent and omnibenevolent being that he would create such a world). But it is false, if (1) is true, that he could. So if (1) is true it is false that He would (that his creating this world can be inferred from his omnipotence and omnibenevolence). So the theist can admit

(L) but must deny (K). He need not admit (L), but he can do so. The set composed of (A-L), minus (K), entails no contradiction.

It is not necessary to show that (1) is true. Philosophers have disagreed profoundly about the logically necessary conditions of freedom.[10] There is no need to discuss their arguments here. The point is simply that it is open to the theist to accept (1)—and also (3) which is equally necessary to the argument. It is open to him in the sense that it is consistent with the other claims that he makes.[11] It is also open to him in the sense that a good many theologians and philosophers have developed powerful conceptual schemes on this basis.

At this point it seems clear that the attempt to make the strong formulation of the problem of evil into a clear refutation of theism is doomed to failure. Immensely complicated problems arise as to the truth of (1) and (3); these ramify into problems of freedom, determinism, theory of agency and agent causality, etc., in metaphysics, and the connections between freedom, determinism, and obligation in ethics. An impasse may well develop and if so it is clear that the theist will not thereby have been refuted. What does emerge, for our purposes, is simply that the theist may assert that (1) and (3) are true. He will then reject (K). He may adopt (L) if he pleases. But only if he adopts (K) does his system become inconsistent, and there seems to be no reason at all why he must adopt (K).

A brief word is in order concerning the concept of a "best (logically) possible world" which occurs in both (K) and (L). There is some reason to doubt that this concept is in fact coherent. It is not coherent unless there is some world W such that there is no good G such that were G to be added to W, W would be a better world. In short, a world is the best logically possible just in case it contains all possible goods. All things being equal, if W_1 contains 1,000 goods and W_2 contains 1,001 goods, then W_2 is better than W_1. But it has been argued that for any world containing n number of goods there is a possible world just like it save that it contains $n+1$ goods. So for any world we can conceive, we can also conceive a possible better one. Namely, a world containing one good more. If all this is so, then there is no logical upper limit on the number of goods a world can contain and so no best logically possible world. Hence the notion of a best logically possible world is incoherent.[12]

This argument does not seem to me to be conclusive. Possibly there are kinds of goods which are logically incompatible in the sense that no universe could contain them both. Perhaps it is good that all human choices be guaranteed to be right ones and also good that all human choices be freely made. No universe could contain both, and if the latter is a greater good then it is better that the former good not exist.

Perhaps, then, there is a finite number of kinds of goods, and/or a finite number of kinds of goods consistent with one another.

But even if this is so, a further difficulty besets the concept of a best logically possible world. There must be, it would seem, a finite number of kinds of compatible goods for this concept to be coherent. Otherwise, for any number n of kinds of compatible goods a universe contains, there is a better universe possible—one just like it save that it contains $n+1$ kinds of compatible goods.[13] Supposing there to be a finite number of kinds of compatible goods, then, must the best logically possible world contain as many instances as possible of each kind of good? Even if an event or entity can be an instance of more than one kind of compatible good, perhaps there is no limit on the number of instances of kinds of compatible goods there can be, and so we run into problems precisely analogous to those already encountered.

To elucidate by means of a single familiar example, suppose it is good that there be free moral agents. Then presumably a world containing 1,001 such agents is better, all things being equal, than one containing only 1,000. But there does not seem to be any logical upper limit on the number of agents that might exist. Nor will it do to say that there would be an infinite number of such agents in the best possible world, for in the present context this is to suggest that the number of free agents be expressed by the highest prime number and there is no such number. So for any number n of free agents in a world, presumably it could have been made better by God having placed $n+1$ such agents in it. But then it would be logically impossible for God to create a world with the highest possible number of agents. Hence it is no objection to say that He did not.

The upshot of this discussion is, I think, that the question as to whether the concept of a best logically possible world is or is not coherent is undecided. Perhaps there is a logical upper limit on the number of instances of compatible goods a universe can contain. To say that there is a logical upper limit on the number of instances of good G a universe U can contain is to say that there is a number n such that the statement "U contains more than n instances of G" is self-contradictory. Perhaps there is not. Very likely, no one knows. So whether there can be a best logically possible world is, shall we say, not something about which we can pronounce with complete confidence. So no objections based on this concept can carry much weight.

It is, of course, clear that if a world consists of just one thing and that thing is good, the proportion of good in that world is perfect. And one might argue that at least we can say that God would create a universe with this sort of proportion of good. This is so just in case it is clear that there is no good G of high value to which some evil E is logically requisite—else a best possible world will contain just such a good, and so also contain its requisite evil and thus not have perfect proportion of goodness. But it is by no means clear that there is no good G of high value to which an evil E is logically requisite.

EVIL AND PROBABILITY

It is by now quite dubious that the strong formulation has much prospect of success. So let us turn now to the "weak formulation" of the problem of evil, namely:

(1) If there is evil, it is probable that God does not exist.
(2) There is evil. So:
(3) It is probable that God does not exist.

As we have noted, (1) is the crucial premise.

We begin our evaluation of (1) by remembering that under certain circumstances,[14] evil was justified in the sense that the fact that evil existed in those circumstances was not evidence at all that God did not exist. But this raises a severe problem about (1), for the evil specified in (1) must include either only justified evil, or only unjustified evil, or evil of both sorts. Thus, letting "P" represent "it is probable that God does not exist," (1) must mean one or another of these things:

(1a) If there is justified evil, then P.
(1b) If there is unjustified evil, then P.
(1c) If there is justified evil, and also unjustified evil, then P.

But none of these is true. (1a) will not do, since the fact that there is justified evil is no evidence at all that God does not exist, and hence does not make it at all probable that He does not. (1b) will not do, for it is too weak. If there is unjustified (pointless) evil, then it follows deductively that God does not exist. The sentence "If there is unjustified (pointless) evil, then God does not exist" is a necessary truth. That is, unjustified evil is logically incompatible with God's existence and so if there is unjustified evil it is not merely probable, it is certain, that God does not exist. And of course (1c) simply combines the defects of (1a) and (1b).

But this does not resolve our problem. It only forces us to alter the weak formulation of the problem. It must now be put as follows:

(A) If there is a great deal of evil, then it is probable that some of it is unjustified.

(B) There is a great deal of evil. So:

(C) It is probable that some of it is unjustified.

(1′) If it is probable that some evil is unjustified, then it is probable that God does not exist. So:

(3) It is probable that God does not exist.

We have thus traded (1′) for (1), dropped (2) altogether, and added (A), (B) and (C). In so doing we provide a valid argument for our original conclusion (3) and it remains only to see if the premises of this argument are true. Since (B) seems unquestionably so, and (C) follows from (A) and (B), it is (A) that must receive our attention.[15]

It would be easy to accept (A) on the basis of its grammatical similarity to these other sentences:

(A1) There are many apples in the orchard, so probably some have worms in them.

(A2) There are many pennies in the box, so probably some of them bear the date 1957.

(A3) There are many children in the school, so probably some of them have poor hearing.

(A4) There are many books in the library, so probably some of them are in a foreign language.

Under quite familiar conditions that we could all specify, these inferences are perfectly justified. It will be worth the effort to briefly note, though, the pattern of reasoning such inferences involve.

Suppose I pick all the apples on one tree, and separate them into two piles: those with worms and those without. Suppose there conveniently happen to be 100 apples on the tree of which 10 have worms. Having counted all the apples, I am able by what is technically called *induction by exhaustive enumeration* to make the claim that 1 of every 10 of these apples is worm-inhabited. If there are 1,000 trees in the orchard, and I count and sort the apples on 600 of them, and find that when I pile all the wormless apples in one stack and all the worm-inhabited apples in another, this ratio of 1 apple in 10 containing at least one worm is sustained, I may wish to infer something about the apples on the other 400 trees; namely, that 1 out of every 10 of the apples on those trees will contain a worm.

Two things stand out clearly from this example. First, I must be able to specify just which apples are worm-inhabited and which are not in order to proceed with my inductive argument. Second, there is no problem at all about what the criterion is for being worm-inhabited or in how to apply it. Analogous remarks would obviously fit any example selected for (A2), (A3) or (A4).

Now let us consider a case relevant to (A). We have already characterized an unjustified evil as one which does not fit any of cases W, X, Y and Z. Let us consider case (Y), a case of an evil E prevention of which will also prevent some good G which is of greater value than the nonexistence of E and for which E is a logically necessary condition. It may be helpful to offer an example of this kind of case. Suppose we grant the following claims for the purpose of illustration.

(1) A world containing morally virtuous men is more desirable than one that does not.
(2) Moral virtue is logically impossible without such things as temptation, pain, and the like.[16]

Therefore:

(3) It is morally more desirable that such things as temptation, pain, and the like exist than that they not exist.

If we grant (1) and (2)—from which (3) follows—then we are saying that such things as temptation, pain, etc., which are certainly evil in case they serve no purpose, are justified insofar as they make possible moral virtue. At least this is so if we assume that moral virtue with the evils mentioned is morally more desirable than the absence of these evils with the consequent absence of moral virtue.

There are some issues that require brief mention in the context of this example. One is whether the chance or possibility of virtue is enough to justify temptation, pain, etc. or whether they are justified only by actually achieved virtue. Either contention will illustrate our case (Y). Again, one might ask if one ought to call justified evils "evil" any more. Here the issue seems purely verbal; we have been using the locution "justified evil" as meaning "anything which would be evil were it to serve no purpose." For an evil to "serve a purpose" in this context simply means for it to fit one of cases W, X, Y or Z. What counts here is not how one uses his words but only that he attach a clear sense to them. Finally, it is not my purpose here to defend or attack the truth of the premises mentioned which provide our illustration.

Now if we consider the task of deciding whether an evil is justified or not in the sense of fitting (Y) or failing to do so, two things stand out clearly. First, I must be able to sort out evils into these classes in order to mount any such argument as that proposed in the weak formulation of the problem of evil. Second, at least often there is no clear-cut criterion for deciding whether a given case of evil fits (Y) or not. Of course if the evil in question is a tidal wave resulting in the death of Brown, that evil will not result in Brown's increased virtue. Then the question will be whether the evil fits any of the other kinds of cases mentioned. Severe pain is a harder case; often it merely produces bitterness but sometimes it produces remarkable depth of character. Whether it could do the latter in cases where it does not is hard to say. If it could, and if providing the opportunity for greater virtue justifies what is logically necessary to provide this opportunity, at least within certain limits, then many or perhaps all cases of severe pain may be cases of justified evil.

The point to be emphasized is that every case of evil may well be a case covered by W, X, Y or Z, assuming these to exhaust the cases where evil would be justified. There is certainly a problem, and likely an insuperable one, in showing that a given case of evil fits none of these cases. But if this is so, then we cannot sort out even a limited range of evils into those which are justified and those which are not. And if this is so, then we have no justification for (A). But this raises an issue worth further reflection.

Reservations concerning this defense of (A) might be expressed along the following lines. We can make sense, it is suggested, of discovering that an evil is justified. We can observe that a man is in great pain over a prolonged period, and that he gains during this period a depth of character he did not previously possess. He recovers, and ever after during a long life is far more compassionate and self-giving than he was before. Given experience of a sufficient number of similar cases, one could argue on inductive grounds that the pain was at least a partial cause, and so a causally necessary condition, of the change of character and on moral grounds that the pain in these cases was justified, providing that producing this change of character was best brought about in this manner. When such features as these are present, we find the rough, but intelligible criteria for justified pain to be satisfied—at least if there were no less costly way of attaining the character development in question. Now when we do not find these rough but intelligible criteria to be satisfied—say, when there is no character change at all, or one for the worse, or where the person dies quickly—then it is reasonable to conclude that the pain in such cases is an unjustified evil. At least, this conclusion is as reasonable as the conclusion that, in the other cases, the pain was justified. This assumes that pointless pain is evil in the sense that a being who permitted it would not be unqualifiedly good; but this assumption seems correct.

The principle underlying this argument is something like this: if the fact that criterion C is satisfied in cases a, b, c, etc. justifies our saying that a, b, c, etc. all are cases of P, then the fact that C is not satisfied in cases x, y, z, etc. justifies our denying that x, y, z, etc. are cases of P. This is patently true, so long as C is exhaustive with respect to the features something must have in order to be P (i.e., disjunctively includes all the P-sufficient conditions). The question arises, however, as to whether one can state any exhaustive criterion for being a justified evil—at least in other than the general terms already suggested. There is no reason whatever to suppose that the only situation which justifies pain is the actual attainment of a better character in the sufferer or in someone else. Of course one can point to cases where a painful death came too quickly for character change to be possible; and there is animal pain as well. But we do not know of any set of sufficient conditions which is possessed by every (or any) case of animal pain and which is such that any state of affairs possessing those conditions is, if evil at all, a justified evil. Of course the theist is at a loss to explain such cases in the sense of showing what God's purposes are in these matters. But why is he at a loss? Perhaps simply because he does not view the world *sub specie aeternitatis*; he is not gifted with God's point of view. There is, however, no reason to suppose that this fact is detrimental to theism. What would be detrimental would be for there to be justified confidence on the critic's part that he had an exhaustive criterion for being a justified evil which some case of evil did not satisfy. But, obviously enough, the possession of such a criterion would also require that its possessor come close to being able to view the world *sub specie aeternitatis*. That anyone does possess an exhaustive criterion for justified evil which he knows not to be satisfied by a case of evil is, to put it mildly, highly dubious.

The response to the reservation under review is this. While we can state some conditions which, when possessed by a case of evil, may be sufficient to justify that case of evil, we cannot state a set of such justifying conditions known to be anything like exhaustive. So while we can know, or have reason to believe, that some cases of evil are justified, we cannot know or have good reason to believe that some case of evil is not justified, though we can know or have good reason to believe that a case of evil does not possess a particular set of conditions which, were it to possess them, would justify it. I have not discussed problems about deciding that a particular set of conditions are satisfied by a case of evil, and about deciding that a particular set of conditions do justify any case of evil possessing them. While important, these are substantially problems of detail; at least, they are less basic than the ones we have been discussing.

One might object to the whole defense of theism against the last objection in some such terms as these. Suppose that in a given case prolonged pain and deepened moral character go together in such a way that the latter is a causally necessary condition of the former. Still, this won't justify the pain, since God is not bound by causal laws and could substitute some other condition for the pain which would result in the deepened moral character. The pain is not, as is required, a logically necessary condition of the deepened moral character, and, it might be suggested, the case can be put in general terms about other evils which are, or are taken to be, causally requisite to goods.

Several points should be made in response. First, as we noted above, pain is a logically necessary condition of fortitude, fear of courage, etc.

Second, it might be suggested, it is not that pain produces a deepened moral character that justifies it. Rather, it is man's (free) reaction to pain. What could be done to give maximal opportunity for that reaction being positive is not limited by logic alone. It is also restricted by what will leave the person in question still free, by what the person has chosen in the past, and the like. This will make the calculations as to what states of affairs will provide maximal chance for moral development in a given case overwhelmingly difficult. This is another circumstance that makes it seem quite appropriate to many theists to be chary of judging an evil to be unjustified.

Third, let us suppose that a given evil E is not a logically necessary condition of G, given the circumstances C. Contrary to the present objection, the theist need not admit that E is unjustified in such a situation. For he can hold that (a) there is a set S of states of affairs such that every member of S is an evil, and S disjunctively contains all of the states of affairs which are necessary conditions of G and that no member of S is less evil than E, or (a') S disjunctively contains all the states of affairs which are necessary conditions of G and there is no member of S which in conjunction with G produces a whole as valuable as the conjunct of E and G. He can add the necessary truth that (b) if G is to exist, then some member or other of S must exist. So (c) the existence of E is justified if (d) there is no good of greater value than G which could, so to speak, replace G with an overall balance of good over evil. So E can be justified, even though E is not a logically necessary condition of G, or of any other good. And while the theist may well be hard pressed to prove, other than by appeal to the truth of theism, that (d) is true or that (c) is, the critic will be equally hard pressed to prove, other than by appeal to the falsity of theism, that (d) is false or that (c) is. It is thus not necessary for an evil to be justified that it be a logically necessary condition of some good.

There is another defense of (A) which is worth considering. It begins by taking exception to the previous account of inductive arguments (i.e., of arguments which lend probability to their conclusion). Thus far we have, in effect, been assuming a frequency theory of probability.[17]

> According to the frequency theory, probability is a matter of statistics . . . Applying the frequency theory to the probability of causes, the statement that the probability of A being the cause of X is 1/n means that X is a member of a class of objects (or events) this proportion of which (namely, 1/n) are known to have been caused by A's.[18]

So if the occurrence of Dutch Elm disease is in 90 of 100 cases fatal to an elm tree, and if the elm tree in my yard has the disease, the odds are nine to one that I lose my elm tree. But there is another view of what it is to lend probability to a conclusion by giving a nondeductive argument for it.

> On this view a proposition is probable, not in isolation but in relation to other evidence-stating propositions. A judgment of probability thus presupposes a corpus of (actual or hypothetical) items of information (p,q,r) such that belief in these prior propositions authorizes belief in a further proposition (x); and the strength or confidence of the belief thus authorized is the measure (although not a measure capable of precise numerical statement) of the probability of x in relation to p, q and r.[19]

Thus to say that Gunkel probably was the one who shot Smith since only he had a motive is not on this account of probability to say that a statistical correlation exists between having a motive to do something and doing it, but to say that on certain assumptions (e.g., a killer always *has* a motive) the fact that Smith was shot by Gunkel explains the fact that Smith was shot. Again, to say that the fact that there is so much evil in the world is evidence against the existence of God is not to claim statistical correlation between the class of all evils and the class of unjustified evils. It is rather to record the fact that the explanation of so many evils seems patently impossible if one assumes that God exists. Many of the evils we encounter do seem absolutely pointless; surely we cannot always be wrong? And if we were always wrong, wouldn't that fact too be inexplicable on the theistic view? So, the argument concludes, belief in God is unreasonable in the face of all the evil the world contains.

We can best appraise this defense of (A) by comparing it to another quite similar appeal to what seems, to others, equally unreasonable. There is a familiar passage in the concluding section of Hume's *Dialogues Concerning Natural Religion* which perfectly illustrates the attitude of those who find the argument from at least apparent design in the universe to a Designer inescapable. It is all the more worth quoting since Hume puts it into the mouth of the avowed sceptic Philo.

> A purpose, an intention, a design strikes everywhere the most careless, the most stupid thinker; and no man can be so hardened in absurd systems as at all times to reject it. *That nature does nothing in vain* is a maxim established in all the schools, merely from the contemplation of Nature, without any religious purpose; . . . and thus all sciences almost lead us insensibly to acknowledge a first intelligent author; and their authority is often so much the greater as they do not directly profess that intention . . . if the infidelity of Galen, even when the natural sciences were still imperfect, could not withstand such striking appearances, to what pitch of pertinacious obstinacy must a philosopher in this age have attained who can now doubt of a Supreme Intelligence?[20]

The regularity of the seasons, the complexity of the human body and the orderly behavior of natural objects have impressed laymen with a sense of the work of a designer, just as the fact that natural science is even possible has impressed many scientists with the sense of "thinking God's thoughts after Him."[21] It is this impression that Hume records in the passage just quoted. It is the same sort of impression that leads others, and sometimes the same persons, to feel that the existence of so much evil is more than theism can bear. In neither case need it be claimed, though it sometimes is, that the evidence entails or in a precise sense makes probable the existence or non-existence of God. Rather, in the sense required by the present defense of (A), after considering the evil in the world, much of which has no very obvious point, one is impressed with the unreasonableness of theism. Just so, after considering the wealth of order amongst variety and the phenomenon of genuine human friendship or love one is impressed with the reasonableness of theism. The kind of impression involved here seems to me to be well described by F. R. Tennant.

> Probability, in the last resort, is a matter of the downright alogical, the psychologically inevitable, the vaguely-called instinctive, . . . our corpus of so-called knowledge is at bottom non-cognitive. Reasonableness is thus largely non-rational. If probability be the measure of belief that is reasonable, or one's moral duty to entertain, reasonableness and morality in this connection consist *ultimately* in being alogical in one way rather than another.[22]

Waiving the question as to whether all probability-claims fit this description, it seems obvious that the sort of defense of (A) which has been offered amounts to just this sort of alogical probability or alogical reasonableness. So does the viewpoint expressed in the quotation from Hume.

If this is so, then since, as we have seen, the impressions connected with alogical reasonableness lead us sometimes toward, and sometimes away from, theism, no one impression of this sort has evidential value unless it is clearly superior to any other one of the same sort. But such clear superiority seems to be ruled out by the nature of these impressions. Even upon the most careful reflection, is it at all clear that we can determine which impression—that stemming from the fact of much evil of which a large proportion seems pointless or that stemming from the fact of great order amongst vast variety seemingly evident in natural phenomena and the great value of such a phenomenon as that of genuine love—gives us the right clue as to the nature of the universe? If there is any point at which rational disagreement or at least disagreement which does not make either side irrational is possible, it is in just this sort of case. But of course if this is so, then no defense of (A) along the lines we have been considering which will establish (A) *in such a manner as to refute theism* is possible. If there is room for disagreement among rational and intelligent men with respect to (A), and there patently is, then surely no justification for (A) has been found. It is not the point, on this defense of (A), that there are reasons which some men are blind to which others see, or even that there are impressions that some men have that others do not.[23] It is rather that some men do find such alogical reasonableness compelling in a given case and some do not. Some men find this alogical reasonableness so compelling in one case when they note the order of nature and the values of human experience that they are relatively unaffected by any impressions arising from the fact that there are many evils which seem pointless to us; others are so compelled by the latter that they are relatively unimpressed by the former. Still others may be unwilling to draw any conclusion from such impressions or even fail to have any such impressions. But plainly, under such circumstances as these, it is impossible to correctly say that one group is justified over the other. So (A) is thus far not justified.

There is another question to be raised. Consider a universe slightly different from our own. In it, no man can succeed in committing a murder, although he can attempt it. This might be arranged in various ways. A knife, bullet or poison might enter and exit harmlessly. Or an attempted murderer might go limp at the moment of his attempt. Or God might permit a murder and then cancel it out by resurrecting the murdered person. Nor need such a universe require God's frequent interference, since presumably He could create a world in which these events, or events like them, were as causally inevitable as death inevitably follows decapitation in our present world.

Now consider a second feature of this world. When considering whether to attempt a murder or not, the fact that in this universe no such attempt can succeed does not cross his mind and so does not figure in his calculations. This too could be made causally inevitable. In this manner, there is no lack of moral agency; each potential attempted murderer subdues or submits to his temptation, so far as he is aware, under circumstances identical to those which obtain in our universe. True, he cannot in fact murder. He is, however, morally culpable if he makes the attempt and perhaps praiseworthy if he resists the temptation to do so. Even if men having no choice with respect to attempted murder would restrict human moral agency in some undesirable way, the creation of a universe differing from our own in the two indicated respects would not have this effect. One could make similar alterations with theft, adultery, and every other morally wrong action. Why not have this sort of universe rather than our own?

This raises a crucial but difficult question. Would a universe in which wrong actions could be attempted but not performed be one in which there was in fact the most valuable sort of moral agency? One could put the question in this manner: Let the sort of moral agency which exists in our world where evil actions can be performed be moral agency$_1$, and the sort of moral agency which would exist in an altered universe such as the one just noted moral agency$_2$. One is, perhaps, inclined to regard moral agency$_1$ as hardly worth the high price of the actual opportunity for wrong actions as opposed merely to attempts at the same. On the other hand, one may be impressed with an apparent artificiality which attaches to moral agency$_2$. Are agents who can attempt but never perform evil actions really "full-blooded" moral agents?

We have now, in effect, raised two distinct questions. (1) Is moral agency$_2$ superior to moral agency$_1$ in the sense that an omnipotent, omniscient, omnibenevolent being would have created a world containing persons with moral agency$_2$ rather than moral agency$_1$? (2) Would it be in the same sense better that persons have only moral agency$_2$ with respect to some actions (e.g., murder) but perhaps moral agency$_1$ with respect to others?

It is important to notice an ambiguity in the suggestion that it would be better were there no murders. It could mean either (a) it would be better were all men to freely choose to refrain from murder, or (b) it would be better had God not placed the power of murder in anyone's hands. While (a) obviously expresses a state of affairs that would be better, but not one that God could guarantee was brought about, it is not obvious that (b) expresses a state of affairs that would be better than the present one. If (b) is true, it is true in virtue of another universe that God could have created putatively containing more value than this one. But (a) is possibly true without God altering the consequences of free choices; all men could have refrained from choices to murder, or from acts of murder, insofar as they were free in such cases, without anything being altered. That (a) is obviously true is no aid for (b).

One thing should be fairly obvious. The answers to these questions are paradigmatic cases of debatable issues—issues about which men of reason and common sense may disagree. These are questions concerning what may be called second-order moral issues—about whether the possibility of actual murder and its correlative possibility of refraining from actual murder are sufficiently valuable as relevant to moral agency to justify their existence.

One conclusion which follows from this consideration is that no answer to either (1) or (2) is likely to be a plausible candidate for a statement which is a necessary or an obvious truth. Perhaps a theist is committed to the superiority in the indicated sense of moral agency$_1$. But then the superiority of moral agency$_2$ is no tenet of theism, so this produces no problem. Nor is the superiority of moral agency$_2$ a necessary or an obvious truth. Any given answer to (1) or (2) seems an unlikely candidate for producing a refutation of theism.

We have not discovered any formulation of the problem of evil which does in fact refute theism. Not all aspects of the problem, of course, have been discussed; nonetheless, enough has been said to make it clear that turning the fact of evil into a refutation of theism is no easy task. It is by no means obvious that it can be done at all.

One other matter deserves brief mention. It is traditional in discussing the problem of evil to divide evil into two sorts, *moral* and *natural*. Moral evil is evil which results from free human choice, and natural evil is any evil that is not moral. We have not made much use of this distinction for the simple reason that making it seems unnecessary in appraising the success of various formulations of the problem of evil as an attack on traditional theism. It is true that the free will defense is usually at most taken to be adequate as a solution of the problem (i.e. as providing an adequate theistic rebuttal to the problem) only insofar as it concerns moral evil and not as also dealing with natural evil. This limitation of the scope of the free will defense has recently been challenged, and it has been argued that the free will defense can be so developed as to rebut at least the strong formulation of the problem of evil for both sorts of evil.[24] In any case, the crucial question is whether it is certain, or at least more probable than not, that there is unjustified evil, whether natural or moral, and it is on this issue that we have centered our attention.

FOOTNOTES ⌒ II

1 David Hume puts the problem in essentially these terms. See his *Dialogues Concerning Natural Religion*, ed. N. K. Smith (Indianapolis: Bobbs-Merrill, 1947), p. 198.

2 More carefully, it is invalid on any interpretation of its premises which makes those premises true.

3 On the so-called "paradox of omniscience," see J. L. Mackie, "Evil and Omnipotence," *Mind*, Vol. LXIV (1955); G. Mavrodes, "Some Puzzles Concerning Omnipotence," *Philosophical Review*, Vol. LXXII (1963); Alvin Plantinga, *God and Other Minds* (Ithaca: Cornell U. Press, 1967), p. 168ff.

4 Cf. the discussion of Ramsey's view in Chapter One.

5 It is, of course, far from clear that no good father will, under any conceivable conditions, knowingly say what is false to his children or permit them to suffer. This will be discussed shortly; for now, I simply wish to indicate how the problem of evil arises.

6 That evil is "only apparent" plainly will not do as an objection. "Appearances of evil," if this phrase is intelligible, will themselves be evil.

7 (I′) ought actually to read: It is permissable to prevent evil E if preventing E will not entail any evil E′ such that E′ is worse than E or entail the non-existence of any good G such that G's existence is better than E's nonexistence. It is good to prevent an evil E if E's prevention is not merely permissable and if preventing E does not entail the nonexistence of some good G which is of greater value than E's nonexistence nor does E's prevention entail the existence of some evil E′ such that E′ is worse than E.

8 Others are, e.g., fear as logically requisite to courage and pain as logically requisite to fortitude.

9 It is also necessary that (3) be true. Also, the theist might simply point out that there may be some good or goods G of great value to which an evil E is logically requisite, and that no world could be the best possible unless it contained G. He would then be denying that (L) is true.

10 One can sample these disputes in such volumes as S. Hook, ed., *Determinism and Freedom in the Age of Modern Science* (New York: Collier Books, 1961); K. Lehrer, ed., *Freedom and Determinism* (Chicago: U. of Chicago Press, 1966); B. Berofsky, ed., *Free Will and Determinism* (New York: Harper and Row, 1966).

11 One might dispute this on the ground that omniscience entails foreknowledge which entails determinism and so the absence of freedom in the relevant sense. But it is not at all obvious that foreknowledge does entail determinism.

12 On this issue, see G. Schlesinger, "The Problem of Evil and the Problem of Suffering," *Americal Philosophical Quarterly*, Vol. 1 (1964).

13 This assumes that containing as many kinds of goods as possible is a necessary feature of the best of all possible worlds. To the degree that it is unclear that this is a necessary feature, it is unclear just what might count as such a world.

¹⁴ Cf. our cases W, X, Y, Z above.

¹⁵ It is worth noting that (1′) could be defended as follows: (a) It is a necessary truth that: if there is unjustified evil, then God does not exist. Letting "U" be "there is unjustified evil" and "N" be "God does not exist," we can rephrase (a) by saying: (a′) U entails N (N follows deductively from U) (b) If U entails N, and there is a probability *p* that U is true, then there is also a probability *p* that N is true. So: (1′) If it is probable that U, it is probable that N.

¹⁶ For a careful argument for this thesis, see Ninian Smart, "Omnipotence, Evil and Supermen," *Philosophical Review*, Vol. XXXVI, (1961). Reprinted in Nelson Pike, *God and Evil* (Englewood Cliffs, N.J.: Prentice-Hall, 1964).

¹⁷ For brief, clear introductory discussions of inductive arguments, see Wesley Salmon, *Logic* (Englewood Cliffs, N.J.: Prentice-Hall, 1963) and P. F. Strawson, *Introduction to Logical Theory* (London: Methuen & Co., Ltd., 1952).

¹⁸ John Hick, *Faith and Knowledge*, Sec. Ed. (Ithaca: Cornell U. Press, 1966) p. 136.

¹⁹ *Loc. cit.*

²⁰ C. Hendel, ed., *Hume Selections* (New York: Scribner's, 1955), p. 283ff. Hume's own views on the nature of religion will be discussed in Chapter Three below.

²¹ Cf. "We are fearfully and wonderfully made," "The heavens declare the glory of God the firmament shows His handiwork," *Ps.* 19:1; "We know (God) by his most wise and excellent contrivances of things. . . . All that diversity of natural things which we find suited to different times and places could arise from nothing but the ideas and will of a Being necessarily existing." (Newton, *Philosophical Principles of Natural Mathematics*). "Were there no example in the world of contrivance except that of the *eye*, it would be alone sufficient to support the conclusion which we draw from it, as to the necessity of an intelligent creator." (Paley, *Natural Theology*). Note the compellingness expressed in the words "could arise from nothing but" (Newton) and "the necessity of" (Paley).

²² F. R. Tennant, *Philosophical Theology*, 2 vols. (London: Cambridge U. Press, 1928), Vol. 1, p. 284.

²³ This seems to me to undercut any attempt to wed the two impressions mentioned above by use of the thesis that a finite god exists. The evidential status of both impressions is dubious.

²⁴ By Alvin Plantinga in "The Free Will Defense" in Max Black, ed., *Philosophy in America* (Ithaca: Cornell U. Press, 1965); reprinted in G. Mavrodes and S. Hackett, *Readings in the Philosophy of Religion* (Boston: Allyn and Bacon, 1967).

BIBLIOGRAPHY ⌒ II

Aiken, H., "God and Evil," *Ethics*, Vol. 68 (1958).

Flew, A., "Divine Omnipotence and Human Freedom" in *New Essays in Philosophical Theology*.

———, "Are Ninian Smart's Temptations Irresistible," *Philosophy*, Vol. 37 (1962).

Garve, S., "On Evil and Omnipotence," *Mind*, Vol. 65–66 (1956–57).

Hick, J., *Evils and the God of Love*. New York: Harper and Row, 1966.

Hudson, W. D., "An Attempt to Defend Theism," *Philosophy*, Vol. 37 (1964).

Leibniz, G., *Theodicy*, trans. P. Wiener. New York: Bobbs-Merrill, 1966.

Mackie, J. L., "Theism and Utopia," *Philosophy*, Vol. 37 (1962).

McTaggert, J. M., *Some Dogmas of Religion*. London: Edward Arnold, 1906.

Pike, N., "God and Evil: A Reconsideration," *Ethics*, Vol. 68 (1958).

————, "Plantinga on the Free Will Defense: A Reply," *Journal of Philosophy*, Vol. 63 (1966).

Plantinga, A., "Pike and Possible Persons," *Journal of Philosophy*, Vol. 63 (1966).

Smart, N., "Probably," *Philosophy*, Vol. 37 (1962).

Wisdom, John, "God and Evil," *Mind*, Vol. 44 (1935).

Yandell, Keith, "Ethics, Evils and Theism," *Sophia*, Vol. 8 (1969).

————, "A Premature Farewell to Theism," *Religious Studies*, Vol. 4 (1969).

III

SOME ARGUMENTS FOR
THE EXISTENCE OF GOD

ST. THOMAS AQUINAS:
THE FIRST THREE WAYS

The attempt to prove that God exists and has certain properties is the major task of natural theology. St. Thomas Aquinas was one of the greatest natural theologians. He asks "Whether God exists?" and answers that "The existence of God can be proved in five ways."[1] We will discuss only the first three of the famed "Five Ways." These are so intimately related that they can best be discussed together.

The first way concerns things in motion. To be in motion is to change, so that it is not only change of place that is in question, but any sort of change at all. The basic argument runs as follows:

1) Some things change.
2) Nothing can change itself.
3) There cannot be an infinite series of changed and changing beings.

Therefore:

4) There is a first cause of change which is not itself caused to change. In Aquinas' language, the truth of the first premise is "evident to the senses." We constantly observe things that change. This is, in one sense, obviously true. But, as we shall see very shortly, there is an important ambiguity in the word "change." The other two prem-

ises of the argument are each supported by a sub-proof. In support of his second premise Aquinas offers this sub-proof.

   2a)   To change with respect to a quality is to move from potentiality
          to actuality with respect to that quality.

This premise provides us with a definition of change. To actually have a quality is simply in fact to have it. To potentially have a property is to not in fact have it but to be capable of having it. Thus this paper is *in actuality* with respect to being white, and *in potentiality* with respect to being blue since one could color it blue. But it is not in potentiality with respect to writing upon itself or running a four minute mile, for it could not have these properties.

Given the definition of change just provided, premise one of the first way offers more of an analysis of our everyday perceptual experience than a mere report of such experience. This can be seen quite clearly if we note what is required for anything to change in Aquinas' sense of the word. There must, in the first place, be something (say, A) which does not have a quality Q, but which can have Q. Then the capacity of A for being Q must be actualized by something actually having Q. So change can occur only if there is something—namely, one and the same thing—that exists throughout the change. This is assumed by defining change as Aquinas does when he says "motion is nothing else than the reduction of something from potentiality to actuality."[2] Contrast this, however, with the analysis of change given by David Hume.

   A change in any considerable part of a body destroys its identity; but
   'tis remarkable that where the change is produced *gradually* and *in-
   sensibly* we are less apt to ascribe it to the same effect. The reason can
   plainly be no other, than that the mind, in following the successive
   changes of the body, feels an easy passage from the surveying its condition in one moment to the viewing of it in another, and at no
   particular time perceives any interruption in its actions. From which
   continued perception it ascribes a continued existence and identity to
   the object.[3]

Hume's account of change requires only that there be a perceiver[4] who has one sensory experience and then another one similar to the first, and a third similar to the second, and so on. The perceiver will make an easy passage from what he actually perceives to belief in one thing which was supposedly perceived in the various distinct sensory experiences.[5] That there is any one, constant thing which is perceived at both times is, in Hume's view, a belief we can neither escape having nor rationally justify. The relevant point here is simply this:

Hume's view underlines the important fact that Aquinas is at the out-set engaged in philosophical analysis of our sensory experience. What is said to be evident to the senses is really the product of applying certain concepts to our sensory experience—concepts that play an essential role in a complex philosophical scheme. That something remains the same, besides the perceiver, throughout an alteration in a perceptual field, that things have natures which are partially defined in terms of potentialities, that the cause must resemble the effect—these are claims built into Aquinas' account of change.[6] Even if these claims, and others also required, (e.g. that every change has a cause) are all true, they are plainly not evident to the senses. To reply, as a follower of Aquinas might, that the concepts of potentiality and actuality are abstracted from sensory experience, and so of course alone apply appropriately to it, is but to appeal to a further debatable claim: that these concepts are abstracted, that only they can be, and that only concepts abstracted from sensory experience, and perhaps others compatible with these, are applicable to sensory experience. If we can reformulate or replace the first premise so as to avoid these complex issues and yet have a premise which can bear the required weight in the argument, so much the better. For now, however, let us return to the sub-proof for (2). Aquinas supplements (2a) with:

2b) If A changes B with respect to some quality Q, then A must actually have Q.

2c) Assumption: some entity A changes itself with respect to some quality Q.

2d) If A changes itself with respect to Q, A does not, at the time the change begins, have Q.

2e) If A changes itself with respect to Q, then A has Q at the time the change begins.

The justification of (2d) is that if A has Q, then A cannot cause itself to have Q. If I am six feet tall, then I cannot cause myself to be six feet tall by changing myself in some manner. Now (2e) can also be justified, for it follows from (2b) and the assumption made in (2c). The argument continues:

2f) Nothing can both have and not have a quality at the same time.

2g) Only if something can have a quality and not have it at the same time can that thing change itself with respect to some quality.

2h) So nothing can change itself with respect to any quality.

Now (2f) is self-evident. (2g) follows from (2d) and (2e), and (2f) and (2g) together entail (2h). Thus we apparently have a correct sub-proof for the second premise of our original argument.

That there is an important difficulty with this sub-proof can be seen if we consider the one premise not yet discussed, namely (2b): If A changes B with respect to some Quality Q, A must have Q. It is not difficult to propose some counter-examples. The chemist by combining H and O gets H_2O, or water. But the qualities of water are in no obvious way present in the qualities of H or of O. Even if we talk about atomic rearrangement instead of sensible qualities, it is not clear that the rearrangement which is expressed by H_2O is in any precise sense present in the arrangements expressed by H and O separately.[7] Or consider Suzy, who has been courted for many months by Johnny and has almost given up hope that he will ask for her hand. Yet one June evening he pops the question and Suzy faints from delighted shock. What is there in Johnny and his asking the question which constitutes actually having the property of Suzy's fainting? Must a hamburger and shake have the quality of feeling full if they cause me to have this quality? More carefully, what in the total conditions preceding or surrounding Suzy's fainting or my feeling full has the relevant properties? Insofar as (2b) is clear, it seems false. At the very least, it is far too much to say that (2b) is self-evident, or even that one must suppose it to be true. Surely, the second premise of the sub-proof is not intended to entail an affirmative answer to the questions we raised. The problem is that insofar as (2b) is clear in meaning, it does precisely this.

In order to state (2b) in a more acceptable fashion, reference to *eminent* causation is required.[8] God, according to Judeo-Christian doctrine, created the world but is not Himself a material being. He caused the world of material entities by virtue of his capacity to be an eminent cause—to cause something to have a quality which He does not actually have. According to the Thomistic tradition, this can occur only because God does actually have qualities which are more perfect than that of being material. Thus (2b) can be restated in some such manner as this:

2b′) If A changes B with respect to some Quality Q, then A actually has Q or A has some Quality R such that R is more perfect than Q and such that any being having R can cause Q without actually having Q.

God can create a material world without being material and, much more mundanely, hamburgers and milkshakes can cause one to feel full without themselves having the quality of feeling any way at all. But now the weight of the premise's clarity falls on the phrase "more perfect." What quality of the food described is more perfect than my feeling of fullness, and in what respect? It is by no means clear that this sort of inquiry is overly promising. Thus we are led to ask if there is not some way of rephrasing the second premise of our original proof so that it needs no sub-proof. The following seems to me to be the most natural alternative:

2′) Nothing can cause itself to exist.

While one might offer a sub-proof of (2′) analogous to the one considered for (2), it seems clear that any premise of that sub-proof will be no more plausible than is (2′) itself. By restricting the original premise to coming into being, thus replacing (2) by (2′), we have no reason to attempt to provide a sub-proof for it. Tentatively, let us grant (2′) to Aquinas and turn our attention to premise (3) of the first way.

The sub-proof for (3) can be stated in this manner:

3a) Let anything which causes change but is itself also caused to change be designated a "subsequent mover."

3b) Let anything which causes change but is not itself caused to change be designated a "first mover."

3c) No first mover can be a subsequent mover, and conversely.

3d) Were there no first mover, there would be no subsequent mover.

3e) There are, however, subsequent movers.

Therefore:

3f) There is a first mover.

One thing to be noted about this sub-proof is that, if it is correct, no main proof is required, for the conclusion of the sub-proof is exactly that of the main proof. The sub-proof, however, is faulty in a crucial manner. The first two premises are definitions and the third premise follows from the first two. The problem arises with (3d); it is ambiguous. It can be taken as meaning either A) or B):

(A): If there is not an absolutely first mover (as defined in (3b)) there is no other mover.

(B): For any mover M, were there not a mover precedent to M to set M in motion, M could not be a mover at all.

So long as one accepts the claim that there cannot be uncaused change, one must grant (B); but then granting (B) is not to deny that there may be an infinite chain of causes and effects. Or, if it is, this must be proved, and the point of the overall argument was to prove just that.

For the sub-proof to succeed, (3d) must be taken as meaning what (A) means. But (A) simply says, in different language, what (4) of the original argument says. We are offered an argument in which a crucial premise is this: there cannot be an infinite series of causes and effects. When we ask why, we are offered a sub-proof in which the central premise says: if there is no first mover, then nothing changes. But this is only another way of saying that there cannot be an infinite series of causes and effects. Saying something over again does not provide a justification of what is said.

We are led, again, to ask if there is not some other way of stating the premise in question, just as there was in the case of (2). Once again, a plausible alternative suggests itself. Thus we replace (3) by (3′): An infinite series of same-level existence-explanations does not explain sufficiently the existence of any entity. We can explain the meaning of (3′) fairly simply.

To ask why something exists may be to ask for its purpose; the relevant answer is a teleological explanation. Or it may be to ask for the sufficient conditions of its existence. A necessary condition for my existence is anything without which I would not exist. Air, a functioning heart, and a head not severed from my neck are necessary conditions of my existing in my present state. The set of all those necessary conditions will provide a statement of the sufficient conditions of my existing. It is this sort of answer to the question as to why something exists that Aquinas is discussing in the first three ways.

It should be obvious upon a moment's reflection that actually stating the sufficient conditions of my existence is an immensely difficult task. It might well be the case, for example, that had a tree not fallen on the path upon which my great-grandfather rode his preacher's circuit, he could not have turned back to take a buggy-ride with my great-grandmother. Had he not taken the ride, he might not have asked my great-grandmother to marry him, in which case my grandfather would not have been born, nor my father, nor hence me. If this account is fact, not myth, then had the tree in question fallen after my great-grandfather passed I would not exist. The falling of the tree roughly when it did is then one of the necessary conditions of my existence, and thus part of the sufficient conditions for it. It is small wonder that normally when we ask for the cause of there being mountains or speckled trout, we are content with a statement of some of the necessary conditions relevant to the case in question. One of Aquinas' basic axioms is that, for any entity at all, there are sufficient conditions for its existence, though this does not entail that we can ever exhaustively state them. That we cannot state the full set of the sufficient conditions of the existence of any entity, but (at least for Aquinas) can be certain that there is a set of sufficient conditions for the existence of every entity, shows clearly that certainty about this axiom is not based on empirical evidence. Aquinas would agree.

To return explicitly to our reformulation of premise (3) of the first way, we now know what a sufficient explanation of the existence of an entity is. It is an explanation which specifies all the necessary conditions of that entity's existing, thus giving us the sufficient conditions of its existing. A same-level explanation is one which explains the existence of A by reference to the existence of B, where B's existence also requires explanation. We are not given a sufficient explanation in the sense that we are left with the same question with respect to the new entity that we had with respect to the old one. With these changes in mind, we can offer a reformulation of the First Way of Aquinas which is in accord with the initial alterations already proposed. Before doing so, however, it will be well to consider the second and third ways in which Aquinas argues for God's existence.

The second way is very similar to the first but is developed in terms of efficient causality rather than in terms of change. Aristotle has distinguished four types of cause: material, efficient, formal and final.[9] To take an instance in which the doctrine of four causes seems eminently plausible, consider the sculptor creating a bust of Socrates. The clay in his hands is the material cause, the plan by which he sculpts the formal cause, and the finished bust the final cause. There is something changed, a set of rules by which the change is effected, and a goal toward which the change is geared and in which it results. There must also be a changing agent or agency; this is the efficient cause. In our examples, the sculptor's hands, or the sculptor himself, is the efficient cause. The wind will be the efficient cause of the fall of a leaf from a tree and the current the cause of the motion of a drifting raft, so efficient causes need not be conscious beings. It is hardly necessary to stress that Aristotle's doctrines concerning change are complex, and that this is not the place to discuss them. Enough should have been said, however, to explain how Aquinas is using the term "efficient cause." His argument begins with a claim about efficient causes.

(1) The world is an order of efficient causes. (evident to the senses)[10]
(2) Nothing can be an efficient cause of itself.
(3) There cannot be an infinite series of efficient causes.

Thus:

(4) There is a first efficient cause.

There is a sub-proof for (2) which is very brief but exactly parallels the sub-proof for (2) in the first way. Our comments on that sub-proof carry over exactly to the sub-proof for (2) in the second way. There is no need to repeat them here. There is also a sub-proof for premise

(3) of the second way which exactly parallels the sub-proof for premise (3) of the first way. Our comments on the sub-proof for premise (3) in the first way thus carry over exactly to the corresponding sub-proof in the second way. We can safely conclude, then, that no further discussion of the second way is required. It emphasizes the efficient cause of change whereas the first way emphasizes the change that is efficiently caused. Precisely the same reformulations of premises (2) and (3) which we offered in the first way will apply for a reformulation of the second way. The reformulation of the second way is necessary for precisely the same reasons that necessitated a reformulation of the first way. We turn, then, to the third way of Aquinas.

Any entity is contingent if it depends for its existence on something else. Any entity is necessary if it does not depend for its existence on anything else. Any being will thus be either contingent or necessary and no being can be both. With these definitions, the third way should be intelligible.

(1)   There are contingent entities.

Aquinas regards this as evident to the senses in that we observe things which come to be and pass away. Plant life, pets, and our fellow human beings fit into this category, as well as much else. This claim, as opposed to the initial premise of the first way, seems unexceptionable. Some things do depend for their existence on that of others.

(2)   Whatever can fail to exist does at some time not exist.

In other words, if something A depends for its existence on something else, then at some time A will not exist.

(3)   There was a time at which no contingent entity existed.
(4)   Something can be brought into existence only by something else that already exists. (self-evident)
(5)   If everything were contingent, nothing would exist now. (from 3 and 4)
(6)   There is something now. (from 1)
(7)   Not everything that exists is contingent. (from 5 and 6)
(8)   Whatever is not contingent is necessary. (by definition)
(9)   There is at least one necessary entity. (from 7 and 8)

Since the positing of more than one necessary entity will explain nothing more than the positing of one, we can move from (9) to (9′): There is only one necessary entity. It should be noted that (9) is what follows from the argument just offered, and the move to (9′) requires appeal to considerations of parsimony. In other words, (9) plus, It is a mistake to posit more entities than those strictly required to explain the relevant data, entails (9'). While the law of parsimony is widely accepted, it does not seem, at least to the present writer, anything like a necessary truth.[11] Aquinas has three other arguments, however, to the effect that there is but one such being.[12] Each of them is stated in terms of the system of philosophical categories with which Aquinas worked and to spell them out in sufficient detail would take a chapter in itself. Nonetheless, their thrust can be put briefly. The gist of the first argument is that there is no distinction in God between His nature and his haecceity. In Socrates, there is that in virtue of which he is a man at all (his *essence*) and that in virtue of which he is the particular man he is (his *haecceity*). One man is to be distinguished from another though they share the same essence. This is possible because of two things: (a) two men differ with respect to their matter; (b) in the case of a man, his *essence* (defining properties) and his *existence* (the fact that something has those properties) are distinct. But God has no body[13] and His essence and existence are identical.[14] His existence is included in His essence. So we cannot distinguish between the essence of God and that which makes God the particular Deity he is. "Deity" does not name a *genus* or a *species*.[15]

The second argument depends on the difficult notions of privation and perfection. God, as perfect being, has all perfections. Suppose A and B are both Gods. Then neither can have a privation, since then he would be imperfect. Thus they cannot be two beings, for if two beings are in fact distinct then there is some property possessed by only one of them. God has no spatial or temporal properties and no accidental properties, no properties He could lose and still be God; but only essential ones.[16] Were a being not to possess any one of these properties essential to being God, it would obviously not be God. So no being which is God can have a property not possessed by another being who is also God. So there can be only one God.

The premise in this argument which is most in need of defense is the claim that God can have no accidental properties. In particular, that God is a creator is, from Aquinas' point of view at least, not something that follows from His nature but is a product of His free choice.[17] It is not clear, at least to the present writer, how this problem is to be resolved.[18] At *Summa Theologica*, Book 1, Question 3, Article 6, all potentiality is said to be absent from God; God is pure actuality. This is one basis for denying that God has any property that He might not have had. Another is that "God is whatever He has." Existence and essence are identical in God, and thus God is identical with each of His properties. Hence no property of God can be accidental. The claim that God is identical to each of His properties rests on the thesis that God is not complex, but simple.[19] It should be clear by now that further appeal to this argument for proof that there can be only one necessary being would involve us in a perusal of much at least of Aquinas' system. This argument may well enmesh its proponent in more, not less, difficulties than he had when he began to defend his case.

The third argument rests on the thesis that there is but one order of things, one universe, and that "many are reduced into one order by one better than by many."[20] This thesis comes very close, in fact, to Aquinas' "fifth way" which is a version of the teleological argument. We will not discuss this argument specifically, though the considerations which we will develop relevant to the first three ways are, *mutatis mutandis*, applicable to the fifth. However, we must now ask whether the third way does indeed justify either (9) or (9').

I think that it is plain that it does not. For one thing, why should one accept premise (2)? That something is contingent in the sense that it depends for its existence on something else does not entail that it will at some time or other not exist. Aquinas is here appealing to the Aristotelian doctrine of contingent or possible beings.[21] That is contingent or possible which exists only for a limited time. In this sense, however, there is no reason that I am aware of to suppose that, for example, an elementary particle is contingent. It is certainly not evident to the senses that everything in the physical universe is contingent in the sense required by (2). But suppose we grant Aquinas (2) for a moment. Still, premise (3) is not at all self-evident. It plainly does not follow from premise (2). Premise (2) says that for every contingent thing there will be some time or other at which that thing does not exist. Premise (3) says that at some time or other there will be nothing contingent that exists. That (2) does not entail (3) is evident; the following example should make it clear if it is not already so. Suppose that it is true that, for anything at all, at some time during its existence it will not be colored blue. It does not follow from this that at some time there will be nothing colored blue; it only follows that at some time or other not everything will be colored blue. Analogously, it follows from (2) only that at some time or other any particular thing will cease to exist and therefore there will be a time at which some things which have existed will not any longer exist.

The reply might be made that unless new things come into being then if everything that exists will sometime cease to exist, then there will be a time at which nothing exists. This is true but irrelevant. For one thing, nothing in the premises does assure us that something will always exist. For another, the argument requires the claim that at some past time nothing would have existed if everything were contingent, not the claim that this will be so at some future time. Yet again, the argument does not show that the number of existing things is static or that contingent beings cannot beget other contingent beings who beget yet others so that the universe has always been and will always be populated. So this reply will not help Aquinas.

A sub-proof is provided, however, which is relevant to both (2) and (3). The interpretation of this sub-proof is a debated issue.[22] The question before us, however, is simply this: what interpretation of the sub-proof will permit us to derive (2) and (3)? Only such an interpretation will be philosophically relevant as opposed to merely raising an interesting issue about what Aquinas meant. The relevant sub-proof runs as follows:

S1) In an infinite time, all possibilities will be realized.
S2) It is possible that there be no contingent things.
S3) It is the case that past time is infinite.

So:

S4) At some time or other, nothing contingent existed.

"Nothing contingent exists," while not something that could ever be known by a human mind, seems neither nonsense nor self-contradictory. If it is neither of these, we must grant Aquinas (S2). We can grant him (S3) or not; it makes no difference to his argument. If we do not grant (S3), we say that past time is not infinite, so that time had a beginning. So this alone gives him the conclusion he desires.[23] Two things should be noted in this connection. (S3) concerns only past time; there was no beginning to time—time is infinite toward the past. This is what (S3) asserts. Aquinas does not believe for theological reasons that (S3) is true, but he does not claim to be able to show that it is not. So he argues dialectically: either time is infinite toward the past or not.[24] If not, then time and thus contingent entities, has a beginning. Nothing can come from nothing. So not all beings are contingent. Or it is the case that past time is infinite. Then we grant (S3) and offer the sub-proof now under consideration. Let us grant, then, (S3). (S1) through (S3) entail the conclusion (S4). It only remains to consider (S1). (S1) is clearly sufficient to play the role required of it in the argument (sub-proof) in which it occurs.

(S1), it seems, contains a fatal defect. It is self-contradictory. This can be seen if we take care to examine some actual cases. "The only typewriter owned by Yandell is being used by him at time T," obviously enough, is a contingent statement. Involving no contradictions, it expresses a possible state of affairs. So, however, does its denial.

But this sentence and its denial, though they each express a possibility, cannot both be true. But according to (S1) they can be both true if time is infinite. But even in an infinite time self-contradictions cannot be true. Since (S1) entails that a contradiction can be true, it itself is necessarily false. It will not do to say that (S1) only entails that one or the other of these possibilities will be realised. If all that (S1) said was that one or another of all contradictories, a statement *or* its denial, would be true, then it would not rule out the possibility that at every time some contingent thing exists, for that is logically possible. It would only tell us that either it is false that there is always some contingent being or it is not false that there is always some contingent being, which is true but not helpful to Aquinas' cause.

To avoid another possible misunderstanding, it should be noted that our criticism does not require that we include a specific temporal clause in our examples of sentences including possibilities. One might object that all that (S1) entailed was that at some time or other I use my typewriter, and that some time or other I not use it, and that both these possibilities can be realized because they have in fact been realized. This, too, misunderstands (S1) in that (S1) in order to play the required role of supporting (2) and (3) in the original proof (the third way) must be stronger. It must entail that all possibilities will be realized. Now one possibility is that I never use my typewriter, and another is that I do use it at some time. Both cannot be realized, but either can be. That the latter statement (that I have used my typewriter, is true is a contingent fact. The former, that I never use my typewriter, expresses, in itself, as genuine a possibility as one could wish. Analogously, that there always be some contingent thing or other in existence is just as much a possibility as that at some time there not be any contingent beings in existence. But both cannot be the case. So one possibility will not be realized, and we have been offered no cogent reason for thinking that it is the one that Aquinas' argument requires, namely that at some time in the past there were no contingent beings. In order to be fully fair to Aquinas, we must ask if there is not some way of dealing with (S1), or a premise very like it which will serve his purposes, which does not entail a contradiction. We can best answer this question by considering what seems to be the source of this strange premise.

The probable immediate source is not hard to identify; in his *Guide for the Perplexed*, Maimonides offers a very similar argument[25] and Aquinas was acquainted with this work.[26] The ultimate source is doubtless Aristotle. In *De Caelo*,[27] Aristotle offers an argument for a premise quite similar to (S1). Aristotle's argument can be stated as follows: Suppose (1) that entity A has capacity C (2) that A exists at each of an infinite series of times (3) that A never exercises C. Let C be the capacity not to exist. Now it is logically impossible that anything ever meet all of these conditions. For suppose that A does meet (2) and thus also meets (3). Then A cannot have exercised C. But if anything cannot have exercised a capacity, it cannot have had that capacity. So if (2) and thus (3) are true of A, (1) must be false of A.

The fallacy of the argument, interpreted in this manner, is obvious and can be stated in terms of Aristotle's own distinctions. He notes a difference between a proposition which is hypothetically impossible, a proposition which, on the assumption that some other proposition is true, cannot itself be true, and a proposition which is absolutely impossible (i.e., which is self-contradictory).[28] Thus on the assumption that a man is always only five feet tall it is impossible that his height reach seventy-two inches; though there is nothing inherently impossible in anyone reaching this height. But that a man both exist and not exist at the same time is absolutely impossible. Aristotle's contention is that "If A cannot exercise a capacity, it cannot have that capacity" is true. In one sense, it indeed is true, for if "A exercises C" is absolutely impossible in virtue of involving a contradiction, then of course A cannot have capacity C. For example, "This set of eleven apples can be evenly divided between two boys without any apple being itself divided" is self-contradictory or absolutely impossible; hence the set does not have the capacity in question.[29] But the fact that if "A has C" is contradictory, then A cannot indeed have C is not in need of defense; nor will it make good Aristotle's case. His claim is that A cannot have C because A *ex hypothesi* has never in an infinite time exercised C. But if the only reason offered that A cannot have C is that, in all time, A does not exercise C, then the obvious question arises: why can't there be capacities which something has, but never exercises and would in fact never exercise even were it always to have existed in the past and always to exist in the future?

Aristotle offers an argument that such unrealized capacities are spurious which seems to run as follows.

Let C be the capacity of being able to exist and also being able not to exist. (i.e., the capacity of being and of not being).[30] Suppose (1) that A has C. Then it is also true that:

(1a)　At some time, A can exist.
(1b)　At some time, A can fail to exist.

Now suppose that

(2)　At all times, A can exist.
(3)　At all times, A can fail to exist.

But, the argument goes, (2) entails that (1b) is false, and (3) entails that (1a) is false. So (1) is incompatible with each of (2) and (3) singly, and thus is also incompatible with their conjunct. Given (1), (2) and (3) are both false. So if A has C, it is false that A can exist at all times, thus at some time it won't exist. It is also false that A can fail to exist at all times, thus at some time it will exist.

This argument, however, fails since the truth of (2) above is not incompatible with the truth of (1b), nor is the truth of (3) incompatible with that of (1a). There is no obvious reason why something can't always exist but always be capable of not existing. One can easily provide a premise which will serve Aristotle's purpose. Consider (4): If anything has a capacity, it will exercise it in infinite time. This premise, together with (2), entails that (1b) is false and, together with (3), entails that (1a) is false. But now, since the argument was to prove (4), a dilemma develops. With (4) as a premise, the argument is valid, but worthless since (4) is identical with the intended conclusion. Without (4), the argument is invalid. And no premise besides (4) which will serve the same purpose seems to be available.

Is there any other support, then, for (S1) or something like (S1) which is available to Aquinas within the resources of his system, or at least compatible with his views insofar as they are relevant to the third way?

There is a somewhat plausible answer to this question. In line with the overall system of Aquinas, one could appeal to the principle of plenitude[31]—that it is better that there be many kinds of thing than that there be just one kind, and perhaps, though Aquinas is not explicit here, best of all that there be an infinite number of kinds, and even an infinite number of things of each kind.[32] But this appeal will not really help. First, one needs (roughly) not the claim that an infinite number of individuals exists, or an infinite number of kinds of things, but the claim that, for each thing that does exist, it passes through an infinite variety, not merely an infinite number, of states. Second, as reference to the passages cited will clearly reveal, the principle of plenitude can be assumed only if we already accept among other things the existence of God. So appeal to this principle in the course of arguing for God's existence would make the argument viciously circular.

A final paragraph may serve to make utterly clear how dubious the premise under discussion really is. Consider a dry match which lights when struck. Lighting is a capacity, striking one but not the only relevant stimulus, and such matters as the match being dry and the presence of oxygen are necessary background conditions. Now consider the capacity C of failing to exist. There can be no question as to the propriety of the example insofar as the argument of Aristotle is concerned; it is his example. If failing to exist is not a capacity, there is an immediate end to his argument.

If, given each logically possible set of background conditions relevant to C, and each logically possible C-triggering stimulus under each such set of background conditions, A fails to exercise C, then given that the absence of countervening conditions is included in each set of background conditions, A does not have C. Indeed, this is a necessary truth. But what possible reason can be given for thinking that, in an infinite time, all the possible relevant backgrounds and stimuli will be exhaustively conjoined in this manner in A's infinitely long life-history? Unless we assume that only if this occurred could an infinite time elapse, there would seem to be no reason whatsoever to grant this ambitious but bizarre thesis. Since it is patent that an infinite time could be filled, so to speak, by a series of events no more varied than, say, a red and a blue object reversing left-right positions against a black background as perceived by an unblinking perceiver, the precariousness of claims about the connection between an infinity of time and the variety of events becomes quite lucid.[33] Thus a justification of (S1), or anything very like it, seems not to be available.

REFORMULATION OF AQUINAS' ARGUMENTS

One might ask what reformulation of the third way could be offered. If we claim that only a non-contingent entity, a necessary entity, can provide a sufficient explanation for there being contingent entities we can produce an argument which makes use of the reformulated premises of the first two ways. Thus we are now in a position to offer a reformulation of the first way which also captures whatever force the second and third ways possess. I waive the question as to what degree the following is precisely what the "Angelic Doctor" meant.[34]

Let the question, with respect to any given entity E, "What caused E to exist?," be abbreviated by "Q." Further, let us say that any answer to Q asked about some entity E will be an "existence explanation" of E. The refurbished argument runs as follows, with justifications of premises noted in parentheses.

1) There are contingent entities.
2) No entity can cause its own existence. (self-evident)
3) For anything that exists, if Q is an appropriate question with respect to that entity, there is a sufficient existence explanation for that entity. (self-evident)

4) Q is an appropriate question with respect to any entity E such that E does not meet either of the following conditions:
   C1) "E does not exist" is self-contradictory
   C2) "E depends for its existence on something else" is self-contradictory. (see comments)

5) No contingent entity meets C1 or C2. (self-evident)

6) Q is an appropriate question with respect to any contingent entity. (from 4 and 5)

7) No existence-explanation of entity E is sufficient if that explanation refers to something else which itself is such that Q is appropriate to it. (self-evident)

8) If every entity is contingent, there is no sufficient existence-explanation for anything. (from 6 and 7)

9) Not every entity is contingent. (from 3 and 8)

10) If E is not a contingent entity, Q is not appropriate with respect to E. (since in this case E is not caused—i.e., it is impossible that E be caused if E exists)

11) There is some entity E such that Q is not an appropriate question with respect to E. (from 4 and 10)

12) Some entity meets C1 or C2. (from 4 and 11)

13) Any entity that meets C1 *a fortiori* meets C2. (for if E is such that to deny that E exists is self-contradictory, then there is nothing on which E depends for its existence)

14) Some entity meets C2. (from 12 and 13)

15) There is an entity which does not depend for its existence on anything else, and the fact that it does not is not contingent. (restatement of 14)[35]

I think it quite clear that if the argument above is valid and has all true premises, then the Thomist has the proof which he sought. I wish to make two comments about this argument before offering an evaluation of it. It is assumed, in premise (4), that only C1 and C2 will do as sufficient conditions of Q not being appropriate. That is, it is assumed that for any entity that satisfies C1, Q is inappropriate and for any being satisfying C2, Q is inappropriate, but that there is no logically independent third criterion C3 such that anything satisfying C3 is also such that it is not appropriate to raise Q with respect to it. The assumption would, I think, be hard to prove and if there might be some such C3, then the remainder of the argument should be altered. Thus premise 12 would have to be restated as: There is some being that satisfies C1 or C2 *or C3* (the italicized words being added), and the remainder of the argument would have to be analogously altered. On the positive side of the ledger, however, I think that it is hard to think of any plausible further condition. One seemingly promising candidate for C3 is this: "E began to exist" is self-contradictory. The claim would be that if an entity E met C3, "Why does Q exist?" would not be an appropriate question with respect to E. So C3 should be added to premise (4), and also to premises (12) and following.

That this suggestion will not do is evident. Consider the description of a logically possible entity E which occurs in (a) through (c) below.

(a) E has always existed
(b) E depends for its existence on E′
(c) E′ has always existed.

Now (a-c) could be true of an E of which C3 was also true. But (a-c) could not be true of any being which was not contingent. Hence C3 can be true of a contingent being, and thus need not be added to the argument. If we add (d): E′ depends for its existence on E, to our description, we will have a case of mutual dependence of two contingent, but always existent, beings. Aquinas would say that even if there are such co-dependent beings which have always existed, something further is needed to explain their existence than the fact that they are co-dependent.[36] This requirement is built into the characterization of a sufficient explanation on which the reformulated argument hinges.

It should be clear in what way this reformulation is related to the third way. Rather than requiring that all possibilities be realized, Aquinas can claim that if all things are contingent, no existence-explanations are sufficient. Rather than claiming that past time cannot have been infinite, he can argue that an infinite series of existence-explanations, all of which are offered at the same level, provides in fact no philosophical explanation at all. Rather than argue that everything contingent must at some time fail to exist, he can claim that no contingent thing contains the reason for its own existence. Nor does the totality of contingent things. I shall assume that the reformulation of the first two ways is also and equally a reformulation of the third way. A comparison of the third way and the reformulation we have offered of crucial premises in the first two ways will reveal significant parallels and our discussion of the third way should offer sufficient justification for making the indicated alterations. We are left, then, with the task of evaluating the reformulation. It is worth mentioning that the reformulation is what a good many followers of Aquinas have taken him to have meant.

The crucial element of Aquinas' argument as it now stands is the characterization of a sufficient existence-explanation. By way of exposition, we suggested that any relevant answer to "Why does entity E exist?" was an existence-explanation of E and that if the answer was that E was caused to exist by E′ which was also something about which we could appropriately ask "Why does E′ exist?" we have been given a same-level existence-explanation. We are left with the same question about E′ that we originally had about E. Not even an infinite number of same-level explanations provides a sufficient explanation. Indeed, if one same-level explanation was not sufficient to explain the existence of the entity being explained, there is no reason to think that an infinite number would be. A necessary being was any being with respect to which Q was patently an inappropriate question. Such a being must exist, since only if one does can any sufficient existence-explanations be offered and there is a sufficient existence-explanation for every contingent thing.

It is, however, at just this point that a good many philosophers, and others as well, would question Aquinas' claims. Why, it is asked, is it not a sufficient explanation of the existence of E to say that E′ exists and caused E? If the entity whose existence is to be explained is a child, surely reference to its parents is sufficient explanation. We do not ask why children exist, at least normally, because we already know. There was a time when we did not, and we asked, and ultimately we were answered. The answer gave us a sufficient explanation, not only in the psychological sense that we were satisfied with the answer, but in the further sense that we knew the conditions under which children come to be.

This objection can be more formally put in terms of two sorts of explanations which are accepted as adequate in science and in everyday life. We shall call one sort *theoretical*[37] and the other *teleological*. An adequate or sufficient theoretical explanation of E's existence has been given if (1) a general statement or set thereof of the form "Whenever A, E" has been well verified; and (2) It is well verified that A. occurred. Given (1) and (2), I can deduce that E occurred. So I have provided a sufficient explanation of E. Suppose, for example, I wish to explain why a certain king ceased to rule at exactly 3:06 p.m. on the third Wednesday of August, 1724. I offer as explanation the fact that there is overwhelmingly good historical evidence that he was decapitated at just that moment and provide you with the well-verified general statement that decapitated kings never thereafter reign. I have thereby offered all the explanation that can be required. I can go on to ask why he was decapitated, and why decapitation has such debilitating effects. The point, however, is that his no longer reigning seems quite nicely explicated. Further theoretical explanations can be offered as to the other matters just mentioned. If some phenomenon p is to be explained, that "whenever q, p" is a general law and that "q occurred" is a well verified claim provides exactly what the scientist desires in terms of an explanation of p. Perhaps phenomenon q, too, can be explained in terms of a general law of the form "whenever phenomenon r, q" and "r occurred." We may not at the present stage of scientific knowledge and theory be able to explain phenomenon r. Perhaps, for example, that there are elementary particles is presently inexplicable; they are the givens of present mathematical physics. But no sort of entity occupies the position of theoretical inexplicability with tenure. It may always be displaced and some other kind of entity posited to explain it, and so on so long as science progresses and theories alter.

Let us review the objection. A theoretical explanation of the existence of E is provided if from a well-established general law of the form "whenever E', E" and the well verified claim "E' occurred" we can deduce that E occurred. For some sorts of entity this kind of explanation cannot now be provided; for anything of this sort it will be true to say that it must now appear in only an *explicans* and never in an *explicandum*. Perhaps there must always be some kind or other of entity that can only appear in an *explicans*. No kind of entity is guaranteed this status forever, for given the progress of scientific investigation and the likelihood of conceptual revolution what is now primitive may become derivative and be replaced by some other primitive. For anything not primitive in our present conceptual framework in the sciences, a theoretical explanation can be in principle provided. For anything primitive in that conceptual framework it is true that no theoretical explanation can now be provided, but also the case that none is required. To ask for more explanation than this is not even unreasonable; it is to ask for what we cannot even conceive.

But this is only part of the reply to the argument of Aquinas. It can be further developed. Suppose, we can say, that it is held that not everything can be even in principle explained theoretically in the sense just defined. It is highly plausible that human choices and actions, human creativity, and the like, cannot be so explained. Nonetheless, there is another sort of explanation that applies here, namely teleological. An adequate teleological explanation of E is provided if (1) it is well established that E is, or is taken to be, a means to a goal G that person S possesses (i.e., that S has goal G and takes E to be a means to G) or that E is itself a goal that S possesses, and (2) it is well verified that S brought about E in order to attain G. Suppose, for example, that Da Vinci desired to paint a masterpiece of religious devotion in order to express profound feelings of reverence. Suppose further that he took painting a certain figure of a certain description to be the means to that end. Suppose further that he painted a

Madonna in order to express just those feelings of reverence. Surely this gives us a sufficient explanation of why he painted the Madonna. Other explanations of this sort would also be sufficient; for example that he wanted money and believed that this sort of painting would sell for a great price; or that he loved a woman greatly and that she asked to pose for a painting of the Virgin Mother. The point is that we can have evidence in this sort of case as to which explanation is correct, and that if any one is correct it does provide a sufficient explanation of the existence of the painting.[38]

While the characterizations of theoretical and teleological explanation are fairly rough, they will do for present purposes. The purpose is this: while explanations of these two sorts are often provided, and while it may be true that for any entity, except those presently theoretically primitive and hence presently theoretically inexplicable, there is such an explanation in principle available. Though we may never in hosts of cases discover it, why should one expect anything more than this? Further, what sort of explanation model can be provided besides those falling into one or the other of the already characterized classes?

It is these issues among others that motivate philosophers to reject the argument from contingency. The crux of the impasse between those who find the argument under discussion persuasive and those who do not can be exposed by considering a crucial case. It is clear, any convinced Thomist must maintain, that the universe, the set of all existents, might not now exist.[39] Thus its existence requires explanation. Obviously, the explanation cannot be of either sort just described. We have no well-verified general statements of the form "Whenever A, a universe exists" nor any well-verified teleological statements of the form "The existence of the universe is a means to goal G which person S possesses." But Q is appropriate, the Thomist insists, with respect to the universe, for "If there is a universe, then it does not depend for its existence on anything else" is not a necessary truth, nor is "The universe exists" a necessary truth. If I say that the universe does not exist, I say what is false but not what is self-contradictory. But explanations are only adequate in case the sentences which express them are not all contingent. True sentences do not alone an explanation make, even if they are relevant and adequate in the sense that a theoretical explanation in science is adequate. The inadequacy, then, of scientific theoretical explanation for the Thomist is that its general statements are contingent rather than necessary.[40] But those whose standards for explanation are restricted to theoretical and teleological ones must regard the question "Why is there something rather than nothing?" as unanswerable because unintelligible.

AN IMPASSE CONCERNING EXPLANATION

With respect to the argument from contingency, then, it seems that one must recognise a philosophical impasse. What is for one side an intelligible question the answer to which can only be found in something which necessarily exists, is for the other side not intelligible at all and hence not answerable even in principle. Here is basic philosophical disagreement.

On the one hand, it is perfectly clear to some philosophers that the existence of a universe is something which calls for explanation. Richard Taylor writes:

> There seems to be nothing in the world, then, concerning which it is at all plausible to say that it exists by its own nature, or contains within itself the reason for its existence . . . While this might be true of everything in the world, is it necessarily true of the world itself? . . . must we also say that the world itself, or the totality of all these perishable things, is also contingent and perishable? Logically, we are not forced to, for . . . it is not logically necessary that a totality should share the defects of its members . . . it is possible that the world is in itself a necessary thing . . . This is logically possible, but it is not plausible. For we find nothing whatever about the world, any more than about its parts, to suggest that it exists by its own nature . . . It would seem, then, that the world, in case it happens to exists at all—and this is beyond question—is contingent and hence dependent on something other than itself for its existence, if it depends on anything at all. And it must depend on something, for otherwise there could be no reason why it exists in the first place . . . either . . . the world depends for its existence on something else, which in turn depends on another thing, this depending on still another, *ad infinitum* or . . . the world derives its existence from something that exists by its own nature . . . The first of these alternatives is impossible, however, for it does not render a sufficient reason why anything should exist in the first place. Instead of supplying a reason why any world should exist, it repeatedly begs off giving a reason. Ultimately, then, it would seem that the world . . . must depend on something that is necessary . . . and which accordingly exists . . . by its own nature.[41]

Taylor takes it as at least reasonably obvious that "Why is there something rather than nothing?" is an intelligible question. Further, he takes it as at least reasonably obvious that this question must have an answer, and that this answer must be in terms of a noncontingent or necessary being.

On the other hand, it is perfectly clear to other philosophers that explanations involving necessary being are quite suspect. Thus Paul Edwards rejects any such argument as the one proposed by Taylor.

The contingency argument rests on a misconception of what an explanation is and does, and similarly on what it is that makes phenomena
"intelligible." Or else it involves an obscure and arbitrary redefinition
of "explanation," "intelligible," and related terms. Normally, we are
satisfied that we have explained a phenomenon if we have found its
cause or if we have exhibited some other uniform or near-uniform
connection between it and something else. Confining ourselves to the
former case, which is probably the most common, we might say that a
phenomenon Z has been explained if it has been traced back to a group
of factors, a, b, c, d, etc. which are its cause. These factors are the full
and real explanation of Z, quite regardless of whether they are . . .
necessary or contingent . . . If it is granted that, in order to explain
a phenomenon or to make it intelligible, we need not bring in a necessary being, then the contingency argument breaks down.[42]

Edwards and Taylor, who are but representative in this respect of
many other philosophers, seek quite different sorts of explanation.
What Taylor requires, Edwards rejects—not on the ground that explanation in terms of a necessary being is mistaken, but that such
explanation is at best unnecessary and at worst meaningless. The latter
alternative is strongly suggested by Edward's claim that the contingency argument "rests on a misconception of what explanation is and
does." How is such an impasse to be resolved? Perhaps we can see at
least the beginnings of an answer to this question if we momentarily
forget the dispute and approach the matter from a different direction.

Ancient materialism made the ambitious claim that all events in
natural and human history were explicable given only that we assume
that an infinitude of eternal, simple material atoms fall in infinite
space according to fixed laws.[43] As this simplistic model has little
appeal to contemporary philosophers, there is no present need to canvass its defects. Assume, however, that a contemporary Lucretius were
asked to explain why there are material atoms rather than nothing at
all. His answer would be presumably that we asked what could not
be answered; the atoms in question are eternal, so they have no beginning. Collections of atoms and the relations between these collections
into which the events of natural and human history are said to be
analyzable in principle are explicable in terms of these simple atoms
and the laws which govern or describe their movement. But within
the system, it is a necessary truth that atoms appear singly only in an
explicans. To doubt that is to doubt materialism, and to deny it is to
reject materialism.

The difference between Taylor and Edwards, and they are merely
representative of many other philosophers who have taken opposite
sides in this dispute, lies in part in their disagreement concerning the
maxim that only in case there is a necessary being is there sufficient

explanation of the fact that something exists. Underlying this disagreement is another one. They do not agree as to whether the question "Why is there something rather than nothing?" is intelligible. I take it that Edwards would grant that this question is intelligible if it is asked about any particular thing, but deny that it is intelligible if it is taken as asking why space-time is not completely empty. Explanations according to Edwards can occur only insofar as the terms in the *explicans* refer to entities within the same framework as the entities to which the terms in the *explicandum* refer. To refer to something outside the spatio-temporal-causal nexus as being the cause of anything within the nexus is to have a misconception of what explanation is and does.[44] And now it seems clear that we must add, "according to a given view of the nature of explanation." On the view of the nature of explanation which is today widely held by philosophers and scientists, among others, the contentions of Edwards are plainly correct. They are plainly not correct if one takes Aquinas' view of this matter or that of Leibniz, or Spinoza, or Taylor. So the question arises as to whose account of the nature of explanation is correct, and each man's reply seems obviously correct in its own systematic context.

Here, however, we seem to exhaust our resources. Appeal to the majority opinion hardly seems satisfactory, nor is it clear that if we permit philosophers of the past as well as those of the present to be counted that one side would win over the other. To what can we appeal to decide what can legitimately count as an explanation or to decide which questions are in fact intelligible?

POSSIBLE RESOLUTION OF THE IMPASSE

The impasse reached has certain obvious features. It is not merely a dispute over words in the sense of simply being a disagreement over how to use the word "explanation." The dispute as to whether a certain border-line color is to be called blue or green may be a purely verbal dispute. Whether a claim is even intelligible is a philosophical dispute. When a man says "Your idea of what an explanation is, is literally absurd" he is claiming that the proffered criteria for counting anything as an explanation are unintelligible or incoherent. Far from being merely verbal, this sort of claim requires careful defense and argument.

Equally obviously, the dispute is not capable of empirical test. The procedures which are results of empirical testing occur already within a set of assumptions as to what explanation is; further, that a criterion for being a sufficient explanation is unintelligible or at best unnecessary, cannot be decided by appeal to what happens in a Wilson cloud chamber; it requires appeal to incoherencies present in the criterion or to a system of explanation which satisfies less questionable criteria and is sufficient for all the data we have. There is nothing suspicious about nonempirical grounds for making rational decisions. The criteria of consistency, coherence, and simplicity, which are constantly appealed to by both philosophers and scientists, are nonempirical in character. That is, the consistency, coherence, or simplicity of a system is not a sensorily observable feature of the system.

But if the dispute is neither verbal nor empirically decidable, is there any way to resolve it? One possible way will be suggested here. If we can find a pattern of argument which is plainly cogent and which appeals to the principle of sufficient reason, the principle that no series of same-level explanations is rationally sufficient, then at least one appeal to the principle, namely, the one made by the patently cogent argument, is legitimate. Then any other appeal to that principle sufficiently analogous to the one in question will also be legitimate.

Although the problem of evil was discussed in the previous chapter in some detail it is useful to deal here with one attempt to solve the problem which seems quite clearly inadequate. The point of doing so is to note carefully the criticism by which the attempt is shown to be inadequate; this criticism, patently a cogent one, appeals to the principle of sufficient reason. Thus if the appeal to the principle of sufficient reason in the reformulation of Aquinas' argument is sufficiently analogous to the appeal made by this criticism, the appeal to the principle of sufficient reason in the reformulation of Aquinas' argument is also legitimate. Then the dispute will be resolved in favor of Aquinas, Taylor *et al.*

Let us grant that pain is evil, and pleasure good, for the sake of developing an attempt to solve the problem of evil. Other examples would also serve but these are convenient. Let us ask why pain is permitted by God, who is omnipotent, omniscient, and omnibenevolent. One answer sometimes offered is that pain is a logically necessary condition of higher-order goods.[45] Let pain-alleviation be a good. Suppose, for the sake of the argument, that the existence of pain-alleviation is a good sufficiently great to justify the existence of pain. It is also suggested that pain is a logically necessary condition of certain moral virtues, etc., but we need not develop this point here. It is plain that to say that pain-alleviation occurs, but that no pains occur is logically contradictory; pain is a logically necessary condition for the occurrence of pain-alleviation. So the existence of pain is explained; it makes possible the great good of pain-alleviation (e.g., mercy).

Let us grant for the sake of the argument that this does explain the existence of pain in a way fully adequate to show why God permits pain. A problem still remains. The existence of pain is also a logically necessary condition of pain-aggravation. No one, for example, could increase a man's embarrassment when he committed a social blunder by loudly publishing the blunder to all those in the room unless there was already some embarrassment to increase. So there is an evil, pain-aggravation, for which pain is also a logically necessary condition. How, then, do we explain the evil of pain-aggravation?

One way of doing so is by noting that the existence of pain-aggravation is a logically necessary condition of the existence of pain-aggravation-prevention. If, as we can grant for the sake of the argument, the existence of pain-aggravation-prevention is of great enough worth, then the existence of pain aggravation will be explained in a way consistent with the existence of a fully benevolent God. But the existence of pain-aggravation is also a logically necessary condition of pain-aggravation-promotion.

By now, the schema of the attempt to answer the problem of evil begins to become clear. Let pain be a first order evil. We can then map out a hierarchy of goods and evils in this manner:

	Good	*Evil*
First Order:	(pleasure)	pain
Second Order:	pain-alleviation	pain-aggravation
Third Order:	pain-alleviation-promotion	pain-aggravation-promotion

The principle for ordering the hierarchy, once the first order of pleasure as good and pain as evil is granted, is simply that the evil of order n is a logically necessary condition of both the good and the evil of order $n + 1$. I am not concerned with whether the examples are the most *apropos*, but wish only to make clear the type or schema of argument under discussion.

There is an important and obvious reason why no argument of this type can succeed as an attempt to solve the problem of evil. It is this: for each evil of order n that is *ex hypothesi* adequately explained, there is an evil of order $n + 1$ of which no explanation has been given. So the problem of why any evil at all is permitted by God is not solved, for that problem remains so long as there is one evil of any level which is unexplained. Of course if one could find a good of level $n + 1$ which had an evil of level n as a logically necessary condition and which was of great enough value to justify the existence of that evil, and if the good of level $n + 1$ was accompanied by no evil of the same level, then the existence of evil of level n would be adequately explained. The same will hold if a good G of level n is good enough to outweigh the evils of levels n and $n + 1$. But this is not an argument which fits the schema we have been discussing.

The reason why this sort of argument fails to solve the problem of evil can be put succinctly by saying that if any evil is left unexplained then the problem of evil is unsolved, and it is a feature of this sort of argument that some level of evil is necessarily always left unexplained (i.e., unjustified).

Now suppose we consider once again the argument which explains the existence of one contingent thing by appeal to another contingent thing. The problem is why anything at all exists. This is analogous to the problem as to why any evil exists. Just as there might be no evil, there might be no contingent things. If the existence of contingent being A is left unexplained, and the existence of contingent being B is explained in terms of the existence of A, we've no sufficient explanation as to why contingent being B exists. This is analogous to the fact that if evil of level $n + 3$ is unexplained, where the existence of evils of level n, $n + 1$, and $n + 2$ are explained in terms of goods of levels $n + 1$ and $n + 2$, and where the existence of evil of level $n + 2$ is a logically necessary condition of the existence of evil of level $n + 3$, we have no sufficient explanation as to why evil exists. Just as the schema of the attempt to solve the problem of evil solves it in such a way as necessarily always to leave a certain level of evil unaccounted for, so the schema of the argument explaining the existence of one contingent being in terms of the existence of another contingent being (and so on) necessarily leaves the existence of some contingent being unaccounted for.

One might point out disanalogies between the two argument-types. One possible disanalogy is that the attempt to explain the existence of evil deals with value terms whereas the attempt to explain the existence of contingent beings does not. While I agree that "causes to exist" is not a value term, this disanalogy hardly seems an important one in the present context. Another disanalogy that might be proposed is that the argument concerned with the problem of evil deals with a hierarchical order whereas all contingent beings are on the same order. This too is true, but hardly relevant. If we have contingent beings A and B and explain B's existence by reference to the existence of A, then we are saying that the existence of A is sufficient to explain the existence of B (and not conversely). A, with respect to B, is a causally sufficient condition. If we explain the existence of A by reference to the existence of Z, then we are saying that Z is causally sufficient for A (and not conversely). So there is a series of explanations of the existence of contingent beings which involves the connection of each such being to another as causally sufficient for its successor. This is not, indeed, a hierarchy; but the point of analogy between the arguments in question is that in the one case we have terms of a series connected such that each is logically necessary for its successor in the series whereas in the other series each term of the series is causally sufficient for its successor in the series. The analogy is between the relations of "being logically necessary to the existence of" and "being causally sufficient for the existence of" in the two arguments. This analogy is not affected by the fact that the terms in one series occur in a hierarchical series of levels whereas the terms in the other series occur in a non-hierarchical sequence.

What we need to notice in connection with the criticism of the attempt to solve the problem of evil is that it fails because it produces a new and unexplained case of the same sort of thing, albeit of a higher level, that it was intended to account for. For each *explicandum* to which the solution offers an *ex hypothesi* satisfactory *explicans*, that very solution provides a new *explicandum* built into the *explicans* for which all presently available *explicans* are inadequate.[46] But a same-level explanation is precisely one that leaves another *explicandum* by the fact that it offers the *explicans* that it does.[47] That such explanations are indeed insufficient is just what the principle of sufficient reason affirms. So the criticism of this particular solution to the problem of evil makes explicit appeal to the principle of sufficient reason.

The concluding contention is easy to anticipate. The appeal to the principle of sufficient reason made by the criticism of this solution to the problem of evil is, as we have attempted to make clear, quite analogous to the appeal to the principle of sufficient reason in the reformulation of Aquinas' arguments. There, too, we have the rejection of the explanation of the existence of contingent beings via an infinite series of such beings in which each is causally sufficient for its successor. The ground offered for that rejection is the same as that in the preceding case. For each *explicandum* to which the explanation offers an *ex hypothesi* sufficient *explicans*, that very explanation provides a new *explicandum* built into the *explicans* for which all presently available *explicans* are inadequate. If the appeal to the principle of sufficient reason in the evil case is legitimate grounds for rejecting the purported solution, the appeal in the contingency case to the same principle is legitimate grounds for rejecting the purported explanation. Since the former appeal is legitimate, so is the latter appeal. Hence Aquinas and Taylor are right after all.

But one qualification must be made. The argument in defense of appealing to the principle of sufficient reason rests on the similarity of two reasonably complex arguments. In short, it is as strong as the analogy between the arguments compared. If the attempted solution of the problem of evil is indeed very similar to the attempt to explain the existence of contingent beings via an infinite series of such beings, and if the criticisms of each attempt are indeed very similar to one another, and if one criticism is conclusive, it is highly reasonable to conclude that the other is. But as is always the case with analogies or "parity of reason" considerations, we are left with the questions "how similar are the cases?" and "how similar is similar enough?." Absolutely definitive answers in such instances are not easy to come by. Also, the critic of Aquinas and Taylor could, after all, deny that either criticism is adequate.

Before briefly remarking on the relevance of our conclusion to religious belief and practice, one final matter requires attention. Suppose, it might be asked, one grants that a necessary being exists; so what? How is this religiously relevant, particularly, for example, to the Judeo-Christian tradition? Aquinas was well aware of this problem, and offered other arguments to attempt to show that a being who was all-wise and all-good exists. He argued from the fact that non-sentient beings behave as if they consciously pursued ends, the acorn always, if not obstructed, producing an oak tree, to the existence of an all-wise being. The attempt to prove that the orderly and end-oriented behavior of organic bodies and the design manifest in all bodies proves that an all-wise, more carefully, omnipotent and omniscient, being exists is not dealt with here. The reason is that philosophic dispute about this argument ends in precisely the same sort of impasse as the one we have discussed. But this must be left, as the logic texts say, as an exercise for the reader.[48]

It seems that a conclusion follows from all this as to the relevance of the argument from contingency to religious belief.[49] The entire discussion has reflected a conviction that the issues raised by the argument from contingency are not simply those expressed in "Is the argument valid?" and "Are the premises true?." The argument, as stated, is indeed valid, an advantage not to be despised. But issues of importance arise even about the intelligibility of its premises, let alone their truth. They concern the very criteria used for rational appraisal of an argument. Whereas one's views about such matters may be influenced by, or even deduced from, theological beliefs independently held,[50] the disputes in question are rather plainly philosophical, not religious, in character. I think that one can say this much without providing (what may in any case be impossible) a clear criterion for being a religious, versus a philosophical topic. At least this much may be said: one would look long and hard in, say, either the Old or New

Testament to find anything that committed one to one position as opposed to the other with respect to the propositions in dispute between Taylor and Edwards.

This is not to say that the argument from contingency is of no religious relevance. If there is demonstrably a necessary being, then if we can also justify Aquinas' confidence when he says "and this everyone calls 'God,'" theism will be rational in the sense of having been, in part at any rate, proved. But the proof is apt to be one that only the intellectual elite can follow, as Aquinas acknowledged.

It is sometimes said that if God's existence could be proved, there would be no room for faith. This claim rests on a certain conception of what faith is, and this topic will be discussed in a later chapter. For now, it will suffice to point out that it seems obvious that one could in fact prove that God exists and still live as if he did not. As St. James has it, "The devils believe and tremble."[51]

ANSELM'S ONTOLOGICAL ARGUMENTS

If impasse may arise upon consideration of the argument from contingency, perhaps more conclusive results can be reached with respect to some other argument for God's existence. One of the most interesting attempts to prove that God exists is the ontological argument[52] formulated by St. Anselm in his *Prosologion*.[53] It is fashionable to distinguish two Anselmian arguments; one is in *Prosologion*, Chapter Two and the other in *Prosologion*, Chapter Three.[54] Since this procedure reflects much of the contemporary discussion of the ontological argument, it will be adopted here. Each of these Anselmian arguments has been discussed in detail, and I shall select just one treatment of each argument for analysis.

The argument found in *Prosologion*, Chapter One can be stated as follows. It consists of a prologue and a main argument. The prologue is expressed by Anselm in these words.

> . . . 'the fool has said in his heart: there is no God.' (Psalm 13:1; 42:1) But certainly that very fool, when he hears what I say, viz., 'something than which nothing greater can be thought,' understands what he hears; and what he understands is in his intellect, even if he does not understand that it exists.[55]

He adds

> . . . he understands this when he hears this, and whatever is understood is in the intellect.[56]

Anselm offers an argument which assumes that if a phrase is understood by a person, say Jones, then there is something in Jones' understanding which corresponds to the phrase which he understands.[57] But consider the phrase, "the square circle." We understand this phrase, at least well enough to know that it does not, and cannot, refer to anything. It is certainly not clear, however, that there is anything in the understanding to which the phrase corresponds. Again, consider the phrase "the number one higher than that ever actually thought by any human being." We understand the phrase, but it is again far from clear that something in our understanding is referred to by this phrase. There is reason, then, to question the prologue to Anselm's argument. For present purposes it is not necessary to follow up this line of criticism. Suffice it to say that it emphasizes the model of linguistic term-mental entity-external referent (e.g. the word "God" —the concept of God—God, the eternal being) with which Anselm apparently operates.

The argument itself relies on the distinction between existing in the understanding and existing in reality, and on the claim that to exist both in concept and reality is greater than to exist in concept alone.[58]

Anselm puts his argument in this fashion.

> Now certainly that than which a greater cannot be thought cannot exist in the intellect only. For if it exists only in the intellect, it can be thought that it exists also in reality which is greater. If therefore, that than which a greater cannot be thought exists only in the intellect, that very thing than which a greater cannot be thought is something than which a greater can be thought. But certainly this cannot be. Hence beyond doubt there is something than which a greater cannot be thought both in the intellect and in reality.[59]

The argument can be stated simply.

1. God is that being than whom no greater can be conceived.
2. God exists in the understanding.
3. To exist in both understanding and reality is greater than to exist in the understanding alone.
4. God cannot exist in the understanding alone, for if He did then we could conceive of a greater being (one just like God except that He exists in reality also).
5. But we cannot conceive of a being greater than God.
6. Thus God exists in reality as well as in the understanding.

Numerous objections have been raised to any kind of ontological argument. As famous as any is the claim that whatever can be conceived to exist can also be conceived not to exist.[60] Another is that we cannot move from mere concepts which exist in man's understanding to what exists in reality. The former simply begs the question, leaving us asking why this is so. If the ontological argument is correct, then there is one being, God, whose existence is conceivable but whose nonexistence is not conceivable. The latter objection is not clearly true. In addition to leaving us asking why we cannot ever move from concepts to reality, it neglects that fact that we do go from the fact that a concept is inconsistent to the fact that nothing can correspond to it.[61] The concept "round square" is inconsistent; therefore there can be no round squares. That we can never move from mere concepts to the existence of something referred to by those concepts needs proof.

Another objection, also frequently made, is that the most that the ontological argument could prove is that if God exists, then He necessarily does.[62] The reason why this move seems plausible is not far to seek. Generally, modal statements[63] can be treated as conditionals. Thus "All triangles necessarily have three angles" means "If anything is a triangle, it has three angles." But quite plainly "God necessarily exists" does not fit this model.

This can be seen if we consider the following argument. Supposedly, (1) "God necessarily exists" is identical to (2) "If God exists, then God necessarily exists." If so, then the truth conditions of the one sentence are identical to those of the other, and conversely. Now by an elementary rule of transformation,[64] (2) is identical to (3) "God does not exist or God necessarily exists." So if (1) and (2) are identical, so are (1) and (3). Now (3) is true if God does not exist. But (1) is false if God does not exist. So (1) is not identical to (3)—they do not have the same truth conditions. Since (3) is identical to (2), (2) is not identical to (1).

Another traditional criticism of the argument under discussion is that existence is not a predicate. As Walter Alston comments,

> Where the support for this denial goes beyond pious asservation, which is less often than one would like to think, it usually takes the form of pointing out logical differences between admitted subject-predicate statements and statements which differ from these only in the substitution of "exists" for the predicate. But it is never shown that these differences are such as to prevent "exists" from being a very special sort of predicate, . . . After all, there are very great logical differences between admitted subject-predicate statements too.[65]

Nonetheless, Alston believes, this objection can be developed so as to constitute a refutation of the first formulation of the ontological argument.

The usual presentation of the familiar claim that existence is not a predicate argues that in order to say of an entity E that E has a property, one must assume that E exists. Of course, Jones, who is broke, may deceive Smith into thinking that he is wealthy by speaking of his large bankroll. In so doing, Jones is not deceived by his own lie into thinking that he really has such a bankroll. Nonetheless, were it not the case that "I (Jones) have a large bankroll" entailed "I (Jones) have a bankroll," the lie could not possibly succeed in making Smith think Jones is wealthy. The point is that "E, which does not exist, has property P" is contradictory.

Suppose, now, we regard existence itself as a property. Then, the traditional presentation goes, unhappy results immediately follow. Suppose E does exist. Then to predicate the existence of E will give this result: "E exists." But that E exists is also a condition of predicating anything at all of E. So we have "E (which exists) exists." Next suppose that E does not exist. Now if existence is a predicate, so is nonexistence. So we can predicate nonexistence of E, with this result: "E does not exist." But existence is a condition of predication. Thus we have "E (which exists) does not exist." So the net result of making existence a predicate is that all affirmative existential statements (i.e. all statements saying that something exists) are necessarily true and all negative existential statements are necessarily false.[66]

Alston offers counter-examples to this thesis.[67]

(A)   There are centaurs in Greek mythology, but no such creatures exist.

(B)   In many old legends, there is a British king named Arthur . . . and, according to some scholars, he really existed.

(C)   That ghost exists only in your imagination.

(D)   Perfectly unselfish people exist only in literature.

In these cases, and others like them, we have in some cases affirmative and in other cases negative existential statements which are not either necessarily true or necessarily false.

In order to make good his case against the traditional objection, Alston has to assume that there are different modes of existence: existing in literature, existing in the imagination, existing in reality, for example, are all modes of existence.[68] Granting this assumption, it would seem to follow that:

> . . . the standard argument against treating "exists" as a predicate collapses. If I can say, without redundancy, "There is in many old legends a British King named Arthur . . . and the evidence is that he really existed," it would seem that I can just as well set up a subject

on the presupposition of the first conjunct, and then, without triviality, predicate real existence of this subject.[69]

That is, granting the assumption just mentioned, I can say "King Arthur (who exists in legend) exists (in fact)" without saying anything that is either necessarily true or anything which is contradictory.

Analogously, admitting at least two modes of existence (in the understanding; in reality) I can say "God (who exists in the understanding) exists (in reality)." This will have the form "God (who exists$_1$) exists$_2$." The traditional objection rehearsed above gives us no reason to deny that exists$_2$ is a predicate. As Alston puts it,

> We can use one mode of existence to set up the subject, and another mode of existence as the predicate. At least, once we recognize the diverse modes of existence, the standard arguments are powerless to prevent this. And this means that the ontological argument has not finally been disposed of.[70]

Nonetheless, Alston believes, there are other grounds for rejecting that argument. He points out in detail that to exist in one mode is quite different from existing in another.[71] That is, a statement of the form "x exists in the understanding" has a quite different set of entailments than "x exists in reality."

> Anselm escapes the standard criticism by presupposing existence in the understanding so as to get a subject of which he can show real existence to be necessarily predicated . . . The statement which he is claiming to be necessarily true is a statement about a being in the understanding, and as such exhibits the logical features of statements based on a pre-supposition of mental existence.[72]

One such feature of this statement is that it can be truly tested, if at all, by reflection.

> The person in whose understanding a certain being exists has only to reflect, to ask himself what he means by a certain term, in order to determine whether or not any statement about that being is true.[73]

To verify that I have the idea of God, that God exists in my understanding, I need only reflect in the sense of "examining what is in my understanding."[74] But it is not that the idea in my understanding is really to be "God." Rather, we infer that God exists from our idea of him.

But, Alston continues, this is just the sort of inference we cannot make. Two sorts of inferences can, he says, be made from the fact that an entity E has non-real existence or exists in the understanding.

(1) "There is some real existence of a given sort, which is always of the same sort for a given non-real mode, the existence of which is entailed by the non-real existence of the thing in question."[75] E.g., a real dream-state, or a real state of imagining.

(2) that we can describe something which has the properties which are included in our idea and which may really exist.

But neither of these inferences will serve Anselm's purpose. Since they are purportedly the only inferences which can be made from the fact that something exists in the understanding without obliterating the distinction between the two modes of existence, Anselm's first formulation of the ontological argument fails.[76] As Alston summarizes his conclusion:

> This means that if "The being than which nothing greater can be conceived exists in reality" is to be interpreted as the attribution of a predicate to a being in the understanding, it can have no implications with respect to the real world other than the fact that Anselm, or whoever else forms this concept, had a certain idea in his mind. But it is plain that . . . this sentence . . . implies much more than this about the real world.[77]

It will be helpful to distinguish various sorts of non-real existence. By so doing we can enter into the spirit of Alston's criticism as we appraise it. Let us distinguish between the following sorts of non-real existence: in the understanding (exists$_1$), in fiction (exists$_2$), as a figment of the imagination (exists$_3$). And let us use "exists" without a subscript to mean (exists in reality). There are important differences between existence$_1$, existence$_2$, and existence$_3$. That X exists$_3$ entails that X exists$_1$ and that X does not exist. That X exists$_2$ entails that X exists$_1$, and has no entailments about whether X exists$_3$ or whether X exists. That X exists$_1$ does not entail that X exists$_2$ or that X exists$_3$. Normally, that X exists$_1$ does not entail that X exists.

The fact that X exists$_3$ entails that X does not exist is a counter example to Alston's rigid claim that the non-real existence of X cannot have entailments about X's real existence. So does the fact that "The concept of X is an inconsistent concept" entails "X does not exist," for presumably if the former statement is true then X exists$_1$. Or, if one holds that no one can actually have contradictory concepts, then the fact that X cannot exist$_1$, entails that X cannot—and hence does not—exist. But perhaps all that Alston wishes to say is that no affirmative existential claim of the form "X exists" can follow from any statement ascribing non-real existence to X, though the existence of something other than X may follow from this statement.

Part of the plausibility of Alston's argument rests upon certain features of exists$_2$. These features are nicely expressed by Everett Hall when he says concerning one sort of non-real existence,

> . . . the accomplished fiction-writer uses *all* the resources of ordinary language for his creative purposes . . . any commitments involved in the serious use of various linguistic forms and devices are exactly the same in the imaginative writing save that they are *all* set aside by the authors telling the reader in some way, "This is fiction," thus psychologically disengaging himself . . ."[78]

Thus whereas "X is P" normally presupposes "X exists," if it is the case that "X exists$_2$," is the assumption upon which "X is P" is made, obviously "X exists" is not entailed by "X is P."[79]

It would not do to simply assume that this disengagement occurs with respect to all modes of non-real existence. While it occurs when one writes fictionally about X, it does not occur when one simply thinks about X. Assertive disengagement is a feature of exists$_2$ usage, but not necessarily of cases of exists$_1$ which are not also cases of exists$_2$. To think of X is not to always presuppose that X does not exist. If this were necessarily a feature of all cases of exists$_1$ usage, we could be fully confident that Alston's restrictions on the possible entailments of "X exists$_1$" were justified. Since it is not, and since Alston seems to provide no other basis for such confidence, it looks as if—for all Alston proves—an ontological argument has not been shown to be an impossibility. It is still possible that for some value of "X," "X exists$_1$," does entail "X exists."

Nonetheless, our original formulation of the argument is not without problems of its own. What might it mean to say that if X exists$_1$ and exists, it is greater than Y which is just like X save that Y does not exist? The argument requires this premise, but the premise is certainly neither at all clear nor at all plausible. It is time, then, to consider a second formulation of the ontological argument.

MALCOLM'S FORMULATION OF ANSELM'S ARGUMENT

Anselm's second version of his argument runs as follows.

> If it (the thing a greater than which cannot be conceived) can be conceived at all, it must exist. For no one who denies or doubts the existence of a being a greater than which is inconceivable, denies that if it did exist its non-existence, either in reality or in the understanding,

would be impossible. For otherwise it would not be a being a greater than which cannot be conceived. But as to whatever can be conceived but does not exist: if it were to exist, its non-existence either in the reality or in the understanding would be possible. Therefore, if a being a greater than which cannot be conceived, can even be conceived, it must exist.[80]

Norman Malcolm's statement of this other version of Anselm's onto-logical argument is the clearest I know of. It begins as follows:

1. Either God exists or God does not exist.
2. If God exists, God necessarily exists.
3. If God does not exist, God necessarily does not exist.
4. God necessarily exists or God necessarily does not exist.

The first statement is obviously a logically necessary truth. If the fourth statement is necessarily true, it is not obviously so. For if God exists with logical contingency, then (4) is false, and no necessary truth can, under any conditions, be false. So an argument is needed to show that (4) is necessarily true, and premises one through three provide that argument. If one accepts premises one through three but denies (4), he contradicts himself. So the argument for (4) is valid. Malcolm would say that each of premises one through three is a necessary truth, and that therefore (4) is a necessary truth, since anything that follows from only necessary truths is itself a necessary truth. A crucial question, then, arises about (2) and (3); are they necessary truths, or even true at all?

If we grant (2) and (3) for the moment, thus granting (4) for the moment, it is easily shown that God necessarily exists.

5. God necessarily does not exist if, but only if, "x is God" entails "x has incompatible properties."
6. "x is God" does not entail "x has incompatible properties."
7. It is false that God necessarily does not exist.

Once again, (5) is a necessary truth. Premise (6) can also be granted; the onus would clearly be on the man who denied (6) to show that it is false. We rightly deny that a concept is contradictory if we examine it carefully and find no reason to believe that it is. The concept of God has been carefully examined by many philosophers and theo-logians who have found no reason to suppose it to be contradictory. Neither Malcolm, nor the present writer, knows of any argument to the contrary that succeeds.[81] Thus (6) can safely be granted until some argument shows that (6) is false. To put the point differently, just as one is justified in taking "x is a table" not to entail "x has incompatible properties" until he is shown that it does entail this, so one is justified is taking "x is God" not to entail that "x has incompatible properties" until he is shown that it does entail this. But if "x is God" does not entail "x has incompatible properties," the concept of God is a consistent concept and (6) is true. Together, (5) and (6) entail (7). From (7) together with (4) it follows that:

(8) God necessarily exists.

If we grant Malcolm (2) and (3), then, he has provided a proof that God necessarily exists. But it is not obviously self-contradictory to deny (2), or to deny (3), in the way that it is obviously self-contradictory to deny (1). So a defense of (2) and (3) must be provided. The defense might run as follows:

(2) is true, since a valid argument can be provided in which "God exists" and certain necessary truths entail "God necessarily exists." The argument is this one:
   (a) God exists (assumption)
   (b) N (If God exists, then God always has existed and always will exist) (necessary truth)
   (c) N (God always has existed and always will exist) (from a and b)
   (d) If N (God always has existed and always will exist) then "God does not exist at time t" is self-contradicatory, where t is any time we pick) (necessary truth)
   (e) If for any time we pick, "God does not exist at t" is self-contradictory; then for any time we pick, "God exists" is necessarily true. (necessary truth)
   (f) If God exists, then He necessarily exists. (from a-e)

Thus from (a), which is the antecedent of premise (2), and two necessary truths, namely, (b) and (c)—where (c) follows from (a) and (b), the consequent of (2) follows. So if we expand (2) into "If (a) and (b), then God necessarily exists," (2) is true. The expanded version of (2) will do quite as well for the argument as the original version. So we have an argument for (2).

This attempt to prove (2), however, by deriving (c) from (a) and (b) is fallacious. Consider the following two arguments:

A: The number of planets is nine.
    N (9 = 3 times 3)
    Thus: N (The number of planets is three times three).[82]
B: God exists.
    N (If God exists, then He has always existed and will always exist).
    Thus: N (God has always existed and will always exist).

Argument A is plainly fallacious. The discovery of a tenth planet is not logically impossible, which it would be were the conclusion to A true. But the premises of A are true. So argument A is invalid. Thus argument B, which is exactly analogous to A and the inference from (a) and (b) to (c), is invalid. Further, I can see no way to make B valid which would serve Malcolm's purposes. So this defense of (2) fails; are there any others?[83]

Although a "defense" of (3) could be constructed on lines exactly analogous to those suggested for (2), there is obviously no point in producing it. I am not sure that Malcolm ever offered the sort of defense just discussed; the argument for (2) that I will now analyze, however, is one that Malcolm gives.[84]

a) If "God exists" is contingent, then it is possible, at any time *t* you pick, that God not exist at *t*.

b) If it is possible that, at any time *t* you pick, God does not exist, then the question "How long has God existed?" is an appropriate question.

c) "How long has God existed?" is not an appropriate question.

d) Thus (from (b) and (c)) it is not possible that, at any time you pick, God does not exist at that time.

e) Thus (from (a) and (d)) "God exists" is not contingent (i.e., "God exists" is, if true, necessarily true, and, if false, necessarily false).

The interesting thing about this argument is that it alone, if correct, will prove (4) in the original proof. If "God exists" is not contingent, then it is necessary, either necessarily true or self-contradictory. So this argument must be examined carefully. I grant Malcolm that (c) is true. Just as one who asks "How many blue-berries are square roots of minus 14?" does not understand what blueberries are or square roots, or both; so the man who asks "How long has God existed?" does not understand what "God" means in the Judeo-Christian tradition, the only tradition relevant to Anselm's or Malcolm's argument.

Nonetheless, the argument, though valid, is unsound since (b) is false. This can be shown in the following manner. Premise (b) is true only if its antecedent cannot be true when its consequent is false.[85] The following statement is a necessary truth: (S): N (If God exists, He has always existed and will always exist). Now (S), plus the antecedent of (b) "God exists" taken as contingent but true entail: (T) something, namely God, exists with respect to which the question "How long has it existed?" is inappropriate. Succinctly stated, contrary to Malcolm's assumption that only if God necessarily exists is it true that the question is inappropriate, the question "How long has God existed?" is inappropriate because "If God exists, then He has always existed and will always exist "is a necessary truth.

Thus a necessary truth, S, plus the antecedent of (b), entail that "How long has God existed?" is not appropriate with respect even to a contingently existing God, the denial of (b's) consequent. So the antecedent of (b) can be true while its consequent is false, and thus (b) is false. So we have no proof of (2).

The point is this. Whether one believes that "God exists" is necessarily true or does not believe this, he can agree with Malcolm that "How long has God existed?" is not an appropriate question. But the man who believes that "God exists" is contingent, whether true or false, can account for this fact. He need merely note that "If God exists, He always has existed and always will exist" is a necessary truth. Just as "How happy is a perfect circle?" is clearly not an appropriate question, whether there are any perfect circles or not, so "How long has God existed?" is not an appropriate question whether God exists or not. But Malcolm's argument assumes that this question can be shown to be inappropriate only on the view that "God exists" is a necessary statement. Since this assumption is, for the reason just given, mistaken, Malcolm's argument is unsuccessful. The conclusion would seem to me to be that we must regard this ingenious argument of Malcolm's as at best incomplete unless he, or someone, can offer a successful argument for the claim that "God exists" is either necessarily true or self-contradictory.

With respect to the ontological argument, I think that we can only say this much. One formulation, the one which Alston has shown is very naturally attributed to Anselm's *locus classicus,* is not sufficiently clear to be at all plausible. A different formulation, the one that Malcolm has shown is very naturally attributed to another portion of Anselm's writings, is clear enough. But the two crucial premises of Malcolm's formulation are neither obviously necessary truths nor supported adequately by Malcolm's sub-proof. Nor is it at all clear how one could move from any statement that is obviously a necessary truth about God to either (2) or (3) in Malcolm's main argument. It is not at all clear why anyone ought to accept either of these premises. Equally, however, I am unable to provide any reason why they must be rejected. It is easy to see why the argument continues to fascinate philosophers and provoke discussion. I do not think that the issue as to whether any such argument could succeed is settled, though none that I am aware of does seem to succeed. The conclusion is hence not as clear-cut as one would wish. Nonetheless, it seems to me to be the one required by the facts.

FOOTNOTES ᴄ∾ III

1 *Summa Theologica*, Part 1, Question 2, Article 3. Hereafter references to this volume will be cited *ST* with three numbers following indicating part, question, and article respectively. The passages cited can be conveniently found in St. Thomas Aquinas, *Basic Writings of St. Thomas Aquinas*, ed. A. Pegis (New York: Random House, 1944), p. 21.

2 *Loc. cit.*

3 David Hume, *A Treatise Concerning Human Nature*, ed. Selby-Bigge (London: Oxford U. Press, 1965), p. 220.

4 I waive questions concerning Hume's theory of mind. For this, see *op. cit.*, Part Four, Section Six, and Appendix, p. 633ff.

5 This account of things is obviously crude. What constitutes *distinct* sensory experiences? Is the perceiver constant throughout the perceptual change? These questions, among others, require an answer. More fundamentally, can one give a consistent Humean account of perception? Nothing here hangs on how one answers these questions.

6 For a discussion of Aquinas' theory of sense perception which makes clear that he is committed to these views, see these works plus the passages from Aquinas which they cite: Etienne Gilson, *The Christian Philosophy of St. Thomas Aquinas* (London: Victor Gollancz, Ltd., 1957), Part Two, Chapters 5 and 6; F. C. Coplestone, *Aquinas* (Baltimore: Penguin Books, Inc., 1955); St. Thomas Aquinas, *Philosophical Texts*, ed. and trans. by T. Gilby (New York: Oxford U. Press, 1960), chapter 10.

7 Admittedly a chemist who was a determined follower of St. Thomas might be able, for every chemical counter example offered, to provide an explanation of that counter example consistent with (2b). But this would leave the status of (2b) in some doubt, unless the explanation consistent with (2b) was plainly better than any explanation not consistent with (2b). This would show that one already convinced of (2b) need not abandon it, but would give no reason for anyone else to accept it. This would also leave untouched the other counter examples proposed. Nor is the situation materially improved by making reference to the "total cause" of the effect in question.

8 See *Summa Contra Gentiles*, Book I, Chapter 29, paragraph 2; *ST*, I, 45, 7.

9 See Aristotle, *Posterior Analytics*, Book 2, Chapter 2, 94 a 20ff. Aquinas accepts this doctrine. See *ST*, I, 44, and I, 82, 1.

10 Precisely the same sort of issue as arose about premise one of the First Way arises here too. Does one ever perceive by the senses that causation has occurred? Cf. David Hume, *Enquiry Concerning Human Understanding* (London: Oxford U. Press, 1962), Sections 4 and 7.

11 Aquinas makes exactly this appeal in *SCG*, I, 42, 4 (first sentence). For an interesting discussion of the notion of simplicity, see Section Three of *Probability, Confirmation, and Simplicity*, ed. Foster and Martin (New York: Odyssey Press, 1966).

12 *ST*, I, 11, 3.

13 *SCG*, Book I, Chapter 20; *ST*, I, 3, 1.

14 *ST*, I, 3, 3.

15 *ST*, I, 3 Articles 2, 3, 5, 7, 8; *SCG*, Book I, Chapters 24, 25.

16 *ST*, I, 3, 6; *SCG*, I, 23.

17   *ST*, I, 19, 4, especially under "secondly."

18   Cf. Lovejoy's statement of the problem. A. O. Lovejoy, *The Great Chain of Being* (New York: Harpers Bros., 1960), p. 74ff. See also *SCG*, I, 23, paragraph 6.

19   See *ST*, I, 3, 7 and *SCG*, I, 18.

20   *ST*, I, 11, 3, paragraph three of Aquinas' "answer." On the claim that there is but one order which is best explained by reference to one agent, cf. Alvin Plantinga, *God and Other Minds* (Ithaca: Cornell U. Press, 1967), Chapters 4, 8, 9, 10.

21   Aristotle, *Metaphysics*, Book 14, Chapter 2, 1088b23; *On the Heavens*, Book 1, Chapter 12, 281b26ff.

22   Cf. E. L. Mascall, *He Who Is* (London: Longman's, 1943), p. 47. Mascall's own suggested premise will not, together with (S2) and (S3), yield (S4).

23   Strictly, of course, that time has a beginning will not show that at some time nothing existed. It will show, however, that there cannot have been an infinite chain of successive entities up to the present since such a series would require an infinite time.

24   *ST*, I, 46, 2; *SCG*, I, 13; *SCG*, II, 81, paragraph nine.

25   Maimonides, *Guide for the Perplexed*, Part Two, Chapter 1. The best translation is by Pines, published by the University of Chicago. Cf. E. Gilson, *History of Christian Philosophy in the Middle Ages* (New York: Random House, 1955), p. 649–651.

26   *ST*, I, 13, 2; II, 92, paragraph twelve and III, 97, paragraph fifteen.

27   At 281b26ff.

28   *De Caelo*, 281b3ff.

29   Namely, that it be divided into two equal subsets each of the members of which is a whole apple.

30   Aristotle denies, however, that there is an actual infinite. See *Physics*, Book 7, Chapter 1, 242a20. For the claim cited above, see *De Caelo*, 281a27ff.

31   *SCG*, I, 75; I, 81; II, 45; III, 71, esp. paragraph three. Cf. Lovejoy, *The Great Chain of Being*, p. 73ff.

32   Aquinas is explicit that not all possibilities of participating in God's goodness have been exhausted. *SCG*, I, 81, para. 4.

33   The same point can be seen in another way. Suppose that at every one of an infinite number of moments a person S whose perceptual capacities are unbounded happens to perceive only odd-numbered sets of objects. Since there are an infinite number of odd numbers, there can be an infinite number of odd-numbered sets that he perceives. So S can perceive for an infinitely long time without perceiving even one even-numbered set of objects. Since there can be an infinite number of even-numbered sets of perceivable objects, there are an infinite number of untapped perceptual experiences for S, even though S's perceptual experiences endure infinitely. It is fully consistent with our suppositions that only S exists, so no one, we can suppose, ever perceives an even-numbered set. Analogously to all this, it is logically possible that something A exist forever possessing a capacity C not to exist but never being presented with a stimulus that triggered C even though he experienced an infinite number of stimuli.

34   On this question, see E. Gilson, *op. cit.*, Chapter 1 and E. L. Mascall, *op. cit.*, Chapter 5.

35   It should be mentioned that this way of putting the argument does not leave open the possibility that a necessary entity have once existed but have passed out of existence. Since Q at any time *ex hypothesi* has a sufficient answer, at any time there must be a necessary entity. It should be clear that only our knowledge, not the existence, of this entity depends on there being contingent things. In any case, on Aquinas' view, causation is such that if x causes y, x exists so long at least as y does. Also, I have endeavored to state the argument in such a way as to

allow for the possibility that by "necessary being" Aquinas meant "logically neces-
sary being" but also to offer another sense of this term relevant to the argument.
On this issue, see Patterson Brown, "St. Thomas' Doctrine of Necessary Being,"
Philosophical Review, Vol. LXXIII (1964); P. T. Geach and G. E. M. Anscombe,
Three Philosophers (London: Oxford U. Press, 1961); Alvin Plantinga, *op. cit.*,
Chapter 1; J. Hintikka, "Necessity, Universality, and Time in Aristotle," *Eritainos
Ajatus*, Vol. XX, 1957.

36 Cf. *ST*, I, 2, 3, esp. the discussion of the necessary things which have their
necessity caused by another. These are, in the present sense, contingent. See also
Gilson, *op. cit.*

37 For an elementary account, see Wesley Salmon, *Logic* (Englewood Cliffs,
N.J.: Prentice-Hall, 1963). The concept of "giving an explanation" is of course immensely complex, and the above comments are useful mainly to elucidate the sort
of objection which is often felt towards Aquinas' position.

38 Free human choices and actions, and human "creativity," might not themselves admit of either theoretical or teleological explanations, at least in some cases.
But this would be because, for example, "Why did S choose the way S did?" cannot be answered or even intelligibly asked if one accepts a given theory of agency
which makes free choice possible. Cf. the Chisholm article in K. Lehrer, ed., *Freedom and Determinism* (New York: Random House, 1966) and the Taylor article in
Sidney Hook, ed., *Determinism and Freedom in the Age of Modern Science* (New
York: Collier Books, 1961). See also Richard Taylor, *Action and Purpose* (Englewood Cliffs, N.J.: Prentice-Hall, 1966).

39 Not only Thomists (followers of St. Thomas) hold this position. Cf. Richard
Taylor, *Metaphysics* (Englewood Cliffs, N.J.: Prentice-Hall, 1963). The onus of proof
is always on the man who says that a sentence is self-contradictory when its contradictoriness is not obvious.

40 As we have noted, the necessity in question need not be logical necessity.
"Every event has its sufficient conditions" is a crucial premise in the Thomistic
argument, but its denial is in fact not contradictory. Nor need the necessity of a
being with respect to which Q is inappropriate be logical necessity.

41 Richard Taylor, *op. cit.*, p. 92ff. Cf. Taylor's discussion of the locutions
"self-caused," "necessary being," "first cause," Taylor develops his argument with
respect to the universe. It could equally well be developed in terms of each member of an infinite causal series; the switch to speaking of the series itself is only a
response to the claim that whereas each member of the universe might be contingent it does not follow that the universe itself is contingent. If Edwards is correct in his critique of the contingency argument, to which we shall refer shortly,
then we cannot speak of the universe as either contingent or necessary, as to talk
of the universe is only to talk in a "short-hand" way about each particular thing
that exists. Then the claim that the universe is necessary though each of its members is contingent cannot be made. Either way, one can state the argument from
contingency.

42 Paul Edwards, "The Cosmological Argument" in D. Burrill, *The Cosmological Argument* (Garden City, N.Y.: Doubleday-Anchor, 1967), p. 117.

43 See Lucretius, *Of the Nature of Things* (London: J. M. Dent and Sons,
1923).

44 Cf. the criticisms of David Hume, *Dialogues Concerning Natural Religion*
and Immanuel Kant, *Critique of Pure Reason*, Transcendental Dialectic, Chapter 3.

45 A is a logically necessary condition of B just in case "B exists, but A does
not" is self contradictory.

46 It is not, of course, quite fair to pin the blame on the schema of the argument alone. As already noted, there might be some good of level *n* which explains
(justifies) the evil of level *n* − *1* and which has no balancing evil of level *n*. The

parallel in the contingency case to such a good G is a being which explains the existence of all else but whose own existence needs no explanation.

47 The term "same-level" explanation may by now have become somewhat unfortunate due to the hierarchical considerations involved in the "solution" to the problem of evil, but this should cause no great consternation so long as we remember how we have defined this term.

48 In addition to the works by Hume and Kant cited in footnote 44, see F. R. Tennant, *Philosophical Theology* (London: Cambridge U. Press, 1928); Stuart Hackett, *The Resurrection of Theism* (Chicago: Moody Press, 1957); Peter Bertocci, *An Introduction to the Philosophy of Religion* (Englewood Cliffs, N.J.: Prentice-Hall, 1951); Immanuel Kant, *The Critique of Judgment* (New York: Hafner Press, 1951).

49 Quite a different treatment of the argument has been offered in recent philosophy. The argument has been treated as if it were an intellectualization of our "sense of contingency;" we "see" that we, and our environment, are contingent and thereby gain an insight into ourselves and into the existence of a being who "meets" us in this recognition of our ontological poverty. This approach has been suggested by Ninian Smart in *Reasons and Faiths* (New York: Humanities Press, 1958); H. D. Lewis in *Our Experience of God* (New York: Humanities Press, 1959); and by Ian Ramsey in *Religious Language*. We discussed Ramsey's portrayal of this claim in Chapter One. Some have found a sense of contingency in Aquinas himself, with the stress on the metaphysical, not the existential, status of the purported recognition. Cf. Coplestone, *Aquinas* and Mascall, *He Who Is.*

50 For example, if one, independently of the argument from contingency, held God to exist and to be completely rational (on the model of a Perfect Mathematician) he might accept Aquinas' account of sufficient explanation on the grounds that to explain is to deduce from unquestioned and logically necessary axioms. I neglect the question of alternative axiom systems.

51 *The Epistle of James*, 2:20.

52 Cf. Alvin Plantinga, *The Ontological Argument* (Garden City, N.Y.: Doubleday-Anchor, 1965) for an excellent collection of essays on this argument.

53 Whether it was Anselm's intent to prove that God exists in such a manner as to convince anyone with clear enough mind to follow his argument is a point of much debate. (Cf. *The Many-Faced Argument*, ed., Hick and McGill, (New York: Macmillan, 1967) for a long discussion of this issue. The fact is, however, that it was so regarded by many philosophers of later date (Descartes, Leibniz, Spinoza, Kant) and is so regarded by many contemporary philosophers (Malcolm, Hartshorne, Alston, Findlay).

54 Cf. Hartshorne and Malcolm in Plantinga, *op. cit.* and McGill's discussion in Hick and McGill, *op. cit.*

55 I am indebted to my colleague, Prof. Julius R. Weinberg for the translation of this passage, as well as those cited below and footnoted 56 and 59. Cf. St. Anselm, *St. Anselm's Proslogion*, trans. M. J. Charlesworth (London: Oxford U. Press, 1965) p. 117.

56 *Loc. cit.* The discussion of the prologue to the ontological argument results from discussions with Prof. Weinberg who is translating a work of Gregory of Rimini (*Super Primum et Fecundum Sanctarium* (Franciscan Institute Publications, 1955)) in which Gregory makes substantially these criticisms.

57 Whether this applies to individual descriptive terms or phrases or to entire definite descriptions or to whole sentences is neither clear nor relevant.

58 He may also hold that to exist in reality is greater than to exist in concept alone, but this is not immediately relevant.

59 St. Anselm, *op. cit.*, p. 117.

60 David Hume, *Dialogues Concerning Natural Religion*, Sec. 9.

61   Cf. Richard Taylor's "Introduction" in Plantinga, *The Ontological Argument.*

62   "God necessarily exists" is equivalent to " 'God does not exist' is self contradictory." "God exists" is contingent in case neither it nor its denial is contradictory.

63   I.e., statements of the form "It is (is not) necessary that p" and "It is (is not) possible that p." In this sense of "possible," (logically) "possible" and (logically) "contingent" mean the same thing.

64   Symbolically, the rule is: (if p, then q) = (not–p or q).

65   Walter Alston, "The Ontological Argument Revisited," in Plantinga, *The Ontological Argument*, p. 88. The question is, of course, not whether "exists" can be a grammatical predicate (it plainly can), but whether existence is a *quality.* For a fuller treatment of this topic, see Plantinga, *God and Other Minds,* Chapter Two.

66   Cf. C. D. Broad, *Religion, Philosophy, and Psychical Research* (New York: Harcourt, Brace and World, 1953); A. J. Ayer, *Language, Truth and Logic,* Sec. Ed., (New York: Dover Press, 1946) and W. Salmon and G. Naknikian, " 'Exists' as a Predicate," *Philosophical Review,* October, 1954.

67   Plantinga, *The Ontological Argument,* p. 88ff.

68   *Ibid.,* p. 92 and compare p. 95–97 for Alston's defense of this assumption.

69   *Ibid.,* p. 93.

70   *Loc. cit.*

71   Cf. p. 98–106.

72   *Ibid.,* p. 102ff.

73   *Loc. cit.*

74   I waive problems of interpreting this sort of phrase.

75   Plantinga, *The Ontological Argument,* p. 103. Alston seems committed to Anselm's prologue argument in his discussion of a "real correlate."

76   It is perhaps worth noting that, as Professor Weinberg has remarked, any attempt to symbolize the ontological argument would seem to require quantifying into modal and/or psychological contexts, both of which are, in Quine's phrase, "referentially opaque."

77   Plantinga, *The Ontological Argument,* p. 103.

78   Everett Hall, *Philosophical Systems* (Chicago: U. of Chicago Press, 1960) p. 35.

79   Similar remarks apply to "x exists$_3$."

80   St. Anselm, *op. cit.,* p. 119. Cf. Plantinga, *op. cit.,* p. 145.

81   Attempts have been made to prove N (God does not exist). (N(p) = P is necessarily true.) See the discussion by J. N. Findley, G. E. Hughes and A. C. Ranier of the question "Can God's Existence by Disproved?" in A. Flew and A. MacIntyre, *New Essays in Philosophical Theology* (London: SCM Press, 1955). Findley makes the entirely dubious assumption that God is worship worthy only if His nonexistence is logically impossible. He also assumes that logical necessity merely reflects linguistic convention, which is also highly implausible. On the latter point, see Chapter Seven of Arthur Pap, *Semantics and Necessary Truth* (New Haven: Yale U. Press, 1958).

82   This example is borrowed from W. V. O. Quine, *From A Logical Point of View* (New York: Harper Bros., 1961).

83   For a full discussion of this sort of argument, see Plantinga's discussion of Malcolm in Plantinga, *The Ontological Argument.*

84   *Ibid.,* p. 144.

85   In "if A, then B," "A" is the antecedent and "B" the consequent.

BIBLIOGRAPHY ∽ III

Aquinas, St. Thomas., *Concerning Being and Essence*. New York: Appleton-Century-Crofts, Inc., 1937.

Collins, J., *God and Modern Philosophy*. Chicago: Henry Regnery Co., 1959.

Danielou, J., *God and the Ways of Knowing*. Cleveland: World Publishing Co., 1957.

Farrar, Austin., *Finite and Infinite*. London: Dacre Press, 1943.

Gilson, E. *God and Philosophy*. New Haven: Yale U. Press, 1941.

————, *Elements of Christian Philosophy*. Garden City, N.Y.: Doubleday and Co., 1960.

Maritain, *The Degrees of Knowledge*. New York: Charles Scribner's Sons, 1957.

Murray, J., *The Problem of God*. New Haven: Yale U. Press, 1964.

Pontinfex, D., *The Existence of God*. New York: Longmans, Green and Co., 1947.

Weinberg, J., *A Short History of Medieval Philosophy*. Princeton: Princeton U. Press, 1964.

Wolfson, H., trans. and ed., *Cresca's Critique of Aristotle*. Cambridge: Harvard University Press, 1929.

————, *Philo*. Cambridge: Harvard University Press, 1962.

IV

EXPERIENCE AND TRUTH IN RELIGION

Thus far, we have argued that religious claims such as "God exists" have truth-value, that "God exists" is not proved false by the existence of evil, and that certain of the traditional proofs do not show that this claim is true. We now raise a further question: Does religious experience provide relevant evidence for the truth of religious claims, particularly of the claim that God exists?

We must differentiate three questions concerning religious experience.[1] One concerns whether such experience is qualitatively different from all others, in the way that color experience is distinct in its kind. It needs to be added that we could accept the thesis that religious experience is qualitatively distinct, having, for example, a uniquely numinous quality, without claiming that any numinous object exists, just as we can grant that color experience is irreducible to and qualitatively unlike any other experience without denying that perceived color is a product of the interaction of perceiving organ and perceived object. Just as a world without perceivers would, at least on a widely accepted analysis of color qualities, be void of color, so a world without subjects of numinous experience, it may be suggested, would be void of numinous objects or events. This latter claim neither follows from, nor is it incompatible with, the thesis that religious experience is unique or irreducible to any other sort of experience.

Again, if religious experience is only a particular complex of experiences of other kinds, having no qualitative uniqueness, it does not follow either that God does not exist or that He is not experienced.

There is no impossibility involved in the thesis that He always mediates His presence through ordinary experiences. It is bedrock Christianity that God became man, yet it is granted that He was unrecognized by most of His creatures who saw Him.

A second question arises as to the causal conditions of a religious experience. Is it produced by divine activity, by an overactive thyroid, or by LSD? Or are such experiences caused sometimes by one and sometimes by another? If St. Paul's dream which led him to go to Macedonia[2] were somehow known[3] to be produced by a particular kind of unleavened bread taken with a glass of a certain sort of Palestinian wine, would this refute his contention that God had called him to go to Macedonia? Surprisingly the answer seems to be negative. God could, presumably, cause Paul to dream in a certain manner by so planning the course of the universe that Paul ate and drank what he did when he did, as well as He could directly cause the dream. What our discovery about the cause of Paul's dream would amount to is that, should we know that the immediate cause of Paul's dream was what was in Paul's stomach, we would know that God was not the immediate cause of Paul's dream. This is compatible with, so to say, God's having planned all along that Paul have his dream, and so with Paul's belief that he traveled under divine commission. The issue of the veracity of religious experience seems not to be decisively affected by questions about the unique quality, or the proximate cause, of such experience. But it is just the issue as to whether religious experience is veracious—whether it tells us something about the world besides the fact that people have such experience—that we must now raise as a third question. The answer to this question, it may seem highly plausible to maintain, does not depend on the answer to the others just noted, for the reasons just mentioned.

It is nonetheless true that a man who claims to have experienced God is claiming that what he experiences is not the product of a drug intake or a bodily disorder, any more than he experiences such a product when he notes an oncoming car or devours a sandwich. Different though God obviously must be from cars and sandwiches, He shares their ontological independence from any individual states. The object of the experience is in each case distinct from the experience, and does not depend for its existence on being experienced. Further, it is difficult to see how God could be the object of such an experience were He not also at least part of its cause. Some philosophers, John Locke for example, have maintained that physical objects cause ideas; we directly experience ideas, which resemble physical objects, and indirectly (i.e., by means of these ideas) perceive the objects themselves. Now perhaps one could develop some view by which God is indirectly perceived in an analogous manner, but what such a view would seem to amount to would be the claim that we have experiences of which God is ultimate cause which give us reliable information about God. This view, as we have seen, is compatible with a negative or an affirmative answer to either of our previous two questions.

An experience of which God was cause and object would presumably also be distinct in kind. God is after all conceived of as quite different from physical objects or other persons, though more like the latter than the former. Even given that "no man can see God and live," and given our own finitude so that any revelation of God would be radically short of exhausting God's nature, one might expect the experience, however muted, to fit into a class all its own.

Two kinds of claims concerning God can be based on experience: claims to experience God, or to have experiences of which God is direct, though perhaps only partial, cause and object, and claims to gain truth about God on the basis of experiences of which God is the ultimate cause, or the cause in virtue of His being Creator and Providence. It is usually in this latter sense that moral experience has been said in some sense to reveal God. When we ask whether religious experience provides relevant evidence for the truth of religious claims, we are in the present context asking whether there is good reason to believe that God is the object and direct cause of any human experience, which would then likely be qualitatively unique.

FREUD'S CRITIQUE OF RELIGION

The view that religious experience can be psychologically explained has seemed to many to be a damaging criticism of traditional theism. It is hence worth asking what sort of explanation is in question and to what degree the issues raised by this sort of explanation are crucial. Sigmund Freud's *The Future of An Illusion* provides an interesting case study since it is brief, clearly written, and widely influential.[4]

In an earlier work,[5] Freud claims that man's belief in God results from his projection of his father-image onto a cosmic screen. A child relies on its father for provision of need and protection from danger, but when the child grows up, and even before, he notes his father's grave limitations: he is not all-powerful or all-knowing or even all-good, and he will die leaving the child alone. What is needed is a father without these limitations. Such a being is provided by man's inventing him; man makes the idea and belief in the being of God, not the converse. Of course, men are not aware of this, for were they aware of creating God they would hardly find the comfort they need so desperately. But, fortunately, there are not only psychological mechanisms which invent God but also others which mask the process from the inventor's consciousness. It is against the backdrop of this theory that Freud develops his more detailed account in *The Future of An Illusion*.[6]

In this work, Freud begins his argument by noting that the existence of culture or civilization requires that men's satisfaction of their instincts and desires be to some extent curtailed. Coercion is required to effect this curtailment, since argument is of no avail against the passions. The existence of culture also requires that men work, and men are not spontaneously fond of work. Here is another cause for coercion. Man does have a quite varied set of instinctual dispositional patterns, or tendencies to behave in certain ways, but the course of a man's dispositions is determined by his early childhood experiences and hence the effectiveness of education in radically altering these tendencies is severely restricted. Thus no opportunity for eliminating the need for coercion exists. Men are willing to accept a given culture only insofar as they have made its ideals their own (have "internalized" them) and as it provides them satisfactions. One of these satisfactions is provided by religious doctrine. How, though, is such doctrine satisfying?

Insofar as we view nature as ruled by gods, we can attempt to placate and ingratiate them, extending to nature patterns of behavior that we have found successful in social interaction. We can act to mitigate our helplessness. Even terror, death, and suffering become tolerable. Order is seen as design, and nature is viewed as ruled by powers not altogether unlike us or insensitive to us. Human society is a sub-society under the gods and the natural environment provides the setting for the interaction between gods and men. If one being combines all the powers of the others, he can do more for us, so polytheism gives way to monotheism and security is closer still. Man, destined to remain a child in perpetuity, gains an everlasting father.

Is there, however, any cogent reason for belief in such a being? Freud lists three answers offered as to why one should accept religious claims.

> Firstly, these teachings deserve to be believed because they were already believed by our primal ancestors, secondly, we possess proofs which have been handed down to us from those primaeval times; and thirdly, it is forbidden to raise the question of their authentication at all.[7]

One must admit that these reasons are less than overwhelming, though perhaps only one already committed to the view that religious claims cannot be accepted on rational grounds could be satisfied with sum-ming up the "the case for religion" in this manner.[8] In any case, Freud makes it clear that he is convinced "about the impossibility of prov-ing the truth of religious doctrine."[9] Given this, he asks why people accept religious belief with such firm conviction. He answers that religious beliefs are

> . . . illusions, fulfillments of the oldest, strongest, and most urgent wishes of mankind. The secret of their strength lies in the strength of these wishes.[10]

An illusion is a belief, not necessarily a false one, derived from human wishes. For Freud, religious doctrines are all illusions and none can be proved.

Nonetheless, Freud's view as to the truth of any religious claims is not uninfluenced by his account of their origin.[11]

> To assess the truth value of religious doctrine does not lie within the scope of the present enquiry. It is enough for us that we have recog-nized them as being, in their psychological nature, illusions. But we do not have to conceal the fact that this discovery strongly influences our attitude to the question which must appear to many to be the most important of all. We know approximately at what periods and by what kind of men religious doctrines were created. If in addition we dis-cover the motives which led to this, our attitude to the problem of religion will undergo a marked displacement. We shall tell ourselves that it would be very nice if there were a God who created the world and was a benevolent Providence, and if there were a moral order in the universe and an afterlife; but it is a very striking fact that all this is exactly as we are bound to wish it to be.[12]

Thus Freud does endeavor to assess the truth value of religious doc-trines after all. He speaks of "what I have said here against the truth value of religions" (i.e. against any religious doctrine being true).[13] But what, precisely, has he said in this regard? That one can trace the history of religions? We can trace the development of historio-graphy, physics, and the psychoanalytic movement; does this show these endeavors to be misdirected? But obviously, one will reply, there is a disanalogy between religion on the one hand and historiography, physics and psychoanalysis on the other; the latter are methods or rely on carefully developed methods, while the former consists of substantive beliefs.

> In point of fact, psychoanalysis is a method of research, an impartial instrument, like the infinitesimal calculus, as it were.[14]

And there is no reputable method whose application produces religious beliefs in the way that there is a (set of) reputable method(s) whose application produces scientific results or beliefs. For this reason, Freud claims, religious beliefs must be rejected. He adds that

> . . . in the long run, nothing can withstand reason and experience, and the contradiction which religion offers to both is all too palpable. Even purified religious ideas cannot escape this fate so long as they try to preserve anything of the consolation of religion.[15]

Thus there is, in Freud's view, a conflict between religious claims and reason and experience. No reliable method produces religious data; the data we have gleaned by using reliable methods conflict with religious claims. If these assertions are true, religious experience cannot be said to provide evidence for religious claims. Hence Freud's assertions must be appraised.

Is it true that where there is no reliable method for attaining knowledge there can be no knowledge attained? A reliable method for Freud is simply a scientific method; "an illusion it would be to suppose that what science cannot give us we can get elsewhere." It is worth noting in passing that "illusion" no longer seems to have its technical meaning of a belief arising in some sense from wish-fulfillment. Whether it is intended to have that sense or not, its use here is mere name-calling. That the only possible source of knowledge involves the use of scientific method in some standard sense of that phrase is surely a debatable thesis, whatever its degree of contemporary popularity. Professor M. B. Foster summarizes elements common to various descriptions of science by professional scientists as follows:

> Scientific language is technical, an instrument of man; scientific evidence is communicable to man as man [i.e., is universally communicable]; the experimental method is a method of commanding nature to answer man's questions; the aim of modern science is man's mastery over nature.[16]

As a brief characterization of the method and aims of science, this summary statement seems fair and correct; perhaps its suggestion that the purpose of science is, at least fundamentally, power rather than knowledge for its own sake is debatable, but nothing maintained here will hang on that issue. The point to be stressed is stated nicely by Foster.

> 'Thou shalt not tempt the Lord thy God.' The meaning of the Greek here is 'Thou shalt not put God to the test' and this perhaps includes a prohibition of investigating God by the experimental method, by the

method which science applies to nature. These words are Christ's answer to the Devil when the Devil had said to him on the temple, 'If
thou be the Son of God, cast thyself down. For it is written, he shall
give his angels charge over thee.' The temptation is that of applying
scientific methods to something which is not subject to man. Similar
experiments would be if a man had one twin baptized, and kept the
other as control; or endeavored to ascertain the effects of prayer by
getting large numbers of people to pray for the patients in the North
ward of a hospital but not for those in the South, and then recorded
the comparative rates of recovery for the two classes of patients. This
would be to tempt the Lord our God in the way prohibited. But we
must beware of thinking of this prohibition moralistically, as though
we were standing above God with this frightful weapon of scientific
test suspended in our hands, but were bidden not to subject Him to it.
The point is that this is not a sphere to which it is *possible* to apply
such tests (though it is possible to attempt the impossible).[17]

Surely Foster's point is well taken. God cannot be compelled to
reveal Himself; if there is an Almighty, He will reveal Himself when
and as He wills, not when and as we will. Further, traditional theism
views God as not possessing a body. Hence, were God to be seen by
the naked eye or observed from a Mt. Palomar telescope, theism
would be refuted, not established. Nor will it do to say that this view
of God falls under Freud's remark that

No doubt if they [believers] confine themselves to belief in a higher
spiritual being, whose qualities are indefinable and whose purposes cannot be discerned, they will be proof against the challenge of science;
but then they will lose their hold on human interest.[18]

For, while theism holds that God's purposes cannot be discerned, they
can be revealed. Further, it is just the God who possesses no body who
has held the interest of orthodox Jews and Christians for centuries.
The point to be stressed, however, is not the incorporeality of God,
but the fact that God is not a proper, because not a possible, object
of empirical observation via scientific method. The sum of the matter
on this score seems to be this: if one refuses to accept any claim not
derived by the application of the scientific method, one will reject
the claims of theism, since God cannot be constrained to answer our
questions nor can He be empirically discerned. But this refusal is by
no means easy to justify; it was not derived by the application of
the scientific method(s), and it is not very clear how one would go
about proving it. We can note in an *ad hominem* fashion that Freud
himself does not abide by it. He is fully confident that "a civilization
which leaves so large a number of its participants unsatisfied and
drives them into revolt neither has nor deserves the prospect of a

lasting existence."[19] Freud indeed possessed "the mind of a moralist" and his moral beliefs are not any more derivable from the application of the scientific method(s) than is the belief that God exists.

Freud also claims that religious belief is incompatible with what reason and experience tell us. This claim as it stands is too vague even to be discussed, but at least a hint is offered as to how to make it more definite. Freud says concerning religious beliefs that

> Some of them are so improbable, so incompatible with everything we have laboriously discovered about the reality of the world, that we may compare them—if we pay proper regard to the psychological differences —to delusions. Of the reality value of most of them we cannot judge; just as they cannot be proved, so they cannot be refuted.[20]

Most of this caution, however, has been abandoned by the time Freud reaches the end of his brief book, as the "reason and experience" passage quoted above reveals. One suspects that the (unconscious?) change is caused by this consideration.

> It has been repeatedly pointed out . . . in how great detail the analogy between religion and obsessional neurosis can be followed out, and how many of the peculiarities and vicissitudes in the formation of religion can be understood in that light.[21]

The phrase "obsessional neurosis" perhaps calls for some explanation.

> The core of a neurosis lies at the point where anxiety has blocked or distorted the learning process so that the new learning essential to adjustment cannot take place.[22]

Obsessional or compulsory neurosis is explained by the same contemporary psychologist as follows.

> An obsession is an idea or desire which forces itself persistently into the patient's mind in what he experiences as an irrational fashion. A compulsion is an act actually carried out, which similarly forces itself upon the patient.[23]

Certain symptoms characteristically accompany obsessional neurosis: anti-social and self-punitive tendencies, highly developed secondary defenses, lack of overt but presence of underlying anxiety, concern for orderliness and cleanliness, a tendency to be conscientious and idealistic but also stubborn and stingy, and an awareness of one's compulsions and obsessions as one's own with an accompanying sense that they are somehow foreign to one's being. Freud's argument, then, will be stateable in some such fashion as this.

1. Obsessional neuroses are characterized by certain factors (say, a, b, c, d, e, f) and the beliefs that accompany these neuroses are known to be almost always false.
2. Religious conviction is characterized by certain factors which are very similar, if not identical, to a-f, and is accompanied by certain beliefs.

So:

3. The beliefs which accompany religious conviction are very likely false.

His argument is somewhat similar to one suggested in outline by C. D. Broad.

> Suppose . . . it could be shown that religious experience contains no factors which are not factors in other kinds of experience. Suppose further it could be shown that this particular combination of factors tends to originate and to be activated only under certain conditions which are known to be very commonly productive of false belief held with strong conviction. Then . . . [we would tend] to answer . . . the question of validity in the negative.[24]

How, then, are we to evaluate this argument?

One disanalogy between the beliefs associated with obsessional neuroses and those associated with religious convictions is that those associated with religious belief have not been empirically falsified while those accompanying obsessional neuroses have been empirically falsified. In fact, however, this gives us a way of apparently strengthening Freud's argument. Consider the set S of all religious beliefs. Divide S into S_1 and S_2, where S_1 contains all the members of S that have been empirically falsified and S_2 contains all the members of S that have not been empirically falsified. S_1 will contain such statements as "There are gods on Mt. Olympus" and "Rain gods make it rain." S_2 will contain such statements as "God created and providentially rules the world" and "God loves us." We can now add a further premise to the argument.

2a. Some of the beliefs which accompany religious conviction have been empirically falsified.

The existence of religious beliefs which are appropriately placed in S_1 justifies (2a), and the argument with (2a) appears stronger than the argument without it.

Actually (2a) serves to strengthen the argument significantly just in case the statements included in S_1 are not logically independent of those in S_2. But if S_2 contains, say, the essential tenets of orthodox theism, then these members of S_2 at least are surely quite independent of any member of S_1. Were one to deny this on the ground that some belief included in or entailed by theism has been empirically falsified, then some such argument as those rejected in our discussion of the problem of evil would have to be provided, and shown to be sound. Orthodox Jews and Christians can cheerfully admit that there are no members of Zeus' family and that no god views rain dances with favor. So the addition of (2a) in fact adds nothing to the argument insofar as we are concerned with theism. What then of the original argument?

It is true that belief in God is almost inescapable for many of those who have it, and also that putative contrary evidence is inefficacious in removing it. But unless the evidence against God's existence is cogent, a man who rejected belief in God because of this evidence would be a shoddy thinker, not a paradigm of sanity. Further, even if many of those who believe in God should turn out to retain that belief even when they believed themselves to possess stronger evidence against the belief than for it, that fact would not count against the belief. What counted against the belief would still simply be the contrary evidence.

Freud's point is rather, it would seem, that people assent to the claim that God exists in the absence of anything like overpowering evidence for it (and do so with real fervor). But this shows nothing pathological about the believer unless the notion of pathological belief is to be so widely used as to possess almost no significance. Hosts of people accept all sorts of beliefs without being able to specify any cogent reasons for them. As Socrates says to Crito, "The many believe what they believe by chance." Moreover, to say that belief in God cannot be justified or refuted, whereas other beliefs commonly held without much reflection can be, is to make a substantial philosophical claim for which Freud offers not a shred of evidence. Nothing follows in any case from that philosophical claim about the pathology of believers. What might make their belief pathological, we noted, was that they did not have reason to accept it with anything like the confidence with which they do so; but we have noted that hosts of people, in that minimal sense, are pathological about many of their beliefs. But even if religious believers were absolutely alone in accepting a belief while not possessing adequate evidence for it, assuming for the sake of the argument that they have none, this would go no way at all toward showing that their beliefs were false.

This holds true even given the truth of premise (2) of Freud's argument. That this is so is easily shown. In the absence of any relevant and true premise such as (2a), the only force the argument retains depends on connecting certain psychological features of believers with the truth value of what is believed. The claim is hence:

(c) if a man has psychological features a, b, etc., and believes **B**, then **B** is likely false.

But, while some such claim may indeed tell us that a man does not believe in virtue of adequate reasons, it does not tell us that his belief is certainly or probably false. Even if the majority of beliefs which are accepted by men possessing factors such as a, b, etc., are shown to be false, this does nothing to show that a new belief in a context characterized by a, b, etc., is false. For we have at very best conjunction, but not a law-like connection, between "Belief x arises in a context characterized by a, b, etc." and "Belief x is false." That this connection is not law-like becomes particularly clear when we ask what counter-factual conditional the conjunction grounds. The connection between heating water and water boiling is law-like. We can say of a glass of cool water which has just refreshed me that if it had been sufficiently heated, it would have boiled. We cannot say of a belief held by Jones that if Jones had not been characterized by a, b, etc., his belief would have been true. Nor can we say of a true belief of Jones that had Jones been characterized by a, b, etc., with respect to that belief, it would have been false. With the exception of certain beliefs about a, b, etc., the relevant factors are: (a) belief which is almost inescapable for the believer, but (b) for which he has no adequate evidence. We have seen that even if the majority of obsessive beliefs are known to be false, we are still bound to check out each new case. We are bound to do so simply because an obsessional true belief is neither logically nor causally impossible. That an obsessional belief be true would not counter any well-founded generalization or upset any well-established theory, as would a still-reigning decapitated king or a worm with a developed skeleton. Perhaps one accustomed to testing such matters would be surprised at finding a belief both obsessional and true; if so, that would belong to his autobiography, not his laboratory report. What remains, then, of Freud's argument seems at most only to be an instance of the genetic fallacy.[25] And, of course, that need not detain us.

If the argument hinted at by Broad and Freud does not discredit appeals to religious experience as evidence for the truth of religious claims, what of those appeals themselves? Several subsidiary questions arise in this connection.

(1) Is there one "object" of religious experience, or are there various objects?

(2) Are such experiences necessarily nonconceptual, ineffable?

(3) Insofar as a transcendent being is taken to be the object of such experiences, is the character of this being always the same?

(4) Do all religious experiences, at least insofar as they putatively have a transcendent being as object, include a common element, or some quality which the being is always experienced as possessing?

(5) Are the experiences self-interpretive and/or self-authenticating?

The object of an experience is to be taken as what the experience is, putatively at least, an experience of. Only the first of these questions is easy to answer.

At least if we take them on their own terms, the putative objects of religious experiences are immensely varied. Some religious experiences have God as their object. Thus Isaiah writes,

> In the year that king Uzziah died I saw also the Lord sitting upon a throne, high and lifted up, and his train filled the temple.[26]

But attaining nirvana would also be a religious experience, one of a quite different sort.

> It is to be recognized through freedom from distress, danger and fear, through peace, calm, bliss, joy, abundance, purity, coolness.[27]

While there are various other sorts of putative objects of religious experiences, this makes it clear that the answer to be given to our first question is that the "objects" of such experience are quite varied.[28] This much can be recognized without committing one to any view concerning the veracity of such experiences.

What then of our second question? It concerns a transcendent being as putative object of religious experiences. By "transcendent" we here mean simply a being which exists distinct from and independent of any human experience; and an experience of a being is to be contrasted with an experience of a state of being (e.g., nirvana). There is no question that men have claimed to experience a being, other than human, which existed independently of their experience. Can their claim be sustained? After a detailed examination Rudolph Otto concluded that it can be.

RUDOLPH OTTO'S APPEAL TO
NUMINOUS EXPERIENCE

Otto offers an analysis of religious experience which centers in the concept of the numinous. It is worth asking whether this analysis will help to sort out the varied items which go under the general title "religious experience" in such a way as to make it possible for some of them at any rate to function as nonconflicting evidence for religious claims. Various elements are included in being numinous. Otto mentions absolute unapproachableness, absolute overpoweringness, and living energy. A numinous being is one in whom such attributes are present, and who is in principle incomprehensible.

> The truly "mysterious" object is beyond our apprehension and comprehension, not only because our knowledge has certain irremovable limits, but because in it we come upon something inherently "wholly other," whose kind and character are incommensurable with our own, and before which we therefore recoil in a wonder that strikes us chill and numb.[29]

The attributes of objects of common experience are used as "ideograms" (the term is Otto's) for something in fact ineffable.

Otto explicitly uses this claim as a way of dealing with our problem. He recognizes that seeking for the "void" or for "nothingness," taken literally, seems like lunacy.

> But, in fact, the "void" of the eastern, like the "nothing" of the western, mystic, is a numinous ideogram of the "wholly other."[30]

The necessity for ideogramatic expression for communication, plus the ineffability of the experience itself,

> ... teaches us the independence of the positive content of this experience from the implications of its overt conceptual expression.[31]

Only those who lack the experience will suppose the language used to express it to be other than a way of saying what it is not plus a way of saying what it is more like than anything else.

> ... widely divergent as these states are in themselves, yet they have this in common, that in them the *mysterium* is experienced in its essential, positive, and specific character, as something that bestows upon man a beatitude beyond compare, but one whose real nature he can neither proclaim in speech nor conceive in thought, but may know only by a direct and living experience.[32]

But of course this is not sufficient. If religious experience is ineffable, and that is the end of the matter, one can hardly draw conclusions from it. "Ineffable evidence" is an odd phrase at best. Otto, in any case, offers a theory which puts his account of religious experience in a broader context.

If religious experience or its putative object is supra-rational, it does not follow, for Otto at least, that no claims can be based on such experience.

> Confronted by the fact of the non-rational . . . we cannot be satisfied
> with a mere bare statement, which would be open to all the vague and
> arbitrary phraseology of an emotionalist irrationalism. We are bound
> to try, by means of the most precise and unambiguous symbolic and
> figurative terms that we can find, to discriminate the different elements
> of the experience so far as we can in a way that can claim general
> validity.[33]

Although God is suprarational, or nonrational, he is not irrational.
He is not literally both possessed and not possessed of some attribute,
and no language suggesting the contrary can be taken literally. Some
types of religious language, then, are more appropriate than others.
Otto is quite explicit at this point.

> We maintain . . . following the *via eminentiae et causalitatis*, that the
> divine is indeed the highest, strongest, best, loveliest, and dearest that
> man can think of; but we assert on the other, following the *via nega-
> tionis*, that God is not *merely* the ground and superlative of all that can
> be thought; He is in Himself a subject on His own account and in
> Himself.[34]

He emphasizes that religion is not inherently irrational and that describing God in terms of such predicates as "spiritual," "powerful,"
"purposeful," "one," "good," etc., is not anti-religious.

> Rather we count this the very mark and criterion of a religion's high
> rank and superior value—that it should have no lack of *conceptions*
> about God; that it should admit knowledge—the knowledge that comes
> by faith—of the transcendent in terms of conceptual thought . . . This
> must be asserted at the outset and with the most positive emphasis.[35]

In short, that God cannot be exhaustively described does not mean
that any way of describing God is as good as any other. Some ways
are at least more accurate or appropriate, and we can purportedly
tell which ways these are. Otto's contentions thus far seem quite persuasive and offer a negative answer to our second question. But how
can we tell which ways are in fact more appropriate?

Otto's answer to this question is rather complex. Insofar as religion
is more than mere acceptance of authority it arises, he suggests, from
experiences which man can interpret correctly in virtue of possession
of a special category of interpretation—"the Holy" or "the Numinous."
In responding to an experience to which this category applies, a man
responds to

> . . . an immediate datum given with the feeling of the numen . . . he
> passes upon the numen a judgment of appreciation of a unique kind
> by . . . the category "holy," which is proper to the numen alone, but
> to it in an absolute degree.[36]

The experience is unique, irreducible to any other.

> "Ought" is a primary and unique meaning, as little derivable from another as blue from bitter. . . . The idea "ought" is only "evolvable" out of the spirit of man itself, and then in the sense of being "arousable," because it is already potentially implanted in him. Were it not so, no "evolution" could effect an introduction for it. . . . Now it is just the same with the feeling of the numinous as with that of moral obligation.[37]

According to Otto, there are

> Three factors in the process by which religion comes into being. . . First, the interplay of disposition and stimulus. . . Second, the groping recognition, by virtue of this very disposition, of specific portions of history as the manifestation of "the holy" . . . third, on the basis of the other two, the achieved fellowship with "the holy," in knowing, feeling, and willing.[38]

Men have an innate capacity to interpret certain personal encounters (e.g., those described as mystical) and certain historical events (e.g., the life and person of Jesus) as involving manifestations of a numinous or holy being. When such experiences occur or such events are encountered, this Being is recognized and fellowship with it is achieved. This, in brief outline, is Otto's thesis. What, then, can be said in appraisal of it?

Others besides Otto have suggested that men have at least *a priori* tendencies to interpret some modes of their experience in a religious manner. Thus John Hick writes of "our innate tendency to interpret the world religiously" which he regards as "a tendency to experience it 'in depth,' as a supernatural as well as a natural environment."[39] Both Otto and Hick are theists. Others besides theists have attributed this tendency to mankind.

One who has done so, as we have seen, was Sigmund Freud.[40] Another was Ludwig Feuerbach.

> Whatever is God to a man, that is his heart and soul; and conversely, God is the manifested inward nature, the expressed self of a man— religion the solemn unveiling of a man's hidden treasures, the revelation of his intimate thoughts, the open confession of his love secrets.[41]

He puts his point even more clearly in a later passage: "in religion man contemplates his own latent nature."[42] Thus a religious interpretation of our experiences results from an innate tendency for Freud and Feuerbach as well, but as a projection of ourselves, or of our needs and inadequacies, onto the universe rather than as a recognition (as for Otto) of the existence of a numinous object.

Yet another author has ascribed to man an innate tendency to interpret his experience in a religious manner. David Hume did so, drawing a conclusion different from that of any of the others we have discussed. Hume, in fact, claimed to find in man several propensities to give a religious reading to his experience. Men have a propensity toward anthropomorphism, i.e. to "conceive all beings like themselves, and to transfer to every object, those qualities with which they are familiarly acquainted."[43] But

> Their propensity is equally strong to rest their attention on sensible, visible objects, and in order to reconcile those opposite inclinations they are led to unite the invisible powers with some visible objects.[44]

If the former propensity dominates, theism results. The latter propensity, combined on an equal footing with the former, gives rise to polytheism. Although those propensities are not original (they can for various reasons fail to operate in a given person) they are universal and are the locus of religion's "origin in human nature." Hume does not argue either that these propensities are elicited by experiences for which they produce the correct interpretation or that they provide the basis for a psychological reduction of religious belief to projection or covert self-reflection. Rather, he pronounces the result of his inquiry to be that

> . . . the whole [of religion] is a riddle, an enigma, an inexplicable mystery. Doubt, uncertainty, suspense of judgment, appear the only result of our most accurate scrutiny concerning this subject.[45]

Is, then, there a tendency on the part of men to interpret their experience in religious terms (e.g. in numinous terms), or more modestly as revealing, in Hume's phrase, "intelligent, invisible power"? Otto argues that there is on the ground of the uniqueness of numinous experience; Hick argues to the same effect on the basis of the near-universality of some sort of religious belief. Suppose we grant them their claim. Then we must ask what, if anything, follows from it. One can read this tendency in terms of the capacity to recognize a numinous quality actually possessed by the object of religious experience. One can see it as evidence of projection. Or one can note the great diversity in the religious perspectives to which it gives rise and regard it as an enigmatic feature of an inscrutable being. The sheer existence of such tendency does not, it would seem, show which interpretation of its significance is most accurate. Thus this element of Otto's view has no force in defending the veracity of religious experience.

If the human nature claims that Otto makes by no means provide a source of unambiguous support for his views, neither does his thesis that men recognize the holy in their experience. While Freud's comparison of religious belief to obsessional belief does not serve to prove such belief false, it does undercut any attempt to move easily from what men find themselves incapable of doubting to what is in fact true. Otto's comparison of religious experience to moral experience is illuminating in this regard. A sense of moral obligation—of being morally bound to perform a given action—is not sufficient to show that one is morally obligated. Even granting that there are objective moral obligations, having a sense of being obligated to do x is not identical to being obligated to do x. Nor is having a sense of experiencing the holy necessarily tantamount to experiencing the holy. Such experiences can be interpreted on the model of veridical sensory experience; they can also be interpreted on the model of obsessional belief. Which model is appropriate is not self-evident; that any one having the experience will read it on the model of veridical sensory experience, if this is true, will not show that this fact is not to be interpreted as itself an obsession. Here the issue seems indecisive. Hence, the appeal to religious experience, at least as Otto makes it, does not establish the truth of any religious claims.

Yet another difficulty faces anyone who, like Otto, appeals to religious experience to establish the truth of religious claims. The reports given by the subjects of such experience are by no means obviously consistent. Some examples will make this clear. Contrast the following passages. Meister Eckhart speaks of the still desert of the Deity

> . . . where never was seen difference, neither Father, Son, nor Holy Ghost, where there is no one at home, yet where the spark of the soul is more at peace than in itself.[46]

By way of contrast, St. Theresa relates that

> Our Lord made me comprehend in what way it is that one God can be in three Persons. He made me see it so clearly that I remained as extremely surprised as I was comforted . . . and now, when I think of the Holy Trinity, or hear It spoken of, I understand how the three adorable Persons form only one God, and I experience an unspeakable happiness.[47]

Again, Eckhart writes

> If I am to know God directly, I must become completely He and He I: so that this He and this I become and are one I.[48]

Contrast the words of Isaiah as he describes his experience.

> In the year that King Uzziah died I saw the Lord sitting upon a throne, high and lifted up; and his train filled the temple. Above him stood the seraphim . . . and one called to another and said "Holy, holy, holy is the Lord of hosts; the whole earth is full of his glory. . . . And I said: "Woe is me, for I am lost; for I am a man of unclean lips, and I dwell in the midst of a people of unclean lips; for my eyes have seen the King, the Lord of hosts.[49]

Between man and God there is an unbridgeable gulf, and even when Isaiah is cleansed he is the servant, not the alter ego, of Jehovah.

It is in this spirit that Devendranath Tagore remarks: "What we want is to worship God. If the worshipper and the object of worship become one, how can there be any worship."[50] Turning to a different tradition, consider this passage from *Bhagavad Gita*.

> When I see thy vast form, reaching the sky, burning with many colors, with wide open mouths, with vast flaming eyes, my heart shakes in terror: my power is gone and gone is my peace, O Vishnu![51]

Here, terror is the appropriate response to the purported transcendent being. St. Catherine of Genoa also speaks of a divine fire, but with quite opposite effect.

> O that I could tell you what the heart feels, how it burns and is consumed inwardly! Only, I find no words to express it. I can but say: Might but one little drop of what I feel fall into Hell, Hell would be transformed into a Paradise.[52]

Unspeakable joy or utter terror: which is the appropriate response to the being, if any, which is experienced?

Otto notes that a "mysticism of horror" is distinctively a non-Western phenomenon.[53] Is there some feature of Eastern thought which hallucinates this aspect of horror when the being experienced is loving, or some feature of Western thought that filters out the ferocity actually possessed? How can one decide?

A subdued account of the darker aspects of numinous experience can be found in a Western source:

> As this clear sight of the divine comes like a violent assault upon the soul to subdue it, the soul feels such anguish in its weakness that all power and breath leave it.[54]

He adds

> Therefore He destroys, crushes, and overwhelms [the soul] in such a deep darkness, that it feels as though melted and in its misery de-

stroyed by a cruel death of the spirit. Even as though it were to feel it had been swallowed by some savage beast and buried in the darkness of his belly.[55]

This is neither the bliss of St. Catherine nor the terror of the worshipper of Vishnu. But is it therefore, as something of a mean between our extremes, the appropriate reaction?

Tri-unity versus absence of distinction; obliteration of difference between God and man versus unbridgeable difference; sheer joy and utter terror: In each case, which is to be accepted? Unless some convincing answer is forthcoming, it is dubious that religious experience has evidential value.

In some cases, the contradiction is only apparent. For example, the terror of Vishnu is, so to speak, only a temporary pose on the part of Krishna who is represented close to the end of the *Bhagavad Gita* as saying

> Hear again my word supreme, the deepest secret of silence. Because I love thee well, I will speak to thee words of salvation. Give thy mind to me, and give me thy heart, and thy sacrifice, and thy adoration. This is my word of promise: thou shalt in truth come to me, for thou art dear to me.[56]

The difference between the trinitarianism of St. Theresa and the monism of Eckhart might be reconciled by appeal to some such view as that of Sankara who places any view of God as personal at the level of illusion and Eckart's nonpersonalism at the level of reality. The former is appropriate enough for the novice, but the truth lies in the latter. It seems obvious, however, that this reconciliation is hardly distinguishable from the denial of the veracity of St. Teresa's experience. Further, Sankara's claims rest upon a system of theology which is not self-evidently true. Its correctness can no more be simply "read off" Eckhart's experience than St. Theresa's theological framework can be "read off" her experience. And the difference between experiences in which subject and object are distinct (and in which worship is possible) and those where the distinction is purportedly obliterated (making worship impossible) is particularly acute. In the light of such problems, appeal has been made to a putatively common element to be found in all religious experiences. Otto's candidate, as we have noted, is experience of the numinous. Thus we are required to answer our third question—is the character of the putative transcendent object of religious experience always the same —in the negative, and to raise our fourth question concerning the possibly common characteristics of such experience.

Contrary to Otto's thesis, a numinous element may not be present in all religious or even all mystical experience. Ninian Smart cites Theravada Buddhism as a religious setting from which it is absent.[57] He finds it important, however, that

> . . . though the central content of the Buddhist mystic's experience on the one hand and that of Muhammad's prophetic experience on the other hand differ greatly, there is in both the sense of a transcendent being or state, as though somehow here both had an insight into what lay, so to speak, beyond space and time.[58]

Consider, however, how minimal the agreement is.[59] Of what religious value is it to agree that men in various traditions share a "sense of a transcendent being or state"? Is the "sense" somehow veridical? If so, is its "object" a being or a state? The former could possibly be worshipped, the latter could possibly be attained; reversing the verbs would not do at all. What if there is a transcendent being or state? What are its properties? Does it know or care about human history and about me? Does it love or hate, or both or neither? If it is a state, has it features which make its attainment worthwhile? These questions, and others, must be answered before the agreement has much significance. By itself, the claim that there is a transcendent being or state, even if accepted, is more a curious than a significant fact. In the light of the widely divergent experiences which are viewed as in some sense religious, it seems implausible that anything more detailed or substantial than Smart's offering is available. Thus any common element will, it seems, be so vague as to be unhelpful in offering evidence for the truth of religious claims. Nor, of course, is it clear that a common element in religious experiences is thereby certified as a veridical element—one that justifies inferences concerning a transcendent object of experience. Thus far, we have no reason to suppose that religious experience does provide evidence for religious claims; our results are negative. Also, our question concerning a common element has received an answer.

NINIAN SMART'S REASONS AND FAITHS

Ninian Smart offers another way of answering the question as to whether religious experience provides evidence for religious claims. It is plausible that, on the basis of religious experience alone, one does not have such evidence. One can regard such experiences simply as stimulated by natural phenomena and arising from human need. One can regard them as recognitions of a transcendent being. Or one can reserve judgment. These experiences, then, are not self-authenticating, so our fifth question is answered as well.

In recognition of these alternatives, none of them rationally coercive, Smart offers a set of criteria for evaluating religions which includes, but is not exhausted by, an appeal to religious experience. He suggests that we appeal to

> . . . three elements in the justification of religious doctrines . . . first . . . the bases upon which propositions in the different strands rest . . . second . . . *formal* considerations operative in the formation of doctrines, for example, the requirement of simplicity . . . and, again, the requirement that a divine entity must be concealed . . . third . . . the weaving together of doctrines allows of their being justified by appeals to analogies and similarities, as when the timelessness of a mystical experience helps to cement propositions about the Atman to those about Brahman. Those elements can be named respectively *basic, formal, and organic* justifications.[60]

The third element is, roughly, what has traditionally been designated as "coherence." Smart adds a fourth consideration, which he designates "preferential justification"; "the making of priority decisions between strands."[61] We must now explicate Smart's four sorts of justification.

His reference to "different strands" refers to his insightful separation of different but complementary emphases present in various religions.[62] One is the numinous strand, which emphasizes the holiness of the object of worship—the "otherness" of this being. Another is the mystical strand, in which attaining the mystic goal is emphasized. Those who undertake successfully to attain this goal via a characteristic discipline

> . . . have achieved unspeakable bliss; . . . this experience is timeless and other-worldly; . . . it is gained after a long course of self-mastery and meditation; . . . upon attaining it they acquire a new vision of the world.[63]

The bases upon which these strands rest is, obviously, numinous and mystical experience.

The "formal considerations" need only brief comment. Simplicity has already been mentioned. The requirement "that a divine reality must be concealed" is a quite different sort of consideration. Smart's point is that this thesis is widely accepted; it plays a crucial role in varied religious traditions. It is thus not strictly formal in the sense that it is external to all systems, as, say, consistency seems to be, and as simplicity may be. It is formal only in the weaker sense that it is shared by many religions, and obviously it applies only to religious systems.

The third sort of consideration involves an adaptation by Smart of the traditionally formal criterion of coherence, or mutual relevance of mutually consistent claims. He deals with it by using an analogy with artistic composition. The way of unifying sublime and wonderful phenomena is to show that they are connected in a particular manner.

> since empirical connections between events have no immediate relevance to aesthetic judgments, we cannot produce a causal hypothesis to cover all cases of wonderfulness [being numinous] in a manner which would explain them: indeed the notion of explanation appears discordant here . . . What sort of unification, then, can we expect?[64]

Smart finds at least a hint as to the answer by appeal to artistic composition.

> A work of art is in a sense organic and in roughly the following manner: Elements in a work have a mutual effect evidenced in two main ways: (a) the appearance of each within the whole is not independent, since its appearance would be different with different neighbors or in isolation; (b) the criticism of detail largely involves showing how it does or does not contribute to the general pattern; and so the *reason* for detail lies mainly in its contribution to the whole effect . . . We may expect the same with . . . holy objects: insofar as it is possible to unify them, they will be shown to be part of a . . . pattern.[65]

Thus in orthodox Christianity, the doctrines of the Incarnation, the Atonement, and the Resurrection belong to a pattern. The rejection of any one would entail revision, or more likely rejection, of the others. Each is to be seen in the light of the claims that God is love and that man needs redemption which he cannot himself provide. This set of claims is coherent in the sense that each affects the other, each playing its role in the conceptual pattern.

The fourth element is, Smart notes,[66] in effect a special kind of formal justification. It is concerned with the question, "On what grounds could one strand justifiably be made to be prior to another?" He suggests, as an example, that

> Religion, in its higher forms, aims at being available to all men, directly or ultimately; and so it might be counted a defect in a doctrinal scheme if it concentrates exclusively on the mystical goal, for mysticism is undoubtedly for the few.[67]

Having presented Smart's criteria for evaluation of a religious conceptual system, we must indicate how he applies them and attempt to appraise their adequacy.

Smart, who has a vast knowledge of the history of religions, sorts out the issues in this way.

> How, then, amid the great faiths do we tell where the fullest statement of the truth lies? The choice initially lies between three great systems of belief. First, there is theism, the belief in a personal Creator who reveals himself to men: represented by Judaism, Islam, and Christianity, as well as by certain tendencies in Hindu thought, such as the theology of the *Bhagavad Gita.* Then, second, at the other extreme, there is the agnostic faith of Theravada Buddhism. And third, in the great Hindu Teacher Shankara, there is an intermediate kind of doctrine.[68]

Theravada Buddhism is a religion "which goes back to the Buddha's original teachings; in which there is no belief in a creator God, and the central teaching concerns nirvana, a transcendent state which it is possible for saintly men to reach.[69]

Shankara's doctrines are summarized by Smart as follows.[70] Each man has (essentially, is) an eternal soul, or Atman. This Atman is identical, in some manner, with Brahman, the only independent reality. Each individual thing, including each Atman, is only apparently distinct from Brahman. To regard God as personal, or as Creator, is to think at one level—the level of illusion. At the highest level, that of Reality, there are no ontological distinctions. This position would reduce both the theistic traditions and Theravada Buddhism to the level of illusion.

There are various important differences between religions in which the numinous strand dominates over the mystical and those in which the mystical strand dominates over the numinous. Noting these will provide a basis for the application of Smart's criteria.

One has already been noted. In a religion in which the numinous strand dominates (hereafter, a numinous religion) there is a great gap between man and God. Mystical experience is sometimes described as union with God.[71]

Another is that a numinous religion tends to regard the world as real, non-illusory, while a mystical religion tends to regard it as unreal, illusory.[72]

Still another difference is that religions in which the mystical strand dominates (hereafter, mystical religion) involve the use of such terms as "real," "being," "unity" in the manner of negative theology. Essentially, the Absolute Reality is not describable,[73] and is certainly impersonal. Although not descriptive, these claims stress the value of nirvana or the greatness of Brahman. In the numinous religions God is personal or at least, so to speak, not less than personal and characteristically can be at least minimally described.

Again, a mystical religion will set a high value on mystical experience and the special sort of knowledge it provides.

> Mystical knowledge . . . is a form of knowing what something is like
> . . . though silence is an appropriate way of expressing the knowledge
> gained, the situation is complicated by the fact . . . that the insight so
> gained leads to the expression of a new attitude to the world which is
> figured in the picture of the world as unreal or impermanent.[74]

As St. Gregory remarks,

> The subsequent effect of the divine vision on the Soul is noticed, not
> merely in detachment from the world, and contempt for it, but in the
> experience of being above it and that it is a passing show.[75]

In such a scheme sensory experience loses epistemological primacy and programs to change society are of lesser value than the discipline which leads to nirvana. The works that count are ascetic works. While a numinous religion may also emphasize other experience than sensory, and may also regard the salvation of the soul as the primary goal for each man, moral and social works will be of at least equal value with ascetic. Compare, for example, the insistence on justice for the widows and orphans in the Old Testament Law, or Jesus' saying that when one clothes the naked and visits the imprisoned, it is as if one were clothing and visiting the Son of Man Himself. The *Bhagavad Gita*, in which the numinous strand also dominates, makes moral works as valuable as ascetic.

These differences at least illustrate, but perhaps do not exhaust, the differences between numinous and mystical religions. How, then, can priority decisions be made between the strands?

Smart offers only three explicit comments as to such decisions. One is that monotheistic religion has a formal advantage, in terms of simplicity over polytheistic religion, so long as polytheism is not demanded by cogent data which monotheism cannot assimilate. The same consideration might lead one to opt for a religion involving only one strand—although the application of simplicity seems at this point a bit strained.[76] In any case, as a second consideration, religions involving both numinous and mystical strands seem more appropriate contexts in which to place numinous and mystical experiences. Insofar as the experiences are of two distinct types, each thus irreducible to the other, the complexity of strands can plausibly be claimed as necessary given the experiences to be taken into account. Here, appeal to religious experience as the basis of a religion, in the sense of at least a crucial part of its evidential support, overrides formal considerations. The formal criteria come into play only after the experiential evidence has been dealt with by competing systems. This seems, at least, to be Smart's conception of the matter.

> The strength of a strand ought to rest upon the strength of its bases . . . perception of the strength of the bases depends upon religious experience . . . persuasion will have largely to come from the conduct on the one hand which enlivens and lies behind the doctrines; and from the religious eloquence which points to the bases upon which faith in these matters must rest.[77]

Third, as already mentioned, the mystical religion is for the few and, generally, numinous religion thus seems more acceptable since it provides place for mystical experience but does not regard it as necessary for religious attainment or salvation.

Realizing the difficulty of the appraisal of various religious systems, Smart writes his conclusion with care.

> Illuminating the important features of a piece of music is a task which depends upon insight and is hard to make decisive; so much more difficult then is the task of showing in what respects one doctrinal scheme is superior to another. However, it is by no means true that nothing can be done here; and the pattern of basic, organic, and formal justifications, together with the rather vaguer justifications of priority decisions, give one the material for reasoning (in a special sense of reasoning) about religious matters.[78]

One can agree with Smart that there is no *a priori* reason to suppose that criteria for rational decisions between religious systems are impossible or unavailable. Further, Smart's criteria seem appropriate enough, and he makes no claims that they are the only criteria. Nonetheless, it is not clear that he succeeds in providing us with any very potent justification for preferring a religion in which the numinous strand dominates.

More important still, there is an inherent limitation to Smart's program. At best, it will, as he construes it, provide us with a conclusion of the following sort: religion R is superior to any other religion. Even if we can provide good reason for accepting a conclusion of this sort, with a determinate value given for "R," we still have not shown that the religious system in question is true. Suppose, for example, that a numinous religion is superior to a non-numinous one. Suppose, to push Smart's argument still further, that his criteria, perhaps supplemented by others, shows orthodox Christian theism to be the most plausible religious system. Of course, to find out that a religion in which the numinous strand dominates over the mystical is better than any other sort does not give us knowledge of any sort about whether Judaism, Islam, or Christianity is the proper option.

Still, even if Christian theism is the most viable religion, one has no answer as to whether Christian theism or some variety of atheism is more plausible. To decide between religious systems, even were one to do so in an eminently reasonable and obviously justified manner, is not tantamount to deciding that the superior religious system is superior to every, or even any, nonreligious system.

Smart's reply, of course, is to appeal to religious experience. His view is that such experience is in some way veridical, and the question is to decide in which way it is veridical—which religious system best articulates its significance.

Smart has, in effect, a two-stage reply to the question at hand. At the first stage, he believes it to be more reasonable to view religious experience as in some way veridical than to deny all veracity to it. He asks,

> If the numinous experience, for example, is distinct from other forces of human consciousness, then how can it simply be derived from them, on the assumption that numinous creativity is a kind of self-deception? For if it arises to deal with psychological or social problems, no doubt in an unconscious way, then why does it have its own peculiar character?[79]

He adds that "it is a leap to believe in the transcendent, and it is a leap to believe that somehow in theory religious experience could be given some kind of natural explanation. But then, once the leap is made towards some kind of belief in the transcendent, the importance of religious experience is bound to strike us."[80]

At the second stage, he claims that

> . . . religious experience has its own logic . . . We might put this . . . in another way by saying that the pattern of religious language has its own peculiar and special structure, just as other areas of language, e.g., morals, aesthetics, and so on possess their own characteristic forms of inference.[81]

But if this is so, to judge the claims expressed in religious language in the ways appropriate to judging those expressed in other areas of discourse may be unfair. Smart presses this claim hard in the introduction to *Reasons and Faiths*. He lays great emphasis on it being

> . . . presumptuous and ineffectual to sit down cooly and in a study to excogitate some schemes of salvation or some spiritual theory of the universe. Only extraordinary and spiritually gifted men are the communicators of fundamental doctrines and these, if learnt at all, are learnt in living and experience. Hence it is not amiss—and surely not

cowardice—to count as genuinely important the pronouncements of the great religions: if anything in religion is true it is likely that something like the truth will be found there, and we cannot rely on ourselves to devise novel alternative doctrines.[82]

It is worth noting that even if the origin of religious schemes is different from that of other sorts of conceptual schemes, it by no means follows that they must be evaluated in fundamentally different ways or have a unique "logic"; that question is still open even if we grant the difference in origins. The philosopher of religion, in Smart's view, is thus on neutral ground. He simply notes that there are world religions and finds his task, initially at least, in the comparative study of these religions.[83] He will be primarily interested in how the statements which express a given religion are related to one another and to behavior patterns which are also constitutive of that religion, and how these statements are evidenced and defended. His task is the study of the logic of religious systems—i.e., the description of doctrinal frames in terms of their internal structure of connections between, evidence for, and behavioral consequences of, statements comprising such a frame. He cannot properly discuss one such statement in isolation. To ask whether God exists is to ask about the correctness of a whole theistic perspective. The meaning of "God exists" is not independent of the meaning of such claims as "God is Creator and Providence," "God called Abraham and covenanted with him, and gave the Law to Moses," and "God was incarnate in Jesus Christ."[84] Philosophy becomes the task of drawing comparisons and the philosophy of religion the task of drawing comparisons between religious schemes.[85] Natural theology is no longer viewed as a philosophical task.[86] Philosophy of religion is viewed as in effect, "intellectual comparative religion."

Some questions arise, however, about Smart's approach. For one thing, unless religious experience is somehow veridical the task of studying its intellectual articulation is an exercise in the logic of illusion. We have seen that one can, without logical inconsistency and without flagrantly flying in the face of the facts, view religion in a Freudian or Humean manner or in some refurbished version of the same sort of interpretation.[87] Smart's response to these approaches is inadequate; he insists on the distinctness of numinous experience—its irreducibility to any other sort of experience. But, as we saw at the outset of this chapter, distinct and unique human experience is not therefore experience of something distinct from and independent of human experience. Its own peculiar character might, as Hume suggested, arise from the peculiar character of human beings or of human nature. As Smart himself realizes, this leaves open the question as to whether such experiences or any other sort of religious experience provides evidence for the existence of a transcendent being. Here, Smart speaks of a "leap." If we take it, and thereby assume that some religion or other gives us the truth about the character of reality and the destiny of men, then the application of Smart's criteria may indeed yield us a true or at least most adequate religious system. But this leaves us with the question, "Why take the leap?"

Smart's claims concerning our inability to create new religions are not without point. Nonetheless, they are not as decisive as he takes them to be. Spinoza, for example, excogitated in a study. Yet he developed what can fairly be called a system of personal salvation. His aim in *On the Improvement of the Understanding* is to inquire

> . . . whether, in fact, there might be anything of which the discovery and attainment would enable me to enjoy continuous, supreme, and unending happiness.[88]

He concluded that

> . . . love towards a thing eternal and infinite feeds the mind wholly with joy, and is itself unmingled with any sadness, wherefore it is greatly to be desired and sought for with all our strength.[89]

To attain such perfect happiness one must become cognizant of "the union existing between the mind and the whole of nature" and Spinoza tells us that

> . . . this . . . is the end for which I strive, to attain such a character [as is produced by knowledge of this union] myself and to endeavor that many should attain it with me.[90]

While one might indeed view Spinoza himself as one of the religious geniuses whose reports form the basis for the comparisons philosophers of religion engage in, it must at least be granted that he is hardly to be accounted a founder or a prophet of a world religion. Further, to make this reply would leave it dubious that any counter-example could be provided to Smart's claims; but then the claims are put forth as necessary truths, while their denials seem plainly consistent. Spinoza does operate "within" a Judeo-Christian tradition in that he reacts against the major emphases of that tradition and formulates his own theses as conscious rebuttals to its major doctrines. In that sense, he is dependent upon a religious and philosophical tradition which he inherited. But he also developed what can fairly be called a way of salvation which, if not likely to have wide support and if lacking self-evident truth, nonetheless can be viewed as a religious alternative, or an alternative to religion. To say that covertly the massive conceptual scheme which Spinoza offers is really only an articulation of a religious experience which he had is neither plausible nor consistent with his own claims. If Theravada Buddhism's doctrinal frame forms a religious conceptual scheme, why not Spinoza's? And if one wishes an example independent of Judeo-Christian influence, Plato will do nicely. He, too, offers a way of salvation which is simultaneously a philosophical perspective "excogitated in a study" (i.e., the product of rational reflection). One wonders if the notion of divine revelation, which Smart assimilates or attempts to assimilate to religious experience, is not more fundamental than his comments would lead one to suspect.

Even more fundamental philosophically are doubts concerning Smart's theses about the "logic" of religious discourse. The slogan that each area of inquiry and experience has its own logic or patterns of thought and inference is highly fashionable. One wonders if it is also illuminating. Within a system of religious thought, language is used to assert, to exhort, to express intentions, to inform, to command, to warn, and to evaluate. The same is true within nonreligious systems. Perhaps worship and blasphemy are, or involve, distinctively religious uses of language. Even so, the uses of language in a religious context seem to be fundamentally similar to those which it has outside of any religious system. We can best see if this initial appraisal is effectively countered by Smart's contentions by setting out more fully the analogy he finds between religious and aesthetic discourse.

The grammatical predicate "holy" seems to describe whatever it is predicated of.[91] A sentence of the form "x is red" is grammatically similar to "x is holy," and the former sentence is one in which the predicate describes the subject (if a noun of appropriate sort replaces "x"). Further, there are criteria for applying the word "holy," just as there are for applying the word "red." Sentences of the form "x is holy" are sometimes debated, defended, denied, retracted, and the like. They express claims, make assertions. Sometimes "x is holy" (i.e., a sentence of this form) can be used to mean simply "x fits the criterion for holiness as specified by a certain religion." For these reasons, "holy" is often taken to be a descriptive predicate. Nonetheless, Smart claims that "holy"

. . . does not stand for an observable property . . . there is no property over and above the properties making its application appropriate which it stands for. But this is not to say that there is nothing about the object to make it wonderful apart from the properties that we may mention as conducing to its wonderfulness.[92]

We can correct the tendency to regard "holy" as a descriptive predicate by comparing sentences of the form "x is holy" with sentences of the form "x is beautiful."[93] Smart stresses "holy" and "sacred" on the ground that their use separates religious (at least, numinous) discourse from other kinds of discourse. Both forms of sentences are exclamations. This does not mean that they simply express feelings; "it is the target of wonder, not the observer, which is wonderful"[94] and this is true for being beautiful and being holy as well. Nonetheless, exclamations do express feelings and invite others to share them. They serve to point the hearer to features of an object or situation which justify the use of the exclamatory predicate. Further, there can be disagreement about whether an exclamation is appropriate— a disagreement which concerns the "nature" of the object concerned, not merely the feelings of the discussants. If an exclamation is appropriate, what makes it appropriate would continue to exist even were all sentient creatures to vanish. From the fact that "x is wonderful" is an exclamation, "it does not follow that a lifeless universe would not be wonderful."[95] Again, the same applies to "holy." One cannot teach anyone that something is holy; he must see it for himself. Further, the question "What makes x holy?" is not a request, normally anyway, for the causes of an exclamation but rather a request for a statement of those features actually possessed by the object or situation which makes the exclamation appropriate. Finally, if an exclamation is appropriate, so are certain modes of behavior—worship in the case of "holy," appreciation in the case of "beautiful," etc.

These are important similarities between sentences of the form "x is holy" and those of the forms "x is wonderful" and "x is beautiful"; Smart adds that there are also differences. The former is relevant to a whole way of life; the latter are not. To challenge a statement of the form "x is holy" is to challenge a whole doctrinal scheme. Again, to say that "x is holy," uttered as praise is or can be addressed to its object; "x is beautiful" is not.[96] Smart's contention in this regard is problematic, as "You are beautiful" and "You are wonderful" are also addressed to their "objects." Two quotations can serve to summarize the relevant portions of Smart's view.

> The particular kind of marvelling involved in worship is linked to a doctrinal scheme and it is not possible to understand many of the propositions employed in praise without acquaintance with the scheme.[97] We can set down the main circumstances for the use of such expressions as 'holy' as follows: (a) as part of an exclamatory reaction to a numinous target . . . (b) to give an exclamatory report of such an experience at a later time . . . (c) in the ordinary ceremonial of worship to express the correct religious awe and to give praise, (d) outside the

ceremonial, in order to express praise, etc. . . . in one's daily life . . .
(e) . . . to indicate the way all men ought to react towards the divine.[98]

Taking, then, "God (Brahman, etc.) is holy" as a paradigm of religious discourse, at least in the numinous strand, Smart analyses such discourse as "exclamatory" in the sense elucidated above. This analysis is intended to set out at least a crucial part of the distinctive logic of religious conceptual schemes.

It is dubious, however, whether Smart succeeds in showing that the logic of such systems is unique, or even sufficiently different from that of other systems to justify excusing them from ordinary canons of evidence and inference. For one thing, as we have noted, the same sorts of uses of language occur in religious systems as in nonreligious ones. It may be objected, however, that this is simply not so given Smart's analysis. Religious sentences are fundamentally exclamations, which are subtly different from assertions. And one might recite very familiar warnings about not being misled by grammatical form into supposing similarity of use.

Rather than rebutting criticism, however, this approach leads directly to the most fundamental difficulty with Smart's account. It is difficult to prove that other uses of language presuppose the assertive use. Nonetheless, the claim that this is so is very plausible—so plausible that the burden of proof, at least so it seems to me, lies on the one who denies it. Thus what Austin says about performatives, I want to say about exclamations. When I use language performatively with respect to an action, "in saying what I do, I actually perform that action."[99] Thus "I now pronounce you man and wife," "I apologize," and "I promise to pay you back tomorrow" express performatives in appropriate contexts. These are neither true nor false. Of course there is a condition that is at least necessary to the use of one of these sentences actually being the performance of an action. "The words have to be said in the appropriate circumstances";[100] "the circumstances in which we purport to invoke the procedure must be appropriate for its invocation."[101] Whether a performative is appropriate is a question

> . . . that can only be decided by considering how the content of the verdict or estimate is related in some way to fact, or to evidence available about the facts.[102]

What applies to verdicts and estimates applies, as Austin admits, to other performatives. Indeed, that it does is part of his analysis. Further, performatives often in some sense imply factual statements.[103] All of this, I suggest, applies to exclamations as well.

That these remarks do carry over to exclamations is plausible indeed. For one thing, the argument against Ramsey's view will, I suggest, apply *mutatis mutandis,* to the aspect of Smart's perspective now being considered. For another, and perhaps more crucial to the present context, Smart too grants the point at issue. Holiness, is, in the jargon introduced by R. M. Hare,[104] a "supervenient" quality in the sense that the use of the exclamation "x is holy" is justified or rendered appropriate by actual features of that which is said to be holy.[105] A review of Smart's contentions makes this clear. There are criteria for the application of "holy" and these criteria are not arbitrary (p. 23); it is the object that is holy, not primarily the subject or his relation to the object, and the object would be holy even were there no subjects at all (p. 25). The fact that "holy" is, as Otto pointed out, partially an evaluative predicate only strengthens the argument, for evaluative predicates are applied in virtue of the nonevaluative predicates which are, or at least are believed, applicable to the object. In sum, in religious systems as well as in other systems, the uses of language other than the assertive seem clearly to presuppose the assertive.

Further, "God is holy" presupposes "God exists." Remarkably enough, it has recently been denied by Norman Malcolm that "God exists" expresses a religious belief.[106] It is not, so the suggestion goes, belief that God exists, but belief in God which involves an "affective attitude" which is a religious belief.

> I think, on the contrary, that a 'belief that God exists,' if it was logically independent of any and all ways of regarding him, would be of no interest, even to God.[107]

Malcolm's insistence that anyone taking the issue of God's existence seriously will feel deeply about the matter is well taken. Perhaps it simply follows that belief that God exists has deep affective associations. Disbelief in God's existence perhaps fits this description less fully than belief, though there are atheists with religious fervor about their atheism. Let us suppose that Malcolm's remarks apply equally to disbelief that God exists, and further let us grant him that belief that God exists is not a religious belief, though this is quite gratuitous. Then an element in the religious belief in God will be the nonreligious belief that God exists. The relevant issue is not whether the belief that God exists is a religious belief or merely a belief presupposed by religious beliefs. Surely "God exists" does not express an exclamation. That such words could under exotic circumstances be so used is nothing to the point. That God exists will be one of the facts presupposed by "God is holy." As the author of the *Epistle to the Hebrews* puts the point,

And without faith it is impossible to please him. For whoever would draw near to God must believe that he exists and that he rewards those who seek him.[108]

Exclamations as well as performatives presuppose assertions.

Perhaps the difference between "God exists" and "God is holy" versus other claims will be in terms of the sort of reasons that could in principle be given for the former as opposed to other (e.g., straightforward, empirical) sentences.[109] But even this will not do. The same will apply to "Every event necessarily has a cause," and to any proposition which is essential to and partially definitive of a general conceptual scheme, not merely to religious systems. The sorts of reasons appropriate for any such statement will be more complex and of a different sort than those given for "The ball is round and red." Thus the appeal to the unique "logic" of religious systems seems in fact to reveal, upon careful examination, crucial similarities between basic claims or "axioms" of conceptual schemes of diverse sorts—religious and nonreligious.

The conclusion of our long discussion of Smart's contentions is this: just as his appeal to religious experience as veridical involved a leap which is not required by any evidence we possess, so the attempt to excuse religious systems from the general sort of appraisal appropriate to other conceptual schemes is unconvincing. He admits as much when he stresses the role of formal considerations in evaluating religious conceptual schemes. While the fact that such formal considerations do apply to religious systems, and with what results, is made clearer by his insightful comparative study of world religions, no cogent procedure for justifying religious beliefs by appeal to religious experience has been uncovered. Neither have any reasons been uncovered for excusing religious systems from rational appraisal. The answer to our original query (does religious experience provide evidence for religious belief?) is hence negative.

FOOTNOTES ᕙᕗ IV

[1] Cf. C. D. Broad, *Religion, Philosophy, and Psychical Research* (New York: Harcourt, Brace and World, 1953), p. 191ff.

[2] *Acts* 16:9.

[3] The problem is one of how "The dream was caused by what he ate" would be verified, not simply how one would determine the contents of Paul's stomach.

[4] Garden City, New York: Doubleday and Co., 1964. Rev. Ed., trans. by James Strachey. Quoted by permission of Liverwright Press, New York.

[5] *Totem and Taboo* (New York: Norton Press, 1950).

6 See *The Future of an Illusion*, p. 32, 68 for references to this backdrop.

7 *Ibid.*, p. 39.

8 Freud later adds "the proceedings of the spiritualists" (p. 42) the claim that religious beliefs "must be felt inwardly" (p. 43), and the view that religion is a fiction to be believed because of its importance for the maintenance of human society (p. 49).

9 *Ibid.*, p. 41.

10 *Ibid.*, p. 47.

11 Freud indicates sympathy with the view, discussed below in Chapter Six, that no one has the right to believe in the absence of evidence for what he believes.

12 *Ibid.*, p. 52.

13 *Ibid.*, p. 60.

14 *Loc. cit.*

15 *Ibid.*, p. 89.

16 M. B. Foster, *Mystery and Philosophy* (London: SCM Press, 1957), p. 61.

17 *Ibid.*, p. 62.

18 Freud, *op. cit.*, p. 89.

19 *Ibid.*, p. 16 (my italics). The reference is to a society which is stratified so as to disenfranchise the lower classes from most of their benefits.

20 *Ibid.*, p. 50. See, for example, the passage on p. 61ff. where Freud is eminently confident of his capacity to morally appraise the development of the priesthood.

21 *Ibid.*, p. 71ff.

22 R. W. White, *The Abnormal Personality* (New York: The Ronald Press, 1964), p. 204.

23 *Ibid.*, p. 280.

24 C. D. Broad, *loc. cit.*; the selection is reproduced in Mavrodes and Hackett (ed.), *Problems and Perspectives in the Philosophy of Religion* (Boston: Allyn and Bacon, 1967), p. 180ff.

25 The genetic fallacy is committed whenever one supposes that in discerning the origin of a belief he has discovered whether or not the belief is true.

26 *Isaiah* 6:1ff.

27 Ninian Smart, *Reason and Faiths*, p. 55.

28 Cf. William James, *The Varieties of Religious Experience* (New York: New American Library, 1958 reprint).

29 Rudolph Otto, *The Idea of the Holy* (New York: Oxford U. Press, 1958 reprint) p. 28. He uses "numinous" to indicate " 'the holy' *minus* its moral factor . . . and . . . minus its 'rational' aspect." (p. 6). Its meaning can be evoked, not taught. (p. 7.)

30 *Ibid.*, p. 30.

31 *Ibid.*, p. 34.

32 *Ibid.*, p. 33. Otto takes James to task for neglecting this aspect of religious experience. See *op. cit.*, p. 10, 37.

33 *Ibid.*, p. 59.

34 *Ibid.*, p. 39. Cf. p. 2ff. That claims can be based on religious experience, that such experience is not merely subjective, is stressed by Otto when he speaks of "the object to which the religious consciousness refers." (P. 62.)

35 *Ibid.*, p. 1.

36 *Ibid.*, p. 50, 51.

37 *Ibid.*, p. 43ff.

38 *Ibid.*, p. 176. Cf. Otto's comments concerning "genuine divination," p. 168.

39 John Hick, *Faith and Knowledge*, p. 137.

40 Cf. Erich Fromm, *Psychoanalysis and Religion* (New York: Bantam Books) p. 36ff.

41 Ludwig Feuerback, *The Essence of Christianity* (New York: Harper and Bros., 1957), trans. George Eliot, p. 12ff.

42 *Ibid.*, p. 33.

43 David Hume, *Hume on Religion* (Cleveland: Meridian Books, 1963) ed. Richard Wollheim, p. 40. Cf. his reference to "the universal propensity in mankind to believe in invisible, intelligent power;" *op. cit.*, p. 97.

44 *Loc. cit.*

45 *Ibid.*, p. 98. The complex question as to whether Hume offers any resolution of his own to this enigma is not germane here; I hope to deal with this issue on another occasion.

46 Cited in William James, *The Varieties of Religious Experience*, p. 320.

47 *Ibid.*, p. 316.

48 Cited by Ninian Smart, *Reasons and Faiths*, p. 132. The original is at *Theologica Germanica* xli.

49 *Isaiah*, Chapter Six, verses 1–5.

50 Cited by Smart, *op. cit.*, p. 132. The original is in Tagore's *Autobiography*, p. 72.

51 The *Bhagavad Gita*, ch. 11, Section 24. The translation is by Juan Mascaro (Baltimore: Penguin Books, 1962).

52 Cited by Rudolph Otto, *The Idea of the Holy*, p. 38.

53 *Ibid.*, p. 105.

54 St. John of the Cross, *The Ascent of Mt. Carmel*. Cited by Otto, *op. cit.*, p. 106.

55 *Loc. cit.*

56 Chapter 18: 64, 65, p. 121.

57 Ninian Smart, *Philosophers and Religious Truth* (London: SCM Press, 1964) p. 135. He adds that though the ordinary religion of Buddhist countries has numinous elements, these do not have the centrality which Otto finds them to have elsewhere.

58 *Ibid.*, p. 138.

59 For an interesting analysis of the similarities and differences of various world religions, see Smart, *World Religions: A Dialogue* (Baltimore: Pelican Books, 1966). As to the interaction between cultural and theological contexts, see Smart, *Philosophers and Religious Truth*, p. 138ff. and Broad, as cited in footnote one of this chapter.

60 Ninian Smart, *Reasons and Faiths* (London: Routledge and Kegan Paul, 1958) p. 127. I intentionally neglect Smart's highly debatable (and I think highly misleading) remarks concerning the supposedly unique "logic" of religious discourse. (Cf. *Philosophers and Religious Truth*, p. 158ff. and *Reasons and Faiths*.)

61 *Loc. cit.*

62 Cf. Smart's warning about the limitations of speaking of religious traditions in terms of strands; *op. cit.*, p. 81ff.

63 *Op. cit.*, p. 55ff. A third strand, logically dependent on the numinous strand, is also mentioned—the incarnational in which the deity is spatio-temporally manifest in various manners, or in a single and definitive way.

64 *Ibid.*, p. 40.

65 *Loc. cit.*

66 *Ibid.*, p. 127.

67 *Ibid.*, p. 129.

68 Ninian Smart, *Philosophers and Religious Truth*, p. 154.

69 *Ibid.*, p. 135.

70 *Ibid.* See *Reasons and Faiths*, indexed references to "Sankara." (Smart omits the "h" in this work.)

71 *Ibid.*, p. 131. Cf. *Reasons and Faiths*, p. 131.

72 *Ibid.*, p. 132. Cf. *Reasons and Faiths*, p. 129ff.

73 *Ibid.*, p. 133. Cf. *Reasons and Faiths*, p. 132ff; p. 144ff. Although Smart makes this claim, it seems to me to be dubious. Maimonides, for example, opts for negative theology in his *Guide for the Perplexed*, I, Ch. 55ff. But as a Jew committed to the authority of the Torah, he certainly belongs to a numinous religion.

74 *Ibid.*, p. 135. Cf. p. 137.

75 Cited by Smart, *ibid.*, p. 135.

76 Except for the pragmatic purpose of working with a system easier to handle, it may often be problematic. The justification of applying the criterion of simplicity is also obvious in the cases where one wishes to restrict oneself to the weakest claim one can make on the basis of the evidence at hand, hence to the claim most probably true, given the evidence. But it is not at all obvious that strand-decisions fit this description.

77 Smart, *op. cit.* p. 158.

78 *Ibid.*, p. 159. I waive for the moment reservations about the phrase in parentheses.

79 Smart, *Philosophers and Religious Truth*, p. 148.

80 *Loc. cit.*

81 *Ibid.*, p. 140.

82 *Reasons and Faiths*, p. 6.

83 *Loc. cit.*

84 *Ibid.*, p. 12ff., including the footnote on p. 13.

85 *Ibid.*, p. 16.

86 *Ibid.*, p. 3.

87 Smart retorts bluntly to Freud's views; see *Philosophers and Religious Truth*, p. 144. But the type of explanation Freud offers can be divorced from the aspects of Freud's views which are widely found objectionable. For the latter see A. L. Kroeber, *Anthropology* (New York: Harcourt, Brace and World, Inc., 1948) p. 616ff., and Bronislaw Malinowski, *Sex and Repression in Savage Society* (London: Routledge and Kegan Paul, 1927).

88 Benedict Spinoza, *Works of Spinoza* (Elwes translation), Vol. II (New York: Dover Publications, Inc., 1951), p. 3.

89 *Ibid.*, p. 5.

90 *Ibid.*, p. 6. Cf. *Ethics*, Part V. Prop. 52; *ibid.*, p. 270.

91 Smart, *Reasons and Faiths*, p. 22ff. He discusses "wonderful" and "beautiful" as well as "holy."

92 *Ibid.*, p. 24.

93 *Ibid.*, p. 23. Considering religious and aesthetic uses of these sentences, respectively, not peripheral ones such as "He regards the ground on which she walks as holy" or "He is a holy terror."

94 See *Ibid.*, p. 24–31 for Smart's discussion of these points.

95 *Ibid.*, p. 25.

96 *Ibid.*, p. 30.

97 *Ibid.*, p. 33.
98 *Ibid.*, p. 30ff.
99 John Austin, *Philosophical Papers* (London: Oxford U. Press, 1961), p. 223.
100 *Loc. cit.*
101 *Ibid.*, p. 224.
102 *Ibid.*, p. 237.
103 *Ibid.*, p. 224.
104 R. M. Hare, *The Language of Morals* (London: Oxford U. Press, 1952); *Freedom and Reason* (London: Oxford U. Press, 1963).
105 Smart, *op. cit.*, p. 22, where he admits that "holy" does "characterize" religious entities.
106 Norman Malcolm, "Is It a Religious Belief That 'God Exists'?," in John Hick, *Faith and the Philosophers* (New York: St. Martin's Press, 1964), p. 103–110.
107 *Ibid.*, p. 108.
108 *Hebrews* 11:6.
109 As Smart argues: *op. cit.*, p. 173ff.

BIBLIOGRAPHY ᖾ *IV*

Eliade, M., *Patterns in Comparative Religion*. London: Meridian, 1963.

Hick, J., *Faith and the Philosophers*. New York: St. Martin's Press, 1964.

Hocking, W., *The Meaning of God in Human Experience*. New Haven: Yale U. Press, 1963.

Hook, S., ed., *Religious Experience and Truth; A Symposium*. London: Oliver and Boyd, 1962.

Hutchinson, J., *Paths of Faith*. New York: McGraw Hill, 1969.

Matthews, W. R., *God in Christian Thought and Experience*. London: J. Nisbet & Co., 1963.

Mowrer, E., *The Crisis in Psychiatry and Religion*. Princeton: Van Nostrand Co., 1961.

Noss, J., *Man's Religions*. New York: MacMillan, 1956, revised ed.

Schleiermacher, F., *The Christian Faith*, two vols. New York: Harper and Row, 1963.

Van Der Leeuw, G., *Religion in Essence and Manifestation*. New York: Harper and Row, 1963.

V

RELIGION
AND MORALITY

The topic of the connection, if any, between religion and morality is a vexing one. What does one mean by "religion" and what by "morality"? One's answer to these questions will determine one's view of their relationship.

Let us mean by "religion," the Judeo-Christian tradition. This is not Western prejudice; there are indeed other religions. But in the apparent absence of any essence of religion beyond rather vague and insipid generalities, the only way to profitably approach our topic is to ask in what way, if any, some *specific* religion is related to morality. The content of belief shared by Jews and Christians is rich enough to merit some investigation in this regard. Both religions are concerned with this world as well as with the next though the emphasis may vary. Both contain explicit moral teachings, and in both God is conceived as not less than perfectly good. Further, our topic has been much discussed in connection with this religious tradition. How, then, is the Judeo-Christian tradition related to morality?

RELIGION AND MORALITY:
RELATION BY DEFINITION

A move often made by those who hold that there is a connection between religion and morality is to link them by means of a definition. Thus it is asserted that "x is good" means "God wills x."[1] While this thesis has often been proposed and defended, it has also often been refuted and rejected. The arguments against this view are, in my opinion, conclusive. Two in particular deserve mention.

If "x is good" means the same as "God wills x," then two quite unacceptible conclusions immediately follow. One is that "Whatever God wills is good" is simply a tautology. It, by the principle of substituting equals for equals, simply says "Whatever is good, is good" or "Whatever God wills, God wills." Now since an ethical principle provides a means of sorting out good actions from ones that are not good,[2] it is plain that a tautology cannot be an ethical principle. Knowing that what is good is in fact good does not help at all in deciding whether birth control, or torture for pleasure, is good or evil. So, on this interpretation, "Whatever God wills is good" cannot be an ethical principle.

A reply to this argument has recently been made.[3] Patterson Brown has noted that the following pattern of reasoning is both valid and ethically relevant in the sense of providing a test for good versus evil actions:

(a) If God wills x, then x is good.
(b) God wills x.

So:

(c) x is good.

While this argument is patently valid, it does not suffice to make Brown's point. On his view, (a) is identical to (a′): "If God wills x, then God wills x." Now (a′) and (b) do not entail (c). So it is clear that (a) and (b), as Brown interprets (a), do not entail (c). Only if we interpret the connection between "God wills x" and "x is good" as nondefinitional can we derive (c) from (a) and (b), and it is precisely this interpretation of the connection that Brown denies.

Brown offers an argument for (a) which must also be mentioned. The argument can be stated thusly.

(p) It is a necessary truth that if God wills x, x is good.
(c) If God wills x, then x is good.

But:

(q) If a proposition expresses a necessary truth, then it is true by definition.[4]

So: (r) "If God wills x, then x is good" is true by definition. While (q) is hardly self-evident, I will not question it here. What is not noted, however, is that (r) can be true on the basis of either of two definitions.

(D1) "Good" means "is willed by God."
(D2) "God" means (in part) "a being who is all-good."

Only if (r) is true in virtue of (D1) is (a) a tautology in virtue of the definition of "good." It was precisely by regarding (a) as true in virtue of the definition of "good" that (a) was seen above to be identical with (a′), and thus not to be an ethical principle. So there is good reason to deny that (r) is true by definition of "good." In other words, (D1) is not the definition to appeal to when defending the necessity of (a).

Suppose, however, we defend the claim that (a) is necessarily true by appeal to (D2). Then it will be true in virtue of the fact that "God" is defined in precisely the way in which traditional theism has defined this word. Further, (a) then can function as a fruitful premise in the argument which Brown offers for (c). Since (a) is then not identical to (a′), (a) and (b) will entail (c). Given that we can decide what God does will, and given that we accept (a), we can discern what is good. As Brown notes, we could in principle know what God wills on the basis of His revealing it to us, or on the basis of careful reflection as to what an all-knowing, all-good being might indeed will.[5] In short, "What God wills is good" could then function as an ethical principle. But this assumes that we regard it as true in virtue of (D2), not in virtue of (D1). We will investigate this way of relating religion and morality below.

Our first argument against reading "Whatever God wills is good" as a definition of "good" was that if we do so we cannot interpret it as an ethical principle. There is a second reason. If we take "Whatever God wills is good" as true in virtue of its defining what "good" means, we can no longer say that God is good. If "x is good" means "God wills x," then "God is good" means "God wills God," which is unintelligible. Surely the claim that "God is good" is not identical to any such statement as "God wills God." It might, of course, be said that God is good in an entirely different sense than that in which human actions or agents are good. But then unless this claim is to be empty we must be given some idea of what this new sense is. It is hard to see how God can be said to be praiseworthy or worshipworthy unless the sense in which He is said to be good is at least analogous to that in which the word is used concerning men and their actions.[6]

Since the suggestion that "x is good" means "God wills x" entails that "Whatever God wills is good" cannot function in a theistic system or elsewhere as an ethical principle, and also entails that "God is good" is in fact unintelligible, there seems to be excellent reason to reject it. We have seen how to reject it without denying that "Whatever God wills is good" is a necessary truth, as it seems indeed to be. But we are left the knotty question as to how religion and morality might be related. The easy definitional path leads nowhere;[7] what path can we take?

RELIGION AND MORALITY: NONDEFINITIONAL RELATIONS

It is now time to further specify the content of our question. Let it now read: Is there, in the Judeo-Christian tradition, any basis for an ethical system which is rationally defensible? We will, of course, have to inquire into what sense "basis" may bear in this connection.

There are at least two ways in which one can relate theology and morality without defining "x is right" or "x is good" as "God wills (approves) x." One way is to note that God is omniscient, omnipotent and omnibenevolent. Thus if God issues a command to do x, it is right to do x. This is evident in that God, being all-good, would not knowingly command that a wrong action be performed and, being all-knowing, could not be mistaken about whether an action was right. Given that we can know that God commands that x be done, we know also that doing x is right. This raises the question as to how one identifies a revelation—how one tells a genuine from a merely putative revelation. This would be a problem even if only one religion claimed to possess a revealed text, and the fact that many religions make this claim makes the problem more acute. Nonetheless, this move does not involve the clearly insuperable problems which face any attempt to relate religion and morality via definition.

The alternative just discussed might be called the theological version of the "ideal observer" theory of ethics. Another alternative is available. Man, according to Judeo-Christian theology, is created in God's image. It is thus not surprising that in both the Judaic and the Christian aspects of that tradition, morality has been construed as the *imitatio Dei*. To act rightly is to act in imitation of God, and of course in Christianity this is tantamount to acting in imitation of Christ. By doing so, man realizes his divinely appointed potential. He acts in accord with his own nature as a creature made by God to love both God and fellow man. To imitate God is, essentially, to act from *agape* or self-giving love which acts for the betterment of the other without concern for reward. One delights in the welfare of the other, whether one has contributed to this welfare or not. If one has so contributed, the delight is not primarily in the significance of one's own contribution, but in the welfare of the other which was the contribution's goal. This approach could be viewed as a Judeo-Christian version of the "self-realization" theory of ethics. But just as there is point in the comparison of our first nondefinitional alternative of relating religion and morality to an ideal observer theory of ethics, but also danger of being misleading in that there are differences, so there is point but also danger in making the present comparison. It should be noted that these alternatives are by no means mutually exclusive. One could, for example, view a set of commands, taken as revealed by God, as either partially or fully defining what the imitation of God required.

This is not the place to develop in any further detail these alternatives,[8] either together or separately. Enough has been said to indicate, in general, what moves are open if one wishes to nondefinitionally relate religion and morality. In purely philosophical terms, the next task, I take it, would be to develop such a system of ethics and then appraise it in comparison to the major competing theories to see which best sustained rational appraisal. But that task, even if feasible, would require a separate volume. Our purpose must be more modest.

Two points should be made in concluding this portion of our discussion. The first is that both alternatives mentioned for relating religion and morality are offered within an already-existing view concerning the status of man and the nature of his environment. Man is made in God's image, enjoying a special status among God's creatures. His environment, having been created and existing under the control of God, is safely viewed as not being ultimately recalcitrant to obeying God's commands or realizing one's divinely appointed potential. The universe is viewed as a fitting environment for growth to the maturity of an *agape*-governed life. Second, this has the result of making morality dependent on religion in a dual sense. What is good is determinable by reference to divine commands and/or human nature as created in the divine image. That the commands can be obeyed and the divinely appointed human potential be realized is guaranteed by the power and goodness of God. Of course, this does not mean that the right will be done unless men do it. Thus both the content of morality and the possibility of successful moral endeavor are theologically grounded. In this respect, religion provides a basis for morality on the alternatives presently being elucidated.

Not every philosopher, of course, is content to let morality rest in this or any other manner on religion. Some philosophers have claimed to possess a justified certainty concerning the principles of morality which was quite independent of religious belief. Some among these have then continued by endeavoring to reverse the above procedure by basing religion on morality. This latter has occurred in two ways. In some cases, philosophers have argued that we can be certain that a specifiable set of moral claims are true. They add that this provides relevant or even conclusive evidence for theism. The specific form of their argument varies. Sometimes it is said that just as social law presupposes a law-making body, so a moral law presupposes a Moral Lawgiver. Needless to say, the analogy can be questioned. Or it is argued that true moral principles are eternally or timelessly true, and that their truth is grounded in the existence of corresponding thoughts or propositions which in turn could exist only in an eternal mind. So there must be such a mind. Or it is argued that men are morally responsible, that to be responsible is to be responsible to someone, and that it is not sufficient to say that men are responsible to one another, individually or collectively. Hence there is a Supreme Being to which they are responsible.[9] Now to prove that God exists is to show that a certain statement or set of statements, which are more clearly true than it is clearly true that God exists, entails or makes probable the statement that God exists. It is certainly dubious that a proof of God's existence can be established on the basis of any of the above arguments, since it is certainly dubious that each of the premises of any of these arguments is more clearly true than the statement that God exists or is true at all for that matter.

KANT ON RELIGION AND MORALITY

The other way in which philosophers have endeavored to base religion on morality is exemplified by the writings of Immanuel Kant. Since Kant offered his views concerning religion and morality as a putative exegesis (actually it was a radical reformulation) of Christian doctrine and as a sounder replacement for natural theology, they have considerable intrinsic interest as well as being a peculiarly appropriate topic for reflection given our present concerns. How, then, does Kant conceive of the connection between morality and religion?

Though he rejected the traditional proofs for God's existence, Kant remained a theist. Being unwilling to believe in God in the absence of any rational justification for this belief, he offered his own mitigated version of natural theology. Our present purpose is to analyze and appraise his attempt to provide reasons for theistic belief, or, as he put it, a rational faith.

The rejection of the traditional proofs in the first *Critique*[10] is an essential part of his program. This is so not merely for the obvious reason that were old-style natural theology successful then there would have been no need for a new style. There is the further crucial point that if Kant's criticisms of the traditional proofs are correct, then no conclusion *pro or con* can be reached by the traditional technique of deductively deriving conclusions from self-evident or otherwise obvious premises, one among which is straightforwardly existential. This is so because the categories of human thought cannot be applied beyond the range of possible experience in any manner that will extend our knowledge. This in turn is demonstrated by the putative fact that any argument whose premises involve such an application of the categories can be countered by an equally cogent argument to the opposite conclusion. By thus showing the incompetence of theoretical reason, whose primary task is extending our knowledge, to resolve the traditional problems concerning God, freedom, and immortality, Kant leaves the way open for practical reason to deal with these issues. If the answer to "What can we know about God and immortality?" is "Nothing," perhaps "What may we hope about God and immortality?" can be answered on the basis of our answer to another question, namely "What ought we to do?" Kant, at least, believed this to be so.

The appeal to the results of previous arguments is explicit in the third *Critique*.

> The limitation of reason in respect of all our ideas of the supersensible to the conditions of its practical employment has, as far as the idea of God is concerned, undeniable uses. For it prevents theology from rising in to theosophy (into transcendent concepts which confound reason), or from sinking into demonology (an anthropomorphic way of representing the highest Being).[11]

These results are assumed in the second *Critique* as well, as is made abundantly evident in the preface to that work. In order to make progress in evaluating new-style natural theology we will suppose for the sake of the argument that old-style endeavors have been refuted.

A crucial passage in the development of Kant's argument is the following.

> A final purpose in them [i.e., in men] proposed as duty, and a nature without any final purpose beyond them, in which that purpose might be actualized, would involve a contradiction.[12]

Kant's meaning here can best be made clear by referring to that portion of the *Groundwork*[13] in which he discusses the tests of a maxim relevant to determining whether a maxim embodies the moral law. His position is that a maxim, when universalized, expresses a moral law just in case it is universalizable without contradiction and the opposite maxim is not. Two sorts of contradiction are involved: logical and practical. Any maxim whose universalization is contradictory in either way is morally forbidden, and every maxim whose universalization is consistent is morally permissible. If the universalization of a maxim's contradictory is logically inconsistent whereas its own universalization is not, it expresses a moral obligation.

The test for consistent universalization is then stated in these terms:

> Some actions are so constituted that their maxim cannot even be *conceived* as a universal law of nature without contradiction, let alone be *willed* as what *ought* to become one. In the case of others we do not find this inner impossibility, but it is still impossible to *will* that their maxim should be raised to the universality of a law of nature, because such a will would contradict itself.[14]

A case in point of a maxim whose universalization is, in Kant's view, contradictory is "Let me commit suicide in order to escape from a painful situation." The contradictoriness arises in this manner: the maxim takes escaping from pain as an end and the destruction of human life as a means. "But man is not a thing—not something to be used *merely* as a means: he must always in all his actions be regarded as an end in himself. Hence I cannot dispose of man in my person by maiming, spoiling, or killing."[15] Here is one sense in which a maxim can, for Kant, be logically contradictory. If maxim M, when universalized, can be a moral law just in case a man is treated as a means only, then it is contradictory to assert that M's universalization expresses a moral law, since "Man is an end in himself" is a necessary truth.[16] (In what sense this is so we will investigate later.) The form of the test by which suicide is rejected is this: Let (P) = "man is an end in himself." Then if a maxim M, or its universalization, presupposes or entails not-P, then M does not express a moral law. Since not-P is *ex hypothesi* a necessary falsehood, nothing which presupposes or entails not-P can be a moral law.

Precisely the same considerations hold when we move from a perfect duty to oneself to a perfect duty to others.

> For . . . it is manifest that a violator of the rights of man intends to use the person of others merely as a means without always at the same time taking into consideration that, as rational beings, they ought always at the same time to be rated as ends—that is, only as beings who must themselves be able to share in the end of the very same action.[17]

When we turn to maxims concerning imperfect duties, another sort of test is relevant since another kind of consistency is under review.

> In regard to contingent [meritorious] duty to oneself, it is not enough that an action should refrain from conflicting with humanity in our own person as an end in itself [i.e., be consistent in the first sense]; it must also *harmonize with this end.*[18]

Perfect duties are duties in that not to follow them is to fail to regard man as an end in himself—to refuse to grant to man (oneself and others), as rational agent, the dignity of intrinsic value. Imperfect duties are duties in that not to follow them is to refuse to promote in man (oneself and others) the fullest development of those capacities which are unique to man as rational agent.

As Kant puts it,

> There are in humanity capacities for greater perfection which form part of nature's purpose for humanity in our person. To neglect these can admittedly be compatible with the *maintenance* of humanity as an end in itself, but not with the *promotion* of this end.[19]

To act in accord with maxims which are inconsistent in the first sense would be to act as if man was not a moral agent at all—to deny that there is any moral obligation and any moral dignity, or inherent worth to being a rational agent. To act in accord with maxims which are inconsistent in the second sense would be to act as if man was not capable or worthy of moral progress—to deny that the fullest possible exercise of man's distinctively human (rational) capacities and the consequent development of the predisposition to personality is something worthwhile in itself or intrinsically good.[20]

In giving his example of an imperfect duty[21] to others, Kant offers the duty of a prosperous man to help his less fortunate neighbors. Suppose such a man entertains the maxim "Let me help no one who is in need." Universalized, the maxim will be "Let no one help anyone who is in need." Stated as a moral law, it will read "One ought never to help another who is in need." Now suppose that one adopted the universalized maxim, willing the moral law just noted to hold as if it were a natural law. If a prosperous man wills that the universe be such that no man will help any other who is in need, he must in all consistency will that if he is ever in need, he too will not be helped. But he does not will this; he may be willing to "take his chances" on its happening, but he does not will that it happen.[22]

> If we now attend to ourselves whenever we transgress a duty, we find that we do not in fact will that our maxim should become a universal law—since this is impossible for us—but rather that its opposite should remain a law universally: we only take the liberty of making an *exception* to it for ourselves (or even just for this once) to the advantage of our inclination. Consequently, if we weighed it all up from one and the

same point of view—that of reason—we should find a contradiction in
our own will; the contradiction that a certain principle should be
objectively necessary as a universal law and yet subjectively should not
hold universally but should admit of exceptions.[23]

So a man who wills (1) "Let me help no one else who needs help"
also in fact wills (2) "Let me be helped if I need help." But (1) universalized becomes "Let no one help anyone else who needs help," which
stated as a moral law becomes (A) "One ought never to help anyone
else who needs help." But if this law were followed, the man who
wills to be helped himself will in fact not be helped. So maxim (1)
taken as our duty is incompatible with maxim (2) which all men,
insofar as they are rational, adopt. Thus the person who adopts maxim
(1) in doing so wills contradictory things since he must insofar as he
is rational adopt (2). So by adopting (1) he causes a *practical* contradiction.

Another way of bringing out this contradiction would be to univer-
salize (2) with this result: (B) "One ought always to help another who
needs help." But while either (A) or (B) could be paralleled with
natural laws[24] which held for an actual universe, no actual universe
could exist in which natural laws paralleling both (A) and (B) held.
Such a universe would be logically impossible.

We can now state the second sort of contradiction in a more formal
way. If person S adopts maxims M^1 and M^2, such that M^1 universalized yields moral principle[25] A and M^2 universalized yields moral
principle B, and if there is a natural law statement L^1 which parallels
A and a natural law statement L^2 which parallels B, such that it is
logically impossible that L^1 and L^2 hold at the same time for the same
universe, then M^1 and M^2 are in practical contradiction to one another. Further, if S, insofar as rational, must adopt M^2 (if anyone who
does not adopt M^2 is irrational insofar as he does not) then adopting
M^1 is not morally permissible. (*Ex hypothesi*, this is never true of both
M^1 and M^2.)

This way of putting the test has a flaw, however, in that it rests on
the claim "No rational man fails to will his own happiness," and insofar as consistent and knowledgeable, he wills the means thereto. This
claim is not unqualifiedly true; were one faced with a choice between
sustaining his own happiness and that of his children he might well
opt for the latter and be no less rational for so doing. Further, in the
qualified sense in which it is true, it seems to be morally irrelevant.
It is perhaps as sane, but not as moral, that a man wills his own happiness. Of course, we can alter this test. We can replace "If S, insofar
as rational, must adopt M^2, then adopting M^1 is not morally permissible" by "If S, in adopting M^2, will make possible the further moral

development of himself or another, whereas in adopting M¹ he would not, then adopting M² rather than M¹ is morally obligatory." And we can expand the test to explicitly cover cases in which moral development will be hindered by the adoption of one maxim and not by the adoption of another, and the like. This will have the net effect of saying that treating men as ends-in-themselves requires us to adopt maxims that will further, not hinder, or maxims which will least hinder, the use of their rational-moral capacities, depending on the maxims actually available to us. And this will mean that the basis for tests (1) and (2) are the same—treating man always as an end and never as a means only—but that one can fail to do this in either of two ways: by not treating the creature possessing rational capacities as an end-in-himself or by not treating a creature with the capacity to develop his rational capacities as an end-in-himself. This seems to be the distinction Kant makes in the passage concerning "nature's purpose for humanity in our person" cited above. We will have occasion later to wonder just how sharply this distinction can be made.

For present purposes, however, we can rephrase test two as follows: Suppose that, for all S, if S is moral then S has E as an end. Then if a maxim M¹ will, if followed, result in promoting E, following any maxim M² inconsistent with M¹ is morally forbidden. With qualifications concerning maxims which are such that following them will in various degrees promote or hinder the attainment of E, we can amplify this test to deal with more complex cases. Further, this way of putting the test captures Kant's concern with those ends which men *qua* moral must adopt.

It is worth noting that this version is, in fact, quite in accord with Kant's own views. He distinguishes between physical happiness[26] and moral happiness, the latter being "the reality and constancy of a disposition which ever progresses in goodness (and never falls away from it)."[27] He holds that man is capable of his own

> . . . peculiar kind of contentment—contentment in fulfilling a purpose which in turn is determined by reason alone, even if this fulfillment should often involve interference with the purposes of inclination.[28]

He adds elsewhere that "moral happiness . . . consists of a consciousness of progress in goodness (and this is one and the same act as the forsaking of evil)."[29] The happiness, then, which man (for Kant) must will as a rational being is moral happiness. That is, he must will his own progression in goodness and as a rational-moral being will inevitably find contentment in such progression. The above alteration of our statement of Kant's test is quite in accord with Kant's doctrines concerning moral happiness. Indeed, it is motivated by these doctrines.

We shall see below, however, that another sort of happiness is essential to Kant's argument.

It is important at this juncture to emphasize the role of practical reason in Kant's account of morality. Practical reason, reason concerned with conduct, binds man in an inescapable way insofar as man is a finite rational being at all. It both prescribes my duties and makes me aware of my own dignity and that of others. Just as theoretical reason, reason concerned with knowledge, judges that nothing can have incompatible properties in such a manner that I can (insofar as rational at all) not believe otherwise, so practical reason's deliverances are authoritative and unquestionable.

Before we return explicitly to our passage in the third *Critique*, one further matter deserves brief mention. Kant is often interpreted as treating maxims whose universalization is logically inconsistent as being inconsistent, not externally because they presuppose something necessarily false, but internally. He says

> . . . the universality of a law that every one believing himself to be in need can make any promise he pleases with the intention not to keep it would make promising, and the very purpose of promising, itself impossible, since no one would believe he was being promised anything, but would laugh at utterances of this kind as empty shams.[30]

The point of these comments can perhaps be best put in this manner. The practice of promise-making is possible just in case there is not also a practice of making false promises. The making of a particular promise is no isolated act; it presupposes the practice of promise-making, which presupposes in turn the practice of promise-keeping as a going enterprise. One particular false promise does not bankrupt that enterprise. But the maxim "Let me under duress make false promises" when universalized becomes "Let everyone under duress make false promises" and so stated as a moral principle becomes "One ought to make false promises under duress." Were this principle followed, making false promises under duress would be a practice. But were making false promises under duress a practice, Kant assumes, the practice of promise-making would be logically impossible since the latter practice is logically incompatible with the former practice. Now perhaps all this argument shows is that the practice of promise-keeping under duress, and so the practice of promise-making under duress, is incompatible with the practice of promise-breaking under duress, and that it is sufficiently difficult to tell whether someone else is under duress so that in fact the practice of promise-keeping under any circumstances could not be maintained if the maxim in question were universally adopted. Nonetheless, the *schema* of Kant's argument seems clear enough. Suppose doing any act of kind K presupposes practice P. Suppose that maxim M recommends doing A (which is of kind K) and that the universalization of M if adopted would result in a practice incompatible with P (namely, practice not-P). Now if doing A presupposes P, and M (which recommends doing A) when universalized and adopted will result in practice not-P, then adopting M presupposes P and results in not-P. So M is self-defeating. If there are any such maxims, they are inconsistent in yet a third sense. So we now must ask in which, if any, of these three senses of contradiction is it (as Kant claimed in the passage with which we began this discussion) contradictory that a final purpose as a duty for all men be affirmed but a final purpose for all nature be denied? We can decide this issue only by means of a careful study of Kant's "moral proof," in the context of which our passage occurs.

A good way of seeing what Kant's "Moral proof of God's existence" amounts to is to ask this question: suppose we knew (a) that God did not exist or (b) that the soul is not immortal and indeed does not survive the death of the body, or both. What difference would this make, in Kant's view, with respect to morality?

In one respect, none at all. "Morality can subsist without theology as regards its rule."[31] In another respect, a great deal. Morality cannot subsist without theology (i.e., without knowledge or belief that God exists and that the soul is immortal) ". . . as regards the final design which this [morality] proposes, unless reason in respect of it is to be renounced."[32] What does Kant mean by this strong assertion?

Were God known not to exist, there would be no reason to think that the highest good would ever be attained.[33] There would be no reason to suppose that a good man would ever attain the happiness of which he is *ex hypothesi* worthy, or that an evil man would not escape all judgment. Were the soul known not to survive the death of the body, the same consequences follow. Kant's express claim is that were (a) or (b) known to be true, the highest good—which all men are obligated to seek—would be known to be unattainable. It can easily be shown that Kant's argument that all men are obligated to seek the highest good is at best problematic. Nonetheless, Kant's claims will not have run their full course. He also argues, though quite tentatively, that if we know either (a) or (b) to be true, we also know that man is not, as morality requires, an end-in-himself. We must investigate both of Kant's arguments.

The following seems to be an adequate way of stating Kant's moral proof.[34]

(1) The moral law obliges us to strive toward a final purpose—the highest good in the world possible through freedom.

(2) This highest good is constituted by a perfect proportionment between happiness and worthiness of happiness in rational agents.

(3) The concepts "worthy of happiness" and "possessing happiness" are not analytically connected, and can only be connected by the concept of a moral ruler.

(4) If we are obligated to strive toward a final purpose, which purpose is composed of two elements, A and B, and if A and B can only be connected via concept C, then we must assume that concept C is applicable.

(5) We must assume that the concept of a moral ruler is applicable— i.e., that there is a moral ruler.

Now suppose that a man refuses to assume that there is a moral ruler—because, perhaps, he claims to find a covert contradiction in the concept. He will then deny that the concept has any application. He will then be unable to relate the two elements of the highest good. He will hence be unable to strive for the highest good and so cannot fulfill every obligation the moral law imposes upon him. This, however, does not free him from all his obligations, but only from this one. Essentially, this is Kant's argument.

It has its problems. One concerns the first premise; the connection between being under the moral law and being obligated to strive toward the highest good certainly needs clarification. Further, proof is needed that only by the concept of a moral ruler can the elements in the highest good be other than arbitrarily juxtaposed. Nor is it clear that a man can strive toward an end which involves two components only if he can relate them in some nonarbitrary way.

But supposing that the argument were clearly successful, what would it, in Kant's view, prove?

> This moral argument does not supply any *objectively valid* proof of the Being of God; it does not prove to the skeptic that there is a God, but proves that if he wishes to think in a way consonant with morality, he must admit the *assumption* of this proposition under the maxims of his practical reason. We should therefore not say, it is necessary for *morals* to assume the happiness of all rational beings of the world in proportion to their morality, but rather, this is necessitated *by* morality. Accordingly, this is a *subjective* argument sufficient for moral beings.[35]

The natural tendency to reverse the argument is explicitly forbidden by Kant. From "One of our obligations presupposes that God exists," we cannot infer "That we have obligations proves that God exists." The concept of God (i.e., of a moral ruler) is necessary in order to make sense of our obligation to seek the highest good; that is, to non-arbitrarily relate its diverse elements is a necessary condition of so acting as to produce assurance that anyone satisfying one will also satisfy the other. The assumption of the existence of God is in this sense a conceptual necessity. But the concepts for which the applicability of the concept of God is a necessity are inessential to morality in that the remainder of Kant's moral system remains intact if one sacrifices them. At least, so the official doctrine requires. To say that the existence of God is required as a postulate of morality is to say that the assumption that the concept of God applies is required in order to make sense of our obligation to strive for the highest good. To infer from this conceptual necessity that we have knowledge of the existence of a supernatural being would go beyond anything the moral proof justifies, even if we can resolve the problems which the argument involves. An attempt to resolve them is worth the effort for two reasons. One is that only if they can be resolved has one even the minimal evidence which Kant's moral proof would provide. The other is to see if the official doctrine that the body of Kant's moral system will survive the amputation of one of our obligations is indeed justified.

First, then, what justification does Kant offer for premise (1)? He offers a sub-proof as follows:

(a) Insofar as a man is moral, he necessarily wills (i.e., his reason so forms his will) that the highest good be obtained.

(b) If a man, insofar as he is moral, necessarily wills (i.e., his reason so forms his will) that a state of affairs A obtain, he is obligated to promote A.[36]

(c) Every man, insofar as moral, is obligated to promote the highest good.

That this is his argument is plain from such passages as these.

> We *should* seek to further the highest good (which therefore must at least be possible.)[37]
> The achievement of the highest good in the world is the necessary object of a will determinable by the moral law.[38]
> The moral law . . . determines for us, and indeed *a priori*, a final purpose toward which it obliges us to strive, and this purpose is the highest *good in the world* possible through freedom.[39]

That the highest good is necessarily the object of will of a moral agent explains in what manner the moral law *a priori* determines for us a final purpose toward which we are obligated to strive. Our premise (b) supplies a claim Kant needs to make his argument valid, one to which he can appeal to bridge the gap between what I must, *qua*

moral, will and what I must, *qua* moral, do. Any justification of (b)
will appeal to the status of rational-moral agency; if rational nature
exists as an end in itself, then its necessary objects of will ought to
be promoted. Ends necessarily sanctioned by reason are ends that all
men are obligated to promote. It does not follow that they are ends
any man is obligated to attain; so this version of the argument does
not require that we do what is, for us, quite impossible. Suppose, then,
that we grant Kant premise (1), and turn our attention to premise (2).
Why should anyone suppose that the highest good has precisely two
elements, and those two the exact two that Kant mentions? Tracing
Kant's answer to this question necessitates a small digression.[40]

Reason, whether in its theoretical or practical exercise, seeks the
unconditioned—seeks, that is, what needs no further justification (theoretical) or that which is an end-in-itself and so not a means to some
further end (practical). Practical reason finds the unconditioned, so to
speak, in two places. One is in the unconditional demand of the moral
law. The other Kant expresses as ". . . the unconditioned totality of
the object of the pure practical reason, under the name of the *highest
good.*"[41] The supreme good is that a man always obey the moral law;
this is ". . . the condition which is subordinate to no other." It hence
refers to a state of the individual moral agent. The perfect (i.e., complete) good is that each man be happy in proportion to his virtue. It
thus refers to a state of affairs with respect to each moral agent in his
relation to his environment. Insofar as a man is morally perfect, he
deserves to be happy.

> For to be in need of happiness and also worthy of it and yet not to
> partake of it could not be in accordance with the complete volition of
> an omnipotent rational being, if we assume such only for the sake of
> the argument.[42]

But what could not be willed by a fully rational being cannot be
morally right. What we are owed, but not paid however, is a proof
that a universe in which men are all virtuous, but not happy, is one
which could not be consistently willed by a completely rational and
omnipotent being. If this is true, then a contradiction must be discernible in the maxim, expressed by an omnipotent being, "Let me
create a universe in which all virtuous men are not happy." Such a
universe is plainly logically possible. The maxim is not, then, contradictory in the third sense.[43] What, then, of the second sense? To suggest that God would be unhappy were virtuous men to be unhappy
is either a gross anthropomorphism or a way of saying that for this
state of affairs to exist would be immoral, which is the point under
discussion. More generally, it is difficult to see how any other end that

can plausibly be ascribed to the Deity is incompatible with the unhappiness of the virtuous unless we beg the question and assume the latter to be morally wrong. Thus there seems to be no cogent way of showing that our proposed maxim is self-defeating in sense two. Only the first sense remains.

The proposed maxim is contradictory in the first sense just in case it involves treating men as a means only, and not also as an end. What this amounts to in the present context can perhaps be put in this way. Suppose that God were to create a species S of rational agents such that only insofar as the members of S were virtuous but not happy could the members of species S' of rational agents have happiness proportional to their virtue. This would make the members of S means to the end of a state of affairs which benefitted only the members of S'. So this sort of universe is one that it would be logically impossible for God to create, since necessarily men (i.e., rational agents) ought always to be treated as ends and not as means only and God cannot do what ought not to be done. Nonetheless, this does not show that, in a universe where the fate of men does not influence that of any other species of rational beings (if any), it would be somehow contradictory for God to adopt the maxim in question. We have not shown that it would not be contradictory for a rational, omnipotent being to adopt this maxim, but only that it is by no means obvious that it would be. Thus, Kant's claim that for ". . . the entire and perfect good . . . happiness is . . . required" as well as virtue, and this ". . . not merely in the partial eyes of a person who makes himself his end but even in the judgment of an impartial reason which impartially regards persons in the world as ends-in-themselves"[44] is, apparently, not substantiated by a consideration of what maxims a Deity might, without inconsistency, adopt.

Another endeavor to justify premise (2) could be developed along these lines. Consider the thesis that, if a being B is an end-in-himself, then whatever is not an end-in-itself will, if morally related to B at all, be a means to the self-realization of B.[45] At least, in any world governed by an omnipotent rational being, this thesis will be true. But part of the self-realization of any human rational agent will be that the agent has all the happiness he deserves, since each man, as human, desires happiness just as each agent, as rational, wills his own moral perfection. This argument, however, makes absolute worth reside in human nature, man as both rational and passional, not in man's rational capacity alone. It requires that "happiness" mean more than the "moral happiness" discussed above. On this, more in a moment.

Yet another move is obviously open. That the wicked prosper and the righteous suffer does seem unjust. One can mediate between virtue and happiness (and vice and unhappiness) via the notions of reward and punishment. No just world is a world in which the virtuous are unhappy because of their virtue or the vicious happy because of their vice. Further, since rewarding vice and punishing virtue would be tantamount to promoting immorality, no Deity worthy of the name, remembering that the Kantian model for Deity is that of Moral Ruler, will act in this manner. Nonetheless, this does not show that there being someone who is unhappy and virtuous, but not unhappy because of his virtue, or that there being someone who is happy and vicious, but not happy because of his viciousness, are states of affairs no Deity could consistently countenance. Perhaps virtue is its own reward and vice its own punishment.

I admit that there remains a plausibility to the claim that it is unjust that the virtuous be unhappy. This is perhaps not something which would occur in a morally perfect world. At least, the claim that it would not is perhaps sufficiently plausible to merit serious consideration and to reject only upon receiving good reason against it. But even if this claim has *prima facie* truth, it is not at all clear that one can justify it in a Kantian context. And if one cannot, then it is unclear that, for Kant, there is any morally justifiable connection between virtue and worthiness of happiness. Hence, it is unclear that, for Kant, we are obligated by the moral law to promote the highest good, since it is unclear that any rational agent, *qua* rational and moral, must will that any virtuous man will also be a happy man. In considering premise (2), we find a problem that extends back to premise (1).

I can see only one Kantian rebuttal. It comes in two stages. The first is: whatever a man, as rational, wills is *a fortiori* right. This is true even if what one wills is not something he is obliged to seek. Every man, insofar as rational, wills his own happiness. No man is obligated to seek it. Kant says of a perfectly good will that even were it utterly inefficacious

> . . . it would still shine like a jewel for its own sake. . . . Its usefulness would be merely, as it were, the setting which enables us to handle it better in our ordinary dealings or to attract the attention of those not sufficiently expert, but not to commend it to experts or to determine its value.[46]

On our present reading, rational agents are jewels even more precious. The fact that any agent wills the sort of happiness appropriate to its state (e.g., as possessing or not possessing inclinations) entails that it is right that he attain that happiness, since what a rational agent necessarily wills is *a fortiori* that which will fulfill his nature and whatever will fulfill his nature will produce in its completest form something intrinsically valuable. The second stage is not difficult to anticipate. Insofar as a man violates the moral law, he increases the distance between his own state and the moral ideal; he is less morally perfect and so has less fully realized his nature than he might have. He is hence a less rational agent than he might have been, and so has less value. The capacity for perfection is reduced, so the rightful demand for happiness is mitigated. A man is fully an end-in-himself, a fully rational agent, only insofar as he chooses rightly. The less rational he is, the less perfect he would be even were he granted perfect happiness. Further, when we remember that happiness for Kant is ". . . the state of a rational being in the world with whom in the totality of his existence *everything goes according to his wish and will*"[47] were a man to be granted happiness when he was not morally perfect, his immoral wishes would have to be gratified. There would then be a conflict between what made the agent happy and what was right for the agent, in which case the moral demands of reason would have precedence over the agent's happiness, even though that too is rationally willed. Indeed, the agent would be no longer rational in willing his own happiness in such circumstances, so no injustice would be done by his not receiving it, even granting the ultimate worth of rational agents.

Nonetheless, insofar as he is moral, a man's attaining happiness fulfills his nature and he becomes, actually and not merely potentially, an end-in-himself. As he is obligated to do this, he is obligated to promote the requisite means, among which is his own happiness as well as that of others insofar as his and their reception of it does not require the gratification of immoral wishes. In this way, we can unite "possessing happiness" and "worthiness of happiness" via the concept "fulfilling/realizing the nature of a rational agent," and thus elucidate and defend premise (2). Since such a nature is an end-in-itself, and so something to be striven for, we can now also accept premise (1), which tells us that we have an obligation to seek the highest good, or happiness for all proportionate to their virtue. This is tantamount to promoting the development of rational agents (oneself and others) toward rational maturity or realization of their potential. So "being virtuous" and "being worthy of happiness" are connected via the concept "rational agent."

But if we accent this elucidation and defense of (1) and (2), what about (3), which claims that the concepts "worthy of happiness," and "possessing happiness" are not analytically connected, which is obviously true, and can only be connected by the concept of a moral ruler, which is problematic? We can begin this phase of our discussion by noting Kant's own way of putting premise (3).

> The acting rational agent in the world is not at the same time the cause of the world and of nature itself. Hence there is not the slightest ground in the moral law for a necessary connection between the morality and the proportionate happiness of a being which belongs to the world as one of its parts and thus dependent on it. Not being nature's cause, his will cannot by its own strength bring nature as it touches on his happiness, into complete harmony with his practical principles. Nevertheless . . . we *should* seek to further the highest good (which therefore must be at least possible).[48]

How are we to conceive its possibility? By postulating a cause sufficient to bring it about.

> Therefore . . . the existence is postulated of a cause of the whole of nature, itself distinct from nature, which contains the ground of the exact coincidence of happiness with morality.[49]

Such a cause must be able to discern the degree to which a man has acted out of respect for the law, have the power to give him proportionate happiness, and possess the will to do so. So we have postulated a moral, rational being.

> Now it was our duty to promote the highest good, and it is not merely our privilege but a necessity connected with duty as a requisite to presuppose the possibility of this highest good. This presupposition is made only under the condition of the existence of God, and this condition inseparably connects this supposition with duty. Therefore, it is morally necessary to assume the existence of God.[50]

He adds, "It is well to notice here that this moral necessity is subjective, i.e., a need, and not objective, i.e., duty itself."[51] That is, we need the postulate to make sense of a duty we have to seek the highest good, not to establish that we have that duty.

What is required is that we postulate a moral ruler in order to connect the concepts "being worthy of happiness" and "possessing happiness," since unless there is such a being any coincidence between worthiness and happiness will be fortuitous.

Kant presents the same considerations in the third *Critique*.

> The highest physical good possible in the world, to be furthered as a final purpose as far as in us lies, is *happiness*, under the objective condition of the harmony of man with the law of *morality* as worthiness to be happy.

> But it is impossible for us, in accordance with all our rational faculties, to represent these two requirements of the final purpose proposed to

us by the moral law as *connected* by merely natural causes, and yet as conformable to the idea of that final purpose.[52]

That is, what the moral law requires to be connected cannot be connected merely fortuitously or contingently.

> Consequently, we must assume a moral world cause (an author of the world) in order to set before ourselves a final purpose consistently with the moral law, and in so far as the latter is necessary, so far (i.e., in the same degree and on the same ground) the former must be necessarily assumed; i.e. we must admit that there is a God.[53]

That the highest good be attainable requires that God exist. If it is not attainable, a necessary object of the will of any rational being is unattainable. Since we are obligated to promote any end necessarily willed by a rational being, and since whatever we are obligated to promote must be possible, God's existence must be postulated, since it is a necessary condition of the possibility of an end that reason (i.e., any rational man) necessarily adopts. This, I take it, is the core of Kant's argument for premise (3)—and premise (4) as well. Since (5) follows from (3) and (4), no independent discussion of (5) is required.[54]

The argument quite plainly rests on Kant's assignment to man, *qua* rational agent, inherent dignity or intrinsic worth. Equally clear are the distinctions between the first and second sorts of contradiction in the *Grundlegung* and between the status of what reason legislates as our duty and the status of what reason necessarily wills as an end. Only the former in each case is utterly unquestionable and concerned with the "maintenance" of humanity. The latter in each case is secondary, challengeable, and concerned only with the "promotion" of humanity, or rational maturity, among men. Indeed, the second sort of contradiction arises in connection with imperfect duties, duties with exceptions. Ends necessarily willed by rational beings lead us to postulate God and immortality as necessary conditions of the possibility of the ends ever being realized. Nonetheless, the sort of certitude Kant confidently asserts for the moral law does not attach to the postulates.

In contrast to "objects for concepts, whose objective reality can be proved," which Kant calls "things of fact,"

> Objects in reference to the use of pure practical reason that is in conformity with duty must be thought *a priori* . . . but which are transcendent for its theoretical use, are mere *things of faith*. Of this kind is the *highest good* in the world, to be brought about by freedom. The concept of this cannot be established as regards its objective reality, but its use is commanded by pure practical reason . . . and it consequently must be assumed possible . . . the Being of God and the immortality of the Soul, are *things of faith*.[55]

While these are ". . . of all objects the only ones that can be so called"[56] the net result is that God and freedom are things of faith. They are necessary for the possibility of the highest good.

> A final purpose is merely a concept of our practical reason and can be inferred from no data of experience for the theoretical judging of nature, nor can it be applied to the cognition of nature. No use of this concept is possible except its use for practical reason according to moral laws.[57]

But even this mitigated justification of faith that God exists leaves us with two questions. First, why grant to man *qua* rational agent the central place and unique status that Kant allows him? Second, can one successfully keep separate that which reason as morally self-legislating demands and that which reason necessarily wills, giving primacy to the former alone? If rational nature is an end-in-itself, must they not be of equal status?

Kant is keenly aware of the difficulties involved in our first question.

> Yet in this Idea of the absolute value of a mere will, all useful results being left out of account in its assessment, there is something so strange that, in spite of all the agreement it receives even from ordinary reason, there must arise the suspicion that perhaps its secret basis is merely some high—flown fantasticality, and that we may have misunderstood the purpose of nature in attaching reason to our will as its governor.[58]

One way of putting a crucial portion of Kant's view would be to offer the following syllogism on his behalf: (1) All rational beings are ends-in-themselves. (2) All men are rational beings. So: (3) All men are ends-in-themselves.

A stance quite different from that of Kant is taken by David Hume.[59] Hume challenges Kant's thesis that men are rational creatures in a Kantian sense. Thus, even if it is true that all rational creatures are ends-in-themselves, it will not for Hume, be true that men are rational creatures. He can grant Kant's major premise, since in denying his minor he denies to Kant any rational foundation for his conclusion. Thus he writes

> . . . no truth appears to me more evident than that beasts are endowed with thought and reason as well as men.[60]

He admits in one place that:

> Men are superior to beasts principally by the superiority of their reason; and they are the degrees of the same faculty, which set such an infinite distance betwixt one man and another.[61]

The "infinite distance" (an obvious hyperbole) is not, however, between men and animals, but between men and other men. What concerns Hume in discussing reason is not what concerned Kant.

> The principal reason why natural abilities are esteemed, is because of their tendency to be useful to the person, who is possessed of them. 'Tis impossible to execute any design with success, where it is not conducted with prudence and discretion; nor will the goodness of our intentions alone suffice to produce us a happy issue to our enterprizes . . . All the advantages of art are owing to human reason; and where fortune is not very capricious, the most considerable part of these advantages must fall to the share of the prudent and sagacious.[62]

Reason's value for Hume lies in its utility. He could never say with Kant that:

> Some qualities are even helpful to this good will itself and can make its task very much easier. They have none the less no inner unconditioned worth, but rather presuppose a good will which sets a limit to the esteem in which they are rightly held . . . A good will is good not because of what it effects or accomplishes—because of its fitness for attaining some proposed end: it is good through its willing alone— that is, good in itself . . . Even if, by some special disfavor of destiny or by the niggardly endowment of a stepmotherly nature, this will is entirely lacking in power to carry out its intentions . . .[63]

Rather, Hume insists that

> There are many other qualities of the mind, whose merit is deriv'd from the same origin. *Industry, perseverance, patience, activity, vigilance, application, constancy,* with other virtues of that kind . . . are esteemed valuable on no other account, than their advantage in the conduct of life . . . on the other hand, *prodigality, luxury, irresolution, uncertainty,* are vicious, merely because they draw ruin upon us, and incapacitate us for business and action.[64]

The implication is not difficult to grasp. A good many tasks require instinctual reactions for maximal success; in such matters, many animals have clear advantage.[65] Reason itself is only an instinct[66] and its exercise is only ". . . this little agitation of the brain which we call thought."[67]

Nor will Hume allow that man is superior to the animals with respect to his passional nature. In the concluding section of Book II, Part I (entitled "Of Pride and Humility") Hume concludes his discussion with a section (12) entitled "Of the Pride and Humility of Animals" and Part II ("Of Love and Hatred") of the same Book ends with a section (12) entitled "Of the Love and Hatred of Animals." Hume's frequently stated criterion for success in a theory of reason, or of the passions, is the same. Concerning his theory of the passions, he says

> . . . if we find upon trial that the explication of these phenomena, which we make use of in one species, will not apply to the rest, we may presume that that explication, however specious, is in reality without foundation.[68]

And concerning his account of reason:

> Let us therefore put our present system concerning the nature of the understanding to this decisive trial, and see whether it will equally account for the reasonings of beasts as for those of the human species.[69]

As Marvin Fox notes,

> In all these sections, Hume stresses two points. First, that man is to be understood only by analogy with animals. Second, that there are no essential differences between animal and human psychology.[70]

Nor, we may stress, between animal and human reason.

This should be sufficient to make clear that, and in general on what sort of grounds, Hume denies Kant's minor premise. He does so, essentially, by stressing the similarity between human beings and other features of the natural landscape. Conversely, Kant stresses the differences.

> Man actually finds in himself a power by which he distinguishes himself from all other things—even from himself so far as he is affected by objects, and that is reason.[71]

This issue is obviously complex, and we have certainly not settled it here. Even were it settled in Kant's favor, however, and men agreed to be in Kant's sense rational agents, there would be yet another question. Have rational agents the value Kant attaches to them? And, a related question, can primacy be attached only to what reason necessarily legislates and not equally to what reason necessarily wills, without gross inconsistency? One result of our concluding discussion should be to show that these apparently diverse questions are in fact closely related.

The question is one on which Kant has often expressed himself quite unambiguously. For Kant, the validity of the moral law in no way rests upon either the attainability of the highest good, the existence of God or the immortality of the soul. Each man, as a rational agent, or as a person if one prefers to put the matter that way (i.e. as one whose acts are imputable—who is rationally autonomous and so morally responsible), would be just as obligated to do what is right, were moral virtue always rewarded by severe suffering and moral vice repaid by ecstatic pleasure, were God known not to exist and nature known to have no final purpose, and were physical death known to end consciousness finally and entirely. Men would still be praiseworthy and true to their nature only insofar as they did the right thing, or at least made the right choices, only out of respect for the moral law, and men would still be free agents in the sense that, even if heroically, they could do their duty if they made sufficient effort, and they could indeed put forth that effort. In short, moral autonomy would remain intact and hence the authority of the moral law would continue unabated. This view, in essence, is affirmed at the very outset of the *Religion*, a passage which has numerous parallels.

> So far as morality is based upon the conception of man as a free agent who, just because he is free, binds himself through his reason to unconditioned laws, it stands in need neither of an idea of another Being over him, for him to apprehend his duty, nor of an incentive other than the law itself, for him to do his duty.[72]

This feature of Kant's philosophy—his utter confidence in man's intrinsic worth—is obviously central to his philosophical system. What is the basis of Kant's complete confidence? Is it in fact unchallengeable?

In spite of the confident assertions just noted, Kant comes very close to admitting that the inherent dignity of the moral agent and the binding authority of the moral law are in jeopardy if nature is purposeless. Referring to a "righteous man," his example is Spinoza, who denies that God exists (i.e., who denies a Creator and Providence) and denies that the soul is immortal (it is logically impossible on Spinoza's view that the mind survive the dissolution of the body), Kant remarks:

> . . . he wishes . . . disinterestedly to establish the good to which that holy law directs all his powers. But his effort is bounded; and from nature, although he may expect here and there a contingent accordance, he can never expect a regular harmony agreeing according to constant rules (such as his maxims are, and must be, internally) with the purpose that he yet feels himself obliged and impelled to accomplish. Deceit, violence, and envy will always surround him, although he himself will be honest, peaceable, and kindly; and the righteous men with whom he meets will, notwithstanding all their worthiness of happiness, be yet subjected by nature, which regards not this, to all the evils of want, disease, and untimely death, just like the beasts of the earth. So it will be until one wide grave engulfs them together (honest or not, it makes no difference) and throws them back—who were able to believe themselves the final purpose of creation—into the abyss of the purposeless chaos of matter from which they were drawn.[73]

One is reminded of another passage of equally moving prose in which Bertrand Russell confessed his faith.

> That man is the product of causes which had no prevision of the end they were achieving; that his origin, his growth, his hopes and fears, his loves and his beliefs, are but the outcome of accidental collocations of atoms; that no fire, no heroism, no intensity of thought and feeling, can preserve an individual life beyond the grave . . . all these things, if not quite beyond dispute, are yet so nearly certain, that no philosophy which rejects them can hope to stand.[74]

It is plausible that the dignity of an agent depend, as Kant maintains, on his capacities, not on his source. It is also, however, plausible that the degree to which it is clear that inherent value can be ascribed to an agent is dependent upon the capacity of that agent to attain to an ideal which clearly provides the criterion for having dignity rather than price.[75] Insofar as immortality is required for having the fullest capacity to attain that ideal, it is more reasonable to ascribe inherent worth to an immortal agent with the predisposition to personality than to a mortal agent with the same predisposition. If there is a species of agent for which an omnipotent, omniscient, omnibenevolent deity has created all else, then there is surely good reason for ascribing inherent worth to any member of that species, not only because "x is regarded as having inherent worth by an omniscient being" entails "x has inherent worth" but also because of the role such agents would play in that universe. It is Kant's view that only a rational agent could be such an end.

> . . . it is a fundamental proposition, to which even the commonest human reason is compelled to give immediate assent, that if there is to be in general a *final purpose* furnished *a priori* by reason, this can be no other than *man* (every rational being of the world) *under moral laws*. For (and so everyone judges) if the world consisted of mere lifeless, or even in part of living but irrational beings, its existence would have no worth, because in it there would be no being who would have the least concept of what worth is. Again, if there were intelligent beings whose reason were only able to place the worth of the existence of things in the relation of nature to themselves (their well-being) but not to furnish of itself an original worth (in freedom), then there would certainly be (relative) purposes in the world, but no (absolute) final purpose, because the existence of such rational beings would be always purposeless. But the moral laws have this peculiar characteristic—that they prescribe to reason something as a purpose without any condition, and consequently exactly as the concept of a final purpose requires. The existence of a reason that can be for itself the supreme law in the purposive reference, in other words the existence of rational beings under moral laws, can therefore alone be thought as the final purpose of the Being of a world. If, on the contrary, this be not so, there would either be no purpose at all in the cause of its being, or there would be purposes but no final purpose.[76]

Thus Kant is clearly committed to the thesis that if there are no rational agents then there is no final purpose in nature. In other words, if rational agents have no inherent worth, then no teleological conception of nature is possible. But the converse he will not admit—namely, that if in fact nature has no final purpose then rational agents possess no inherent dignity. It is, for Kant, not the role of final purpose, but the properties or capacities which eminently suit him for that role, which constitute man's unique worth. But why should one set so unique a value on reason, or on the capacities in virtue of which Kant calls men rational agents? It will not do to point out the necessary connection which, at least in Kant's opinion, obtains between reason and morality, for that would only be to appeal again to the Kantian claim that "rational nature exists as an end in itself."[77] It seems quite dubious that the single claim which is for Kant at once noumenal (a claim about how things are, not merely about how they inevitably seem to us to be) and rationally sacrosanct, will bear in splendid isolation the tremendous weight which he places upon it. It is unchallengeable so long as one retains a position within Kant's framework, since that framework assumes it as an axiom. But one can abandon that framework for another—e.g., for Hume's. Then it is surely highly challengeable.

We can now pose what is probably the most important question that Kant or a contemporary Kantian must face. If man is, in fact, only the product of forces which have no intelligence and so no prevision of their effect, if he ends his brief existence by sharing with other animals a common grave and suffers an irrevocable cessation of consciousness, then it is surely more plausible to accept Hume's account of man than to agree with Kant's more austere appraisal of human nature. Consequently, it is more plausible to adopt a prudential, or at least a subjective, account of human morality than a Kantian account. But then not only the postulates, but also the moral law, fall into rational disrepute.

If this is correct, then Kant, or his contemporary defender, must be willing to place the claim that rational nature is an end in itself in a defensible perspective. Such a perspective may well not permit the kind of primacy for man as a bearer of inherent dignity which Kant proposed. One might argue as follows: Only a being which actually fully meets the criterion for a rational nature has inherent value in the deepest sense.[78] But unless something has inherent value in this sense, it is not at all clear that any being, in virtue of having inherent value in the weaker sense, can serve as an end-in-itself. The argument-schema follows the pattern of an argument Kant himself gives in which the distinction is made between purposes which are ends only in the sense that they are also means to still further ends, and purposes which are ends in themselves. Kant's claim is that only a perfectly good will is an end in itself, and unless there are such ends in a universe that universe can contain no final purpose. Is not Kant then open to an argument to the effect that unless there is a perfect Being this universe has no final purpose, and, more crucially, that men since they are not perfectly good wills are only candidates, so to speak, for intrinsic value? But then they have, in one sense, only potential dignity.

To press still further, have they even that? Perhaps the whole story is "a high-flown fantasticality." It is worth nothing how Kant rebuts this suggestion which, it should be remembered, is his own.

> We may have misunderstood the purpose of nature in attaching reason to our will as governor. We will therefore submit our Idea to an examination from this point of view.[79]

Were happiness man's only purpose, instinct would be a better guide or governor than reason. In fact,

> the more a cultivated reason concerns itself with the aim of enjoying life and happiness, the farther does man get away from true contentment. This is why there arises in many . . . a certain degree of *misology* —that is, a hatred of reason . . .[80]

> . . . since reason is not sufficiently serviceable for guiding the will . . . safely as regards . . . the satisfaction of all our needs . . . and since nonetheless reason has been imparted to us as a practical power . . . to have influence on the will. . . . its true function must be to produce a *will* which is *good*, not as a *means* to some further end, but *in itself*; and for this function reason was absolutely necessary in a world where nature, in distributing her aptitudes, has everywhere else gone to work in a purposive manner.[81]

The whole argument rests explicitly on this assumption:

> . . . let us take it as a principle that in it (an organic being) no organ is to be found for any end unless it is also the most appropriate to that end and the best fitted for it.[82]

So far from being a pedagogic tool, Kant's reference in this passage to teleology is a central feature of his argument. Kant, with Hume, appeals, so to speak, to the place of man in the scheme of things. He comes to the verge (and perhaps passes it) of defending his evaluation of a perfectly good will by an argument which makes an explicit teleological assumption. But insofar as he does this, his claim rests, not upon the single thesis that man has inherent dignity, but rather on the plausibility of his teleological way of viewing men and things. A whole philosophic context is in question, not a single premise, and the premise is—contrary to the official doctrine—false if the context is inadequate.

If the preceding argument is correct, Kant failed to establish an autonomous morality. Indeed, it could hardly be otherwise. He argued that man ". . . really finds in himself a faculty by which he distinguishes himself from everything else, even from himself as affected by objects, and that is reason."[83] To be anachronistic for the moment, Hume challenged the factual claim that Kant made; man, for Hume, has no such capacity. Even for Kant, the value of man is not independent of his nonevaluative features. It was ultimately upon this rock that Kant's ship foundered, for claims as to what nonevaluative features man can rightly be said to have depend in part on the sort of world man lives in and on his place in it.

The sort of autonomy Kant wished to allow morality was, in part, autonomy from religious belief. John Smith is, I think, on the right track when he writes

> . . . ultimately, no view of the good life, no . . . doctrine of what man ought to do, is ever possible apart from some view of his final destiny . . . such a view introduces the religious element.[84]

No view of man's obligations is independent of man's nature, or at least of the properties which he possesses. Reference merely to "his final destiny" is too narrow. Nor need this introduce "the religious element"; surely not every view of man's properties and his destiny is a religious one? Nonetheless, Smith is correct when he insists that claims about a man's obligations and claims about his descriptive and evaluative status are by no means unrelated. To the considerable degree that Kant neglects this fact, his views concerning morality are defective.

Were one able to show that a particular moral system was superior to any other—i.e. to argue cogently that set S of moral principles was superior to any competing set—and show that only conceptual scheme C could include S or that C provided, in some sense, the best conceptual setting for S then, it might be suggested, we would have eminently good reason for accepting C. If, for example, the set of moral principles S was clearly superior to any other set, and if, say, Judeo-Christian thought was the conceptual setting into which S fit best, this would provide good reasons for accepting Judeo-Christian doctrine. But, of course, this procedure would, if the argument above is correct, be perverse, for in order to show that a set S of moral principles was in fact superior to others, one would, among other things, have to make claims about the features that human beings possess.

For example, is man "rational" in a Kantian, or only in a Humean, sense? But it is just such claims which are disputed among philosophers of differing persuasions. Deciding which philosophical perspective, if any, is most adequate is, in part, deciding which provides the best basis for a moral system which is superior to competing ones or which best shows why there can in fact be no such moral system. But the tasks are not in fact independent in the way that this suggestion supposes. This in good part explains why many of the formulations of the "moral argument for God's existence" are so remarkably unpersuasive. They appeal to such claims as "If there is a moral law, there must be a moral lawgiver" and "If there are eternal moral truths, then there must be an eternal mind which thinks them." The philosophic context in which they are developed is, in many cases, out of fashion. That ought to make no difference to a philosopher worth his salt. Worse, however, it is far from clear that the philosophic perspectives in question are correct or even viable. To the degree that their perspective or context is questionable, so are the arguments themselves questionable.

We have argued that morality and religion can be related. Religious doctrinal systems are among the possible conceptual settings against which a moral system (a system of moral principles, or a single moral principle considered sufficient in itself) is formulated, clarified, and defended. There are other possible conceptual backdrops. But how can one ever tell what conceptual systems are at least more viable candidates for "telling it like it is"? We will deal with this question, among others, in our final chapter. First, however, another view of the relationship between religion and morality must be discussed.

We have discussed three attempts, one plainly defective and two apparently viable, of basing morality on religion. We have also discussed two ways, both defective, of basing religion on morality. It is now time to consider at least one attempt to construe morality and religion as entirely independent. Although the historical roots of this attempt lie primarily in Hutcheson, it will be convenient to discuss it as presented by David Hume since we have already noted some of the context within which he develops his views concerning morality.

DAVID HUME:
MORALITY WITHOUT RELIGION

In contrast to Kant, as we have seen, Hume does not view man as essentially a rational being; nor is reason central, in Hume's view, to morality. He speaks rather of ". . . the distinguishing impressions by which moral good or evil in known," these impressions being, he continues, "nothing but *particular* pains or pleasures."[85]

> To have the sense of virtue is nothing but to *feel* a satisfaction of a particular kind from the contemplation of a character. The very feeling constitutes our praise or admiration . . . We do not infer a character to be virtuous, because it pleases: But, in feeling that it pleases after such a particular manner, we in effect feel that it is virtuous.[86]

Nonetheless, virtue is not a matter of anything at all that pleases nor vice a matter of anything at all that pains. It is only

> . . . pleasure or pain, which arises from characters and actions, of that *peculiar* kind, which makes us praise or condemn . . . 'Tis only when a character is considered in general, without reference to our particular interest, that it causes such a feeling or sentiment, as denominates it morally good or evil.[87]

If morality is a product of man's passional, not a discovery of his rational, nature we must ask what, for Hume, is the place of reason in morality?

Hume allows reason only two functions relevant to morality.[88] It can inform us of the existence of something which is a proper object of one or another human passion (i.e., is something which humans desire). It can tell us which means is most efficient to the attainment of an end we have already chosen due to nonrational considerations. But it can never either tell us that an action is right or wrong or determine that we shall seek a given end. Ethical decisions arise, for Hume, from our passional nature. In particular, the springs of ethically right conduct are to be found in the sentiment of benevolence[89]—the feeling of compassion for others which, at least on some occasions, leads men to act for the benefit of another without concern for profit to themselves. Without passion or emotion, there would be no action at all. Without the emotion or sentiment of benevolence, there would be no motivation which would yield right conduct. Thus Hume speaks of

> . . . the nature and force of *sympathy*. The minds of all men are similar in their feelings and operations, nor can anyone be actuated by any affection, of which all others are not, in some degree, susceptible.[90]

He adds that

> As to the good or ill desert of virtue or vice, 'tis an evident consequence of the sentiments of pleasure or uneasiness. These sentiments produce love or hatred; and love or hatred, by the original constitution of human passion, is attended with benevolence or anger; that is, with a desire of making happy the person we love, and miserable the person we hate.[91]

He is confident that ". . . sympathy is a very powerful principle in human nature,"[92] that sympathy ". . . produces our sentiment of morals in all the artificial virtues,"[93] and that it is ". . . *extensive sympathy* on which our sentiments of virtue depend."[94] It is with this view in mind that Hume makes his famous claim that ". . . morality, therefore, is more properly felt than judged of."[95]

Naturally conjoined with this account of the springs of morality is a utilitarian view of which actions are good. It is of course true that Hume writes eloquently concerning the centrality of motives in the fixing of praise and blame.

> 'Tis evident, that when we praise any actions, we regard only the motives that produced them, and consider the actions as signs or indications of certain principles in the mind and temper. The external performance has no merit. We must look within to fix the moral quality.[96]

But he supplements this view with a claim as to what sorts of features are actually valued in a man.

> If we examine the panegyrics that are commonly made of great men, we shall find that most of the qualities which are attributed to them may be divided into two kinds, *viz.* such as make them perform their part in society; and such as render them serviceable to themselves, and enable them to promote their own interest.[97]

While Hume admits that occasionally a just act may have bad effects, nonetheless ". . . the whole plan or scheme (i.e., the practice of acting justly) is highly conducive, or indeed absolutely requisite, both to the support of society, and the well-being of every individual."[98]

There is no need to pursue Hume's views further. He offers a moral perspective within which ethical sentences are, strictly, neither true nor false. To regard an act or object as good is to feel in a certain manner toward it, not (even in part) to make a moral assertion about it. To act rightly is to act from a sentiment or feeling of benevolence, not to act from a recognition that doing the action in question is a duty. There is, for Hume, no "rational emotion" which motivates one to perform an action which is recognized as required by a maxim whose denial is contradictory when universalized. Good actions have the feature of promoting human well-being, a matter defined primarily in terms of pleasure and pain. Agents are morally admirable insofar as they act from the feeling of benevolence—a feeling which involves no recognition of duty but rather is constituted by a feeling of approval toward an act performed for another's welfare. There is an intra-subjective constancy as to what is good; men tend, at least within certain limits, to approve or disapprove the same sorts of motivation for action and to desire the same sorts of means to attaining their well-being.

One could endeavor to place this theory within a theological framework by viewing God as having the sentiment of benevolence and having created man in this respect in his image. Or one could regard Hume as offering an account of how survival is effected, reserving morality for an objectivist account along Kantian or other lines. The present point is that it was offered as a view of morality which did not require a theological basis and which made no claims about the intrinsic value of man. In Kant's view, it denied reason its proper place.[99] No orthodox Jew or Christian could, I think, accept it as "the whole story" about morality.[100]

I do not intend at this point to appraise Hume's view or any other version of the sort of position he represents. I wish only to point out what Hume does not deny. His view of man is as central to his account of morality as Kant's was to his quite different account. Hume is explicit at this point.

> 'Tis evident, that all the sciences have a relation, greater or less, to human nature; and that however wide any of them may seem to run from it, they still return back by one passage or another.[101]

Hume's contentions presuppose a view of human nature no less than do Kant's. Hume's view, or any version of the same kind of perspective concerning morality, is flagrantly not autonomous in the sense of being logically unrelated to claims concerning man's nature and capacities, as well as to claims concerning both the remainder of reality and man's relation thereto. To appraise an ethical theory will involve taking into consideration whether it accords properly with what man is. Part, but by no means all, of the issues concerning that topic can be decided on the neutral ground of sheer observation. Even here, interpretation begins very early. In the end, a system of ethics is part of a more general conceptual scheme.

If this is so—and a central purpose of this chapter has been to make the plausibility of this claim clear—then the question changes from "How, if at all, are religion and morality related?" to "How can general conceptual schemes be appraised?" I have argued that one can relate religion and morality in an intelligible and viable manner. I have also noted that one can view morality so as to make it logically independent of religion. But morality is then viewed quite differently from the previous accounts of it. Which is the more reasonable account of morality? This question is tantamount to or at the very least includes the above question concerning general conceptual schemes. We will return to this question in our final chapter.

FOOTNOTES ∼ V

1   G. Clark, *Religion, Reason and Revelation* (Philadelphia: Presbyterian and Reformed, 1961).

2   I shall ignore differences between "good" and "right" in this context, since the argument can be conducted using either of these terms.

3   By Patterson Brown, "Religious Morality," *Mind*, Vol. LXXII (1963).

4   This premise is assumed, but not stated, in Brown's argument.

5   The latter alternative has strong similarities to the "ideal observer" theory of ethics. See R. B. Brandt, *Ethical Theories* (Englewood Cliffs, N.J.: Prentice Hall, 1959), Chapter 7.

6   Cf. Chapter One, especially our discussion of Ramsey.

7   This is why we did not explore it in connection with the problem of evil.

8   See the bibliography at the end of this chapter.

9   For arguments which fill in the schemata just noted, see H. Rashdall, *Philosophy and Religion* (London: Duckworth and Co., 1914); W. R. Sorley, *Moral Values and the Idea of God* (London: Cambridge U. Press, 1921); A. E. Taylor, *The Faith of a Moralist* (London: MacMillan and Co., 1932).

10   Immanual Kant, *Critique of Pure Reason*, trans. N. Kemp Smith (New York: MacMillan and Co., 1958).

11   Immanuel Kant, *Critique of Judgment*, trans. J. Bernard (New York: Hafner Publishing Co., 1966). Hereafter cited as *Judgment*. Kant's *Critique of Practical Reason*, trans. L. W. Beck (New York: Liberal Arts Press, 1956) will be cited as *Practical Reason*.

12   *Judgment*, p. 310.

13   Immanuel Kant, *Groundwork of the Metaphysic of Morals*, trans. H. J. Paton (New York: Harper and Row, 1964) (London: Hutchinson and Co.—*The Moral Law*, 1948).

14   *Groundwork*, p. 91.

15   *Ibid.*, p. 97.

16   *Ibid.*, p. 96.

17   *Ibid.*, p. 97.

18   *Loc. cit.*

19   *Ibid.*

20   On the "predisposition to personality" see Immanuel Kant, *Religion Within the Limits of Reason Alone*, trans. Hoyt and Greene, (New York: Harper and Row, 1960), p. 21 ff.

21   I.e., duties which have exceptions.

22   He would not, for example, endeavor to bring this about.

23   *Groundwork*, p. 91 ff.

24   The laws would be, respectively, (A') "Whenever one is in need, he is not helped by anyone else," (B') "Whenever one is in need, he is helped by someone else." These are to be read as parallel to "Increase in friction causes increase in temperature."

25   Roughly, L is a moral principle if L is of the form "One ought to do X" where "X" is instantiated by the description of an action.

26   Cf. *Judgment*, p. 301.

27 *Religion,* p. 61.

28 *Groundwork,* p. 64.

29 *Ibid.,* p. 69, f. n.

30 *Ibid.,* p. 90.

31 *Judgment,* p. 338.

32 *Loc. cit.*

33 The "highest good" is that state of affairs in which there is perfect proportion, in the case of every man, between his worthiness to be happy and the happiness that he possesses. This concept will be discussed further below.

34 See *Judgment,* p. 310ff.

35 *Judgment,* p. 301.

36 (b) is, in effect, a hypothetical imperative.

37 *Practical Reason,* p. 129.

38 *Ibid.,* p. 126.

39 *Judgment,* p. 301.

40 Cf. *Practical Reason,* p. 111ff.

41 *Ibid.,* p. 112.

42 *Ibid.,* p. 114.

43 By way of review, the different senses were, roughly: (1) M is contradictory if it presupposes that man is not an end-in-himself (2) M is contradictory if to follow M would be incompatible with the pursuit of an end a man must, insofar as rational, adopt as his goal (3) M is contradictory if M is logically inconsistent.

44 *Practical Reason,* p. 114.

45 Except, of course, *other* beings that are ends-in-themselves.

46 *Groundwork,* p. 41.

47 *Practical Reason,* Abbott translation, p. 221. Cited by F. Coplestone, *A History of Philosophy,* Vol. VI (Westminster, Md.; Newman Press, 1964), p. 339. Cf. *Relgion,* p. 61: "*moral happiness* . . . (is) the reality and *constancy* of a disposition which ever progresses in goodness (and never falls away from it) . . . inasmuch as an individual thus minded would quite of his own accord have confidence that 'all things else' (i.e., what relates to physical happiness) would be added unto him."

48 *Practical Reason,* p. 129.

49 *Loc. cit.*

50 *Practical Reason,* p. 130.

51 *Loc. cit.*

52 *Judgment,* p. 301.

53 *Loc. cit.*

54 Nor, of course, independent justification.

55 *Judgment,* p. 321.

56 *Loc. cit.*

57 *Ibid.,* p. 305ff.

58 *Groundwork,* p. 62.

59 David Hume, *A Treatise of Human Nature,* ed., Selby-Bigge (London: Oxford U. Press, 1965 reprint). Cited as *Treatise.*

60 *Treatise,* p. 176.

61 *Ibid.,* p. 610.

62 *Loc. cit.*

63 *Groundwork,* p. 61.

64 *Treatise,* p. 610ff.

[65] See Marvin Fox, "Religion and Human Nature in the Philosophy of David Hume," included in W. Reese and E. Freeman (eds.), *Process and Divinity* (LaSalle, Illinois: Open Court Publishing Co., 1964) p. 561–577.

[66] *Treatise*, p. 179.

[67] David Hume, *Dialogues Concerning Natural Religion*, ed. N. Kemp Smith (New York: Bobbs-Merrill, 1947), p. 148.

[68] *Treatise*, p. 327. Cf. p. 325.

[69] *Treatise*, p. 177. Cf. p. 397ff.

[70] Marvin Fox, *op. cit.*, p. 569.

[71] *Groundwork*, p. 119.

[72] *Religion*, p. 3.

[73] *Judgment*, p. 302.

[74] Bertrand Russell, *Selected Papers of Bertrand Russell* (New York: Random House, 1927), p. 3.

[75] To have price is to be replaceable by an equivalent. To possess dignity is to be above price. See *Groundwork*, p. 102.

[76] *Judgment*, p. 299ff.

[77] *Groundwork*, p. 96.

[78] The "actuality" sense as opposed to the "capacity" sense. Kant does make this sort of distinction. For example, "to become *free* . . . this is the highest prize he (man) can win," *Religion*, p. 85. Again, "complete fitness of the will to the moral law is holiness, which is a perfection of which no rational being in the world of sense is at any time capable. But since it is required as practically necessary, it can be found only in an endless progress to that complete fitness." *Critique of Practical Reason*, p. 126.

[79] *Groundwork*, p. 62. Namely, "this Idea of the absolute value of a mere will, all useful results being left out of account in its assessment."

[80] *Ibid.*, p. 63.

[81] *Ibid.*, p. 64.

[82] *Ibid.*, p. 62.

[83] *Ibid.*, p. 69.

[84] John Smith, *Reason and God* (New Haven: Yale U. Press, 1961), p. 200.

[85] Hume, *Teatise*, p. 471.

[86] *Loc. cit.*

[87] *Ibid.*, p. 472.

[88] *Treatise*, Part I, Book III, Section I. While we will not discuss it here, there is a further aspect of Hume's view which deserves mention. Just as an important part of Hume's discussion of causality is his criticism of competing views held by his predecessors, so also his critique of rationalistic views of morality is important in his discussion of morality. He denies that there is a discernible relation between *de facto* circumstances and obligations, or any perception of moral qualities, or any necessarily true moral propositions, or any way of inferring moral statements from nonmoral ones. He also denies that there is any such thing as "desiderative reason" or "rational desire," here being opposed to Aristotle and Kant. One of Hume's targets was undoubtedly Samuel Clarke, who held that moral relations are as manifest to reason as mathematical relations. Cf. his *Discourse on Natural Religion* in Selby-Bigge, ed., *British Moralists* (New York: Bobbs-Merrill, 1964), Vol. II, p. 3ff.

[89] *Ibid.*, Part I, Book III, Section II; Part III, Sections I and II.

[90] *Treatise*, p. 575.

[91] *Ibid.*, p. 591.

[92] *Ibid.*, p. 577.

93 *Loc. cit.*

94 *Treatise*, p. 586.

95 *Ibid.*, p. 570. Cf. p. 517, "All morality depends on our sentiments."

96 *Ibid.*, p. 476.

97 *Ibid.*, p. 587. Cf. p. 578.

98 *Ibid.*, p. 497.

99 Kant's view was that Hume denied reason its "most important prospects" and so deprived the will of its highest goals. See Kant's *Prolegomena to Any Future Metaphysic* (LaSalle, Illinois: Open Court Publishing Co., 1902), p. 5 f. n.

100 This is so even for Maimonides, who was not an "objectivist" in morals.

101 *Treatise,* p. xix. Hume includes morals in the scope of what he intends by "all the sciences." See *loc. cit.* and p. xxiiff.

BIBLIOGRAPHY ⌒ V

Berkhouwer, G. C., *Man: the Image of God.* Grand Rapids: Eerdmann's, 1962.

Foster, M. B., *Mystery and Philosophy.* London: SCM Press, 1957.

Mitchell, B., ed., *Faith and Logic.* London: G. Allen and Unwin, 1957.

Paton, H. J., *The Modern Predicament.* London: G. Allen and Unwin, 1955.

Ramsey, Ian, ed., *Christian Ethics and Moral Philosophy.* New York: Macmillan, 1966.

―――――, ed., *Prospect for Metaphysics.* New York: Philosophical Library, 1961.

Ramsey, Paul, ed., *Faith and Ethics.* New York: Harper and Row, 1957.

Smart, Ninian, *Reasons and Faiths.* London: Routledge and Kegan Paul, 1958.

Tillich, Paul, *Morality and Beyond.* New York: Harper and Row, 1913.

Books on Kant

Beck, L. W., *A Commentary on Kant's "Critique of Pure Reason."* Chicago: U. of Chicago Press, 1960.

―――――, *Studies in the Philosophy of Kant.* New York: Bobbs-Merrill, 1965.

England, F., *Kant's Conception of God.* New York: Humanities Press, 1929; reprinted 1968.

Gregor, M. J., *Laws of Freedom.* London: Basil Blackwell, 1963.

Paton, H. J., *The Categorical Imperative.* New York: Harper and Row, 1947.

Wolff, R. P., ed., *Kant.* Garden City: Doubleday and Co., 1967.

VI

FAITH
AND REASON

In many circles the concept of religious faith has an unpleasant aura of irrationalism. Theologians who have stressed the transcendence of God to the point where God is indescribable or unknowable, but still for some reason to be worshipped, or have emphasized the power of God to the point of insisting that he can do things whose description is self-contradictory, are doubtless in part responsible. The difficulty of seeing how religious beliefs could ever be established is probably an even more important contributing factor. Whatever the reasons, faith is often taken to be belief which is not based upon evidence, or at least is based upon evidence quite inadequate to justify the degree of certainty the believer possesses.[1] It is thus in some sense taken to involve a culpable abandonment of reason, a reliance on excitation of nerve endings rather than on exercise of intellect. John Locke, himself a theist, notes that at least in the "commonwealth of learning" men profess to love the truth.

> And yet for all this, one may truly say there are very few lovers of truth . . . there is this one unerring mark of it, viz., the not entertaining any proposition with greater assurance than the proofs it is built upon will warrant. Whoever goes beyond this measure of assent, it is plain, receives not truth for the love of it; loves not truth for truth's sake, but for some other by-end.[2]

So men of faith are not lovers of the truth, if faith is indeed irrational and if Locke's account of what love of truth amounts to is correct.[3]

Working along these lines, W. K. Clifford pronounced his famous dogma concerning the ethics of believing—namely, that to believe anything on the basis of insufficient evidence is always wrong.[4]

I propose to examine various accounts of what faith is, hoping thereby to arrive at a concept of faith neither religiously irrelevant nor rationally repugnant. A convenient place to begin is John Locke's analysis of faith. How does he, as a theist, account for his belief consistently with his being, in his terms, a "lover of truth"?

JOHN LOCKE'S VIEW OF FAITH

Locke's account of faith is interesting as much for what it does not say as for what it does. In *An Essay Concerning Human Understanding* he contrasts reason and faith.[5] "Reason" is Locke's term for one kind of basis for accepting a statement, "faith" his term for another kind. When I see that a statement is self-evident, or follows from a self-evident statement, or discover that a statement is empirically verified, or follows from an empirically verified statement, and accept that statement on whichever of these grounds is relevant, I accept it on the basis of reason.[6] If I accept a statement because I believe that God has revealed it to me, or to someone else, then I accept it on faith. Thus Locke's analysis of "S accepts P by faith" is "S believes P because S believes that God has revealed P (to S or to someone else)." God can, in Locke's view, reveal demonstrably true statements to a man who does not know them to be self-evident,[7] or empirically verified statements to a man who does not know them to be empirically verified. But if Jones accepts a statement P on the basis of self-evidence or empirical evidence, while Smith accepts P by faith, Jones has more basic grounds than Smith for accepting P. This follows from a doctrine about which Locke is explicit and emphatic, namely that the claim that a statement is revealed by God is itself one which must be weighed by reason, and which can be accepted only on the basis of reason, not of faith.

> Whatever God hath revealed, is certainly true; no doubt can be made of it. This is the proper object of faith; but whether it be a divine revelation or no, reason must judge.[8]

Jones can accept (A) "God revealed P," and thus accept P by faith, only if (B) "The evidence that (A) is true is greater than the evidence that (A) is false" is true. Otherwise, Jones could accept (A) (and consequently P) only without reason or against reason. And this would not, on Locke's view, be to accept P by faith. Locke leaves no doubt about his condemnation of accepting a statement whose contradictory has better evidence than it has.

> Since a man can never have so certain a knowledge, that a proposition, which contradicts the clear principles and evidence of his own knowledge, was divinely revealed, or that he understands the words rightly wherein it is delivered; as he has, that the contrary is true: and so (he) is bound to consider and judge of it as a matter of reason, and not swallow it, without examination, as a matter of faith.[9]

Faith is not independent of reason. A man can accept a statement of form (A) and thus have faith only in case he is in a position to accept a corresponding statement of form (B) by reason. Belief without such support from reason is not faith. Further, faith can never contradict reason; a statement accepted by faith can never be incompatible with a statement accepted on the basis of reason.

> Faith can never convince us of anything that contradicts our knowledge.[10]

The criterion for rejecting a purported revelation is thus easy to state. "God revealed statement P" is false if P is known to be false. Further, if the evidence for the denial of P is greater than the evidence for P, we have good reason to deny that God revealed P.[11] This leaves us thus far without a criterion for telling that a revelation has indeed occurred. (We will return to this matter shortly.)

There is plainly no possibility of conflict between faith and reason for Locke. For Jones to accept statement P on faith is tantamount to Jones accepting (A) "God revealed P (to me or someone else)." Accepting (A) is appropriate just in case (B) "The evidence for (A) is better than that against (A)" is true. Now a rational man will accept any proposition for which there is better evidence than there is for its denial, if he accepts either. So a rational man will accept any statement of the same sort as (A) if he knows a corresponding proposition of sort (B) is true. Thus a man who accepts a statement P "by faith," in Locke's sense of this term, can argue: there is better evidence that God revealed P than that he did not; so it is more reasonable to accept P than it is reasonable not to accept P, since if God reveals P, P is true. Accepting P on faith is tantamount to accepting a claim about P by reason—namely the claim that God revealed P. The grounds we could have for accepting the claim "God revealed P" are never as strong as those provided by self-evidence or empirical verification. So the acceptance of second-order statements concerning what statements God revealed is always intellectually more risky—always involves more chance of error—than accepting the first order statement in question on more substantial grounds. And it is only where such more substantial grounds are absent that faith is, for a maturely rational man, genuinely appropriate.

Locke was much concerned with the scope and limitation of human reason.[12] There are some things, he suggests, that we simply cannot know by appeal to self-evident axioms, empirically verified statements, and further statements derived from these. That some angels rebelled against God and fell, and that the dead shall rise and live again, are examples of things which cannot be known in this manner. These, ". . . being beyond the discovery of reason, are purely matters of faith with which reason has directly nothing to do."[13]

It is this sort of proposition which must be revealed if we are to know it to be true. Here, the negative criterion for revelation fails, for we cannot by reason know in such cases that what is purportedly revealed is false. This raises quite acutely the problem as to how we can ever tell that it is more likely that God revealed a statement than that he did not. If faith is "assent founded on the highest reason,"[14] how can we discern when the highest reason for accepting a statement (that God revealed it) is available? The crux of his treatment of the topic is expressed as follows.

> . . . we have reason and scripture; unerring rules to know whether it (any statement) is from God or no . . . . Where reason or scripture is express for any opinion or action, we may receive it as of divine authority: but it is not the strength of our own persuasions which can by itself give it that stamp.[15]

But this is both puzzling and unhelpful. It is puzzling in that if reason is "express for" P, then presumably P is self-evident or has empirical support, in which case it is not taken on faith. What Locke means is perhaps that if reason is "express for" "God revealed P" then S can take P on faith. If so, this only underlines the importance of our remaining question: How can one tell that God has revealed a statement? Here, Locke is singularly unhelpful. Besides his appeal to reason, which we have just discussed and found puzzling, he refers us to Scripture (i.e. the Bible). Now if we know the Bible to be a revelation, then nothing which contradicts it will also be revealed. But how do we discover that the Bible was revealed? And what of statements which are consistent with, but not entailed by, anything said in the Scriptures, but which are nonetheless purportedly revealed? Here, Locke leaves us in the dark.

This appraisal may seem unfair in the light of Locke's appeal to the evidential role of miracles, which, when

. . . well attested, do not only find credit themselves, but give it also to other truths, which need such confirmation.[16]

He adds that

Where such supernatural events are suitable to ends aimed at by Him who has the power to change the course of nature, there, *under such circumstances*, that may be the fitter to procure belief, by how much the more they are beyond or contrary to ordinary observation.[17]

Here is a positive criterion for revelation. If Jones claims that God has revealed a statement P to him, then if Jones can credit his case by performing a miracle suitable to ends consistent with those which an omnibenevolent Deity may be presumed to favor, his claim that God revealed P to him is warranted.

What, then, is a miracle?

A miracle I take to be a sensible operation, which being above the comprehension of the spectator, and in his opinion contrary to the established course of nature, is taken by him to be divine.[18]

But of course what appears to a peasant to be a miracle may not appear so to a physicist, and what appears to a man of one generation to be a miracle may not appear so to a man of a later generation if the latter knows scientific laws that the former did not know. Nonetheless, raising a man genuinely dead to life again by a spoken word would seem even nowadays to be miraculous, and at least on Locke's view a man who did that and claimed to possess a revelation would have provided relevant evidence to be a bearer of revelation by performing a miracle.

This raises, of course, the questions as to whether miracles do occur and whether, even if they do, they provide relevant grounds for regarding the one who performs them as a bearer of revelation—if his moral character does not cancel his claim, if his miracle is not for an evil end, if he claims to bear a revelation, and so on. A theistic universe is perhaps a more promising context for events, which serve an ultimate purpose, but do not fall into the range of normal common sense or scientific explanation, than is any other. And perhaps in such a universe the capacity to perform "good" miracles, ones that produce good ends, does, given that other conditions such as the ones mentioned above are fulfilled, provide credence to a claim to possess a revelation. (Though not all miracles mentioned in the Bible were performed by men who were messengers of God.) Even if we grant this, however, the problems that remain for Locke's view of faith are substantial. We must, as already indicated, know that God exists and has a certain character; e.g., He must not be willing to deceive us.[19] Further, we must know that were a man who mistakenly claimed to possess a revelation to perform miracles, his claim to possess a revelation would be accepted, and know that God would never permit this. This rather substantial supply of truths must be established by reason before anything can be accepted by faith. Should proofs of the existence, nature, and providential working of God be in any case unavailable, faith is, on Locke's analysis of it, impossible. Surely this draws the line between reason and faith, if line there be, a trifle late. Nor is it clear that faith must, in order to be faith, depend in the way Locke suggests on rational justification. If it does, the importance of natural theology to which Locke devotes little attention is paramount, and its task enormous.[20] It is at least worthy of inquiry whether there is not an analysis of faith which demands less ability to decide the issues of divine existence, character, and providence by reason alone.[21]

Locke was rather obviously preoccupied with combatting what were for him the gross evils of religious "enthusiasm." Perhaps an essentially similar approach will succeed better if it occurs within a framework less negatively oriented. The views of Thomas Aquinas satisfy this criterion and have been immensely influential. Hence it is worth while to discuss them as, anachronistically, a development and refinement of Locke's position.

ST. THOMAS AQUINAS ON FAITH

St. Thomas Aquinas, in his *Summa Theologica*, discusses faith in some detail.[22] He distinguishes sharply between the preamble to the faith, which can be demonstrated, and the faith itself, which cannot be. For example, that God exists belongs to the preamble, that God is Trinitarian to the faith itself. The substantive "The Faith" stresses that, for Aquinas as for Locke, what is taken on faith is a set of statements believed to have been revealed by God.

> Faith . . . does not assent to anything, except because it is revealed by God.[23]

He adds that

> Faith is a mean between science and opinion. . . . Since, then, science and opinion are about propositions, it seems that faith is likewise about propositions.[24]

This is not to deny that faith is also faith concerning God, since to believe that "God exists" is true is the same as believing that God exists. By "science," Aquinas means simply the class of propositions which are either self-evident or can be derived from self-evident propositions by valid inference, or are "evident to the senses." About any such proposition we have a right to absolute certainty. Often, however, a proposition is accepted which is not part of science in this technical sense. If the belief in such a proposition

> . . . be accompanied by doubt and fear of the opposite side, there will be opinion; while, if there be certainty and no fear of the other side, there will be faith.[25]

To have faith is to choose to believe with absolute confidence that a proposition is true, even though one cannot see from the evidence that it is true.

When should one have faith? Aquinas remarks that

> The believer . . . would not believe [a set of propositions] unless, on the evidence of signs, or of something similar, he saw that they ought to be believed.[26]

What sort of signs Aquinas has in mind becomes clear later when he says

> Faith has not that inquiry of natural reason which demonstrates what is believed, but an inquiry into those things whereby a man is induced to believe, for instance, that such things have been uttered by God and confirmed by miracles.[27]

Thus to have faith is to think with assent about what has been uttered by God and confirmed by a sign to that effect; ". . . the intellect of the believer is convinced by divine authority, so as to assent to what it sees not."[28]

Thus far, Locke and Aquinas follow substantially the same path. Aquinas also agrees with Locke that the ground of faith is more certain than that of science.

> Insofar as science, wisdom, and understanding are intellectual virtues, they are based upon the natural light of reason, which falls short of the certitude of God's word, on which faith is founded.[29]

But it is also true that

> Certitude may be considered on the part of the subject, and thus the more a man's intellect lays hold of a thing, the more certain it is. In

this way, faith is less certain, because matters of faith are above the human intellect, whereas the objects of the aforesaid three virtues are not.[30]

Aquinas, however, adds an element. He asserts that Faith "perfects the intellect" and is meritorious.

> Our actions are meritorious in so far as they proceed from free choice moved with grace by God. (S.T. I–II, Q. 114, A. 3 and 4.) Therefore, every human act proceeding from free choice, if it can be referred to God, can be meritorious. Now the act of believing is an act of intellect assenting to divine truth at the command of the will moved by the grace of God, so that it is subject to free choice in relation to God; and consequently the act of faith can be meritorious.[31]

By having faith, one acts meritoriously, not as compelled by evidence, but as responding to a sign that God has spoken.

John Hick finds an internal inconsistency in Aquinas' position. On the one hand, Aquinas holds that compelled belief is not meritorious.

> The demons are, in a way, compelled to believe by the evidence of signs, so their will deserves no praise for their belief. . . . Rather they are compelled to believe by their natural acumen.[32]

He adds that

> The very fact that the signs of faith are so evident, that the demons are compelled to believe, is displeasing to them.[33]

On the other hand, for the believer, reasons for faith are not rationally compelling.

> The believer has sufficient motive for believing, for he is moved by the authority of divine teaching confirmed by miracles, and, what is more, by the inward instigation of the divine initiation, and so he does not believe lightly. He has not, however, sufficient reason for scientific knowledge, and hence he does not lose the merit.[34]

He adds that while there are reasons for what is taken on faith, these reasons being sufficient to remove obstacles to faith and to make faith not utterly without its supporting reasons though leaving it without demonstrative proof, they nonetheless

> . . . do not always diminish the promptness of the will to believe, and therefore they do not always diminish the merit of faith.[35]

If a man would be equally ready to believe without reasons, his faith is not less meritorious if he has reasons for it.

Hick now raises two problems. First,

> That faith be recognized as involving a responsible act of the human will . . . is not easily reconciled with the claim that the demons are compelled by the visible evidences, even against their will, to acknowledge the Christian mysteries as divine revelations.[36]

He argues that distinguishing, as Aquinas does, between assent based on will for the good (or God), which the believer possesses, and assent based on "many evident signs" which coerce belief, will not solve the problem.

> On the one hand, in discussing human faith he teaches that the historical evidence for the revelatory status of the Church's teaching does not compel assent . . . on the other hand, in discussing demonic faith he teaches that this same evidence does compel assent even in minds which are wickedly resistent to it.[37]

Hick suggests that the only way out of this contradiction would be for Aquinas to adopt the view that demons do not exist and restrict his account to human faith. There seems to be a rather obvious move open to Aquinas, however, which is less drastic: simply claiming that demons have more intellectual capacity or insight for these matters than human beings. Aquinas holds exactly this view. The only knowledge removed from demons because of their wickedness is the affective knowledge which produces love for God.

> Now the divine substance surpasses the proportion not only of the human intellect, but even of the angelic. Consequently not even an angel can of his own nature know God's substance. Yet because of the perfection of his intellect he can of his own nature have a higher knowledge of God than man can have. Such a knowledge of God remains also in the demons.[38]

Thus Aquinas can claim that the force of the evidence, and/or the connection of the evidence to what it supports, is far clearer to demonic intellects than to our own. In another context he also claims that what is true in fact cannot be known by us or, in this case, by angels or demons either. In rejecting the ontological argument of Anselm, he does not deny that Anselm's thesis is true, but only that we have the knowledge of God's essence we would have to have to see that it is true. There are proofs beyond our capacities to attain; only to minds as limited as ours are the evidences merely relevant supports and not coercive reasons.[39]

Even so, Hick finds a difficulty in Aquinas' account of human faith taken on its own.

We can never properly be more certain of the truth of a revealed proposition than of the soundness of our reasons for classifying it as revealed. We cannot (with Newman) claim that the revelation is self guaranteeing, for (as John Locke pointed out) its guarantee is valid only if it is indeed a revelation, and whether this is so must be decided by reason.[40]

The rule expressed in the opening portion of this quotation is not unchallengeable. Nonetheless, by making faith meritorious, indeed, one of the virtues,[41] Aquinas comes dangerously close to making it an intrinsically good thing to believe with greater confidence than any evidence which the believer possesses will justify. He is led almost to apologize that there is any evidence at all for propositions accepted by faith[42]—the evidence is such a danger to the faith being meritorious.

We have seen the many similarities of Aquinas' views to Locke's on the topic of faith. The objections posed to Locke's account apply with equal force to that of Aquinas. The addition of making faith a virtue can hardly be said to alleviate these objections. If anything, it poses a further problem of its own—it makes the presence of evidence for what is believed a danger to the meritoriousness of faith. It will be well, then, to see what other analyses of faith are available.

WILLIAM JAMES' DEFENSE OF FAITH

A quite different approach from that of either Locke or Aquinas is adopted by William James.[43] James does not begin by basing faith on reason; since he does not hold that it is demonstrable either that God exists or that God has a certain nature. He does place matters of faith in contrast, though not in opposition, to what can be decided by appeal to objective evidence. He develops ". . . a defense of our right to adopt a believing attitude in religious matters in spite of the fact that our merely logical intellect may not have been coerced."[44]

The defense requires a series of distinctions which, though not precise, seem useful. A hypothesis, namely, "anything that may be proposed to our belief,"[45] is live if the one to whom it is proposed takes it "as a real possibility." Otherwise, for that person, it is dead. An option between two hypotheses is live if both the hypotheses are live for the person who chooses. An option is forced if the hypotheses exhaust the alternatives of choice and momentous[46] if it is important whether one hypothesis is chosen as opposed to the other. Although no clear criterion for "important" is available, and hence none for "momentous," the choice of a career is in an obvious sense more momentous than what brand of gum one will buy. Implicit in James' use of "momentous," I think, is this rough criterion: the more effects which will follow for an agent upon making a choice in one way as opposed to another, the more momentous the choice is. But James' use of "momentous" seems also to be evaluative or qualitative, as well quantitative.

Assuming that James' distinctions are clear enough at least to permit us, in a rough and ready fashion, to identify options which are at once live, forced, and momentous (e.g., "Will I ask her to marry me?," "Will I agree to marry him?," "Shall I become a doctor?," "Shall I become a Christian?"), James' contention is that in the case of some such options the objective evidence we possess gives us no rational basis for deciding one way rather than another. "Objective" evidence is, roughly, evidence about matters other than how adopting a given hypothesis will affect the life of the one who adopts it. In such cases, he maintains,

> Our passional nature not only lawfully may, but must, decide an option between propositions, whenever it is a genuine option that cannot by its nature be decided on intellectual grounds; for to say, under such circumstances, "Do not decide, but leave the question open," is itself a passional decision,—just like deciding yes or no,—and is attended with the same risk of losing the truth.[47]

Since, in the case of genuine (i.e., live, forced, and momentous) options, the effects of choosing in one way rather than another are crucially important for the person choosing, in a case in which evidence is absent or indecisive it is, James asserts, only reasonable to appeal to the consequences of making one choice as opposed to the other, and to choose in the light of those consequences.[48] The risk of believing something which is false is sometimes less fearsome than the risk of the consequences of choosing not to believe at all. For example, if one agrees with Tolstoi that if God does not exist, then life has no value, and if there is no rational procedure for establishing the truth or falsity of "God exists," then one who wishes his life to have some point, and who does not?, may reasonably choose to believe that God does exist. "Reasonable" belief here means reasonable in the light of the consequences, not reasonable in the light of evidence independent of the consequences.

An obvious objection to James' contentions thus far must be dealt with before we complete our account of his defense. We cannot, the objection goes, decide to believe or not believe a statement, at least in most cases. I can decide that the evidence that Lincoln was our sixteenth president is sufficient, thereby accepting the belief. But the appraisal of the evidence is an appraisal in the light of criteria for good evidence; I do not arbitrarily choose to regard the evidence as reliable, nor is the belief which is a consequence in some sense of my accepting the evidence the product of a fiat on my part. It comes, so to speak, without invitation. This is generally true about our beliefs; they arise without our deliberately choosing them, and we cannot admit or reject them at will. The imperative "Start (or, Stop) believing in God" would be silly, for beliefs are not in that manner subject to our will. James is aware of this point, and comments

> The talk of believing by our volition seems, from one point of view, simply silly. From another point of view [that, namely, of Clifford's maxim], it is vile.[49]

So James grants that in general beliefs cannot be commanded.[50]

Nonetheless, James holds, his defense is acceptable. To adopt a belief in the case of choosing between genuine options is, he suggests, tantamount to adopting a policy of action. It is to adopt a way of life, with the consequent assumptions and ways of acting. He leaves for a footnote what is perhaps the most crucial paragraph in his essay.

> Since belief is measured by action, he who forbids us to believe religion to be true necessarily also forbids us to act as we should if we did believe it to be true. The whole defense of religious faith hinges upon action. If the action required or inspired by the religious hypothesis is in no way different from that dictated by the naturalistic hypothesis, then religious faith is a pure superfluity . . . I myself believe . . . that the religious hypothesis gives to the world an expression which specifically determines our reactions, and makes them in a large part unlike what they might be on a purely naturalistic scheme of belief.[51]

But we can choose to adopt ways of life, which includes adopting beliefs and more besides.

One obvious feature of James' defense is that the behavioral and attitudinal consequences of accepting theism are different from those of rejecting it. Further, at least for some people, adopting theism has beneficial consequences.[52] As cases in point, the description of the "blessed man" who trusts in the Lord in Psalm One, or the man whose Shepherd is the Lord in Psalm Twenty-three, or St. Paul's expressions of gratitude toward God throughout his epistles provide relevant indication that this is the case in the lives of at least some individuals. For any such person, adopting a religious outlook or committing oneself to a religious way of life is patently reasonable, given that the conditions of his choice are those indicated: absence of determining evidence and presence of beneficial consequences.

But there is a further element in James' defense which ought not to be overlooked. He notes that, in some cases, what we desire to be true can be brought about by our own efforts. He who courts a woman often wins a wife, and if a man wishes to have friends, he must himself be friendly. Trusting a man sometimes makes him trustworthy. Within somewhat restricted limits, the claim that "the desire for a certain kind of truth . . . brings about that truth's existence" is true.[53] A relation between two people, or a character trait in one person, can often be elicited by the behavior of an individual who desires to produce just that relationship or trait.

But how does this apply to the case of religious belief? It would be madness indeed were James to suggest that we could make "God exists" true by anything that we did. His point is rather that if a personal Deity exists, being aware that He does may be possible just in case we act as if He did, or adopt a theistic way of life with its attendant beliefs and ways of acting. This might, of course, only produce the illusion that He exists; i.e. create the belief that He does when the belief was false. Or it might, so to speak, establish contact with a Deity who was there all along. But if "God exists" cannot be demonstrated, perhaps nonetheless God can be experienced; if this is a possibility, there is no cogent reason not to try it and see—i.e., not to adopt a religious way of life, including accepting certain beliefs.

We can now succinctly sketch the essence of James' defense. We have no decisive or probable evidence with respect to the claim that God exists. In some cases, at least, belief that He does exist produces beneficial consequences for the one who adopts the belief. If a personal God exists, it is possible that only by worship or meditation or other aspects of a religious way of life, with acceptance of attendant beliefs, can He be apprehended. To refuse to risk error, and hence to refuse to seek that apprehension, would be the reverse of rational. Given that evidence relevant to religious belief is absent or indecisive, and that the adoption or not of such belief is a genuine option, belief is more rational than unbelief.

> A rule of thinking which would absolutely prevent me from acknowledging certain kinds of truth if those kinds of truth were really there, would be an irrational rule.[54]

We can, in James' view, reject any such rule in the light of the foregoing considerations. Indeed, in rejecting such a rule we are faithful to a more fundamental rule of right thinking.

> *We must know the truth, and we must avoid error,*—these are our first and great commandments as would-be knowers; but they are not two

ways of stating an identical commandment, they are two separable
laws.[55]

Indeed, James suggests, they are so importantly different that

> . . . by choosing between them we may end by coloring differently our
> whole intellectual life. We may regard the chase for truth as para-
> mount, and the avoidance of error as secondary; or we may, on the
> other hand, treat the avoidance of error as more imperative, and let
> truth take its chance.[56]

Clifford, James notes, establishes the second priority for his life; James
emphatically establishes the first for his.

Where the force of the evidence is clear, then no conflict between
the rules arises.[57] But, as we have seen, where an option is genuine
and evidence absent or indecisive, the rules do conflict and establishing one priority over another becomes itself a genuine option for
which no decisive or compelling objective evidence is available. James'
case for religious faith is, in effect, equally a defense of the priority
of the rule "We must know the truth" over the rule "We must avoid
error." In this sense, James' defense is a defense of faith against Clifford's critique—against the claim that faith is unreasonable since it
involves holding statements to be true with far more tenacity than the
evidence allows. Appraisal of the success of his defense is now in order.

Even if it is true that, at least for some, religious belief has good
consequences, surely no one could in fact accept it simply for that
reason and yet profess any allegiance to the rules of reason that James
articulates. If adopting religious belief were merely a matter of choosing to act in a specified manner, the defense might well be sufficient.
But we saw the implausibility of that view, at least for beliefs central
to the Judeo-Christian tradition, in our first chapter. Since, at least
in some cases, religious belief involves the acceptance of substantive
claims,[58] what would accepting these claims on the basis of personal
benefit amount to?

As Tennant correctly observes,

> Spiritual efficacy or capacity to promote pious and moral life is one
> thing; reality of the . . . object figuring in efficacious doctrines is an-
> other. It is in asserting the reality of such objects that faith essentially
> consists; not in appreciating the value of statements concerning them
> while their ontological status is left a thing indifferent.[59]

No account of religious belief which makes it an "as if" faith can be
adequate. It simply would not capture the fact that such belief involves accepting substantive assertions confidently as true. Further,
while one might recommend religious faith to others on the ground

that it had beneficial consequences, this would not be tantamount to claiming that it was true. Nor could a follower of James recommend it to himself on these grounds, for if the only thing that makes faith reasonable is the consequences of adopting it, it is reasonable only in the sense of "prudential." But the rule "We should seek the truth" would not then apply, since it is quite distinct from the rule, which James does not discuss, "We should be prudential." Practices, not theses, can be defended on prudential grounds. If religious belief can be commended only as a "cosmic aspirin," no priority of one of James' rules over another will make its adoption more rational or reasonable than its rejection. In short, believing that if one accepts a statement S one will reap beneficial consequences is not the same as believing S, or showing that in believing S one will be seeking the truth.[60]

The element of his defense, however, which James chooses to emphasize is that if a personal God exists, it is plausible to believe that only by a commitment on our part can He be known; only by our anticipating, so to speak, a divine step in our direction can we ever hope to respond to a divine overture if such there be. Only by making the response can we tell, if at all, whether there are indeed any divine overtures. This would be James' way of saying "Taste and see that the Lord is good." That something like this is his intent is suggested when he comments that

> It matters not to an empiricist from what quarter an hypothesis may come to him . . . if the total drift of thinking continues to confirm it, that is what he means by its being true.[61]

Were James' argument intended to prove that a religious position is the correct one, questions would multiply. Which religious position should one adopt among the many incompatible ones available? Does religious experience provide relevant evidence for religious claims? These issues we have, to some degree, canvassed in an earlier chapter. Here, it is only appropriate to remind ourselves that James' intent is only to show that religious faith of a very general sort is not irrational. More specifically, to adopt a set of beliefs regarding which no adequate evidence, pro or con, is available and whose adoption or not is a genuine option, is not irrational. In the case of religious belief, in fact, it is the rational option to believe.

But does James prove even this mitigated claim? His defense in part rests on the claim that there is an important difference between any attempt to verify "God exists" and an attempt to verify, say, "Bodies become expanded by friction." The former hypothesis, it is suggested, can be verified only if God, if He exists, reveals Himself, which He will (*ex hypothesi*) do only to those who, without evidence, accept the thesis that He does. The latter can be tested by anyone with the requisite talent and materials, whether he is initially inclined to accept or to reject the claim, or has no initial view whatever about its truth. One would have to justify the assumptions involved in the claim that there is indeed this difference between the two hypotheses. How can one be so confident about what God will and will not do? But let us grant James this distinction. His proposal then is that verification in religion can only temporally follow religious belief. Even if this is so, the hypotheses will otherwise be substantially similar. Evidence, pro or con, relevant to "God exists" will either be forthcoming or not. If so, then the evidence will decide the matter, with certainty or with probability, and the option will no longer be genuine. If not, then this portion of James' defense will have run its tether and the whole weight of his argument will rest upon the issue of consequences again. We have offered reasons for thinking that an argument resting on this issue will not serve James' purposes. Hence, James' defense seems patently inadequate.

In spite of many obvious differences, there are features common to the analysis of faith proffered by Locke, Aquinas, and James. One shared element is the insistence that statements are the objects of faith; faith is primarily belief that certain statements are true. Another is that faith is involved in such belief only in the absence of coercive or probable evidence. A third common feature is emphasis on the role of the will; since coercive or probable evidence is *ex hypothesi* absent, choice between alternatives is required—a choice not automatic upon inspection of the evidence. Thus faith is quite sharply distinguished, at least apparently, from reason. F. R. Tennant challenges this bifurcation.[62]

F. R. TENNANT: SCIENCE AND FAITH

Tennant shares with James the emphasis on faith as creative, reaching

> . . . beyond the Actual or the given to the ideally possible, which in the first instance it creates . . . and then by practical activity may realize or bring into being. Every machine of human invention has thus come to be.[63]

He also stresses that

> . . . faith may similarly lead to knowledge of Actuality which it in no sense creates, but which would have continued in the absence of faith-

venture to be unknown . . . There is, of course, no necessity as to the issue of faith in either actualization or knowledge.[64]

But if faith, in the sense of taking a statement to be true in the absence of good evidence that it is true, may involve us in accepting false beliefs, as Tennant admits, why make faith-ventures at all? Tennant's answer, in essence, is that any attempt to know involves our initially accepting statements as true in the absence of adequate evidence for them.

> The principle "nothing venture, nothing gain" . . . underlies acquisition of all presumptive knowledge. We might accordingly . . . say: by faith . . . Newton founded physics on his few simple laws of motion; by faith the atomists of ancient Greece conceived the reign of law throughout the material world, and so on indefinitely.[65]

Underlying this suggestion is Tennant's analysis of human endeavors to know anything. His view is that Aristotle is right when he asserts that "all men by nature desire to know."[66] Human behavior is, to a large degree, oriented to this end. Both science and religion arise from this orientation.

> Science postulates what is requisite to make the world amenable to the kind of thought that conceives of the structure of the universe, and its orderedness according to quantitative law; theology, and sciences of valuation, postulate what is requisite to make the world amenable to the kind of thought that conceives of the why and wherefore, the meaning or purpose of the universe, and its orderedness according to teleological principles. Both are necessarily interpretive, anthropic, interested, selective.[67]

Both science and theology require the postulation of entities (e.g. atoms, electrons, God) not directly observable, and the assumption of theses (e.g. that the data we discover will be amenable to interpretation within a unified conceptual scheme, that God exists) not strictly provable. Indeed, ". . . the theistic interpretation of the world is but a carrying to completion, and an explication, of the implicit belief of science in what is vaguely called the rationality of the world."[68] Religion and science are the products of the same activity, and have their essential features in common, so much so that the former merely completes the latter. "Science" names the product of man's attempt to know at a less general or comprehensive level than that to which "religion" applies.

Not surprisingly, then, Tennant claims that the same verification procedures applicable for scientific claims are equally appropriate for religious claims.[69] Tennant's analysis of faith is clarified by the implications he explicitly draws from it.[70] First, science and theology are products of our attempt to know or understand the world. They both posit unobservable entities and make unprovable assumptions; in this sense, they both require faith. As expressions of the same conative activity, science and theology have the same epistemological status; they are the same sort of conceptual endeavor, involving the same kind of reasoning and the same type of verification. Second, science and theology are committed to claims about the existence and nature of actual entities, neither being limited to assertions about subjective states or the behavioral consequences of beliefs. Third, as a consequence of this, neither science nor theology can be derived from, or reduced to, valuational claims (i.e. claims about what ought to be, what is right, what is good, etc.).

The essential feature of faith, in Tennant's view, would seem to be this: in their inevitable attempt to understand their environment, men must assume, or act as if they assume, certain statements to be true. Unless the future resembles the past, unless data are amenable to systematization within a unified conceptual scheme, etc., no knowledge is possible. But any proof of these assumptions would be circular, for it would necessarily presuppose them. To have faith is to accept as true those assumptions which are required by any attempt to gain systematic knowledge.

> The justification of faith is the fact that without it we lack assurance that the world is reasonable, in the sense of not being meaningless.[71]

The assumptions of religion are of no different character than those of science. Hence, if the latter are rational so are the former. These assumptions are justified if the attempts to know for which their acceptance is a necessary condition do indeed provide workable conceptual schemes. In this sense alone can statements accepted by faith be given rational justification. Obviously Tennant's account is not intended to cover lower-level generalizations in science—i.e. those amenable to verification or falsification via appeal to sensory experience or the results of crucial experiments. Hence his comparison of postulating atoms and believing in God must be jettisoned. This seems to be an accurate summary of Tennant's analysis of faith. As it stands, it seems to apply only to claims which must be assumed by *all* attempts to provide a conceptual system intended to interpret men and things.[72] It easily expands to cover the claims assumed by *any* attempt to provide such a scheme, with the corollary that if a system C assumes that a statement S is true, S is justified to the degree to which C is "workable."[73] This expandability is at least somewhat of a virtue in that, while it seems overly ambitious to claim that any attempt to know presupposes that "God exists" is true, plainly there are conceptual schemes whose acceptance does require the assumption that God exists. Thus Tennant's analysis of faith is expandable so as to cover cases of believing religious claims even if he is mistaken in his view, noted above, that religion "completes" science.

Although, as we shall argue shortly, there is merit in Tennant's analysis, it is by no means unexceptionable. Its emphasis on the cognitive and conative aspects of faith is salutary. To have faith is indeed to make an interpretation of the world, and to opt for one possible interpretation when others are available. But is, say, the interpretation of the world shared by orthodox Jews and Christians[74] legitimately described as being essentially the same sort of interpretation as that of, say, contemporary physics? Tennant himself points to important differences between science and religion.[75] Science is concerned primarily with the explanation in some sense of ordinary and laboratory observations; religion is not. Science is value-neutral; religion is not. At least, such religions as Judaism and Christianity explicitly include moral concepts and moral principles, whereas, say, physics has neither. Religious systems involve specific assumptions in the sense of strictly unprovable claims which are not assumed by science. (Perhaps the converse is also true.) The question raised is thus an important one. We can best answer it in the wider context of considering a final analysis of religious faith, that provided by John Hick.

We will begin our discussion of Hick's analysis of faith by considering his treatment of religious faith as putative knowledge of God.

JOHN HICK'S FAITH AND KNOWLEDGE

In Hick's view, knowledge of God is mediated knowledge. One is not, for Hick, aware of God in the way that various philosophers have asserted and others denied that one is aware of himself and his experiences. Nor, for Hick, does one infer that God exists from some other more basic data.

His positive account is more complex. He considers the difference between such statements as:

(a) Jones *recognizes* the object as a dog.
(b) Jones *interprets* the object as a dog.

According to (a), Jones has succeeded in properly identifying an object. According to (b), Jones has drawn a conclusion which may or may not be true. Other interpretations than Jones' are viable. To recognize is to explain something ". . . by disclosing its context, revealing it as a part of a wider whole which does not, for us, stand in need of explanation."[76]

> But in the unique case of the universe as a whole the distinction be-
> tween explanation and recognition fails to arise. For the universe has
> no wider context in terms of which it might be explained; an explana-
> tion of it can therefore only consist in a perception of its significance.[77]

We cannot recognize, but can only interpret, the universe; alternative interpretations are patently possible, as the history of philosophy makes evident. Nonetheless, incompatible interpretations cannot both be correct.[78] For reasons already discussed, no evaluation of competing total interpretations in terms of probability is possible.[79]

The interpretation involved in a theistic reading of the universe occurs at three levels, or in Hick's language contains "three orders of significance."[80] They are the natural, the human, and the divine. In a way that requires no discussion here, our material environment has significance in that it is intelligible to us; we can normally operate in it successfully. That there is a material world, external to us in the sense of being distinct from any experience or set of experiences is itself an interpretation;[81] one, Hick suggests, neither self-contradictory to deny nor amenable to justification by an argument from proba-bility. Again, in the presence of other people, we tend to feel a sense of responsible relationship, or restrictions, obligations, proprieties, and the like. One can more easily escape making this moral interpretation than one can escape, say, believing in an external material world or in other minds. Many more philosophers, for example, have denied the existence of objective moral standards than have rejected the other beliefs just mentioned. No strict proof, and no probability argument, Hick suggests, can be given for the claim that we have moral obliga-tions. A third level of significance presupposes the others, regarding the material universe and the moral and social context as the environ-ment in which God providentially governs so as to provide men the opportunity to freely attain the moral maturity of self-giving love which regards and treats others as divinely created. It is even easier to escape making this interpretation than it is to escape making the moral interpretation, and strict proof and probability arguments are again unavailable. Because of this, some philosophers have claimed that the theistic interpretation does not assert anything different from its atheistic denial. Theism and atheism, it is suggested, are optional ways of looking at the world, analogous to the optional ways of look-ing at a configuration of dots which one moment looks like a rabbit and another moment looks like a duck, and is neither really. Hick rejects this suggestion, claiming that theism can, in principle at least, be verified and atheism, in principle at least, can be falsified.

We have seen[82] good reason to deny that there must be symmetry between verification and falsification, and Hick makes this point clearly. Other portions of Hick's argument are more puzzling. He appeals to eschatological[83] verification, claiming that

> Christian doctrine postulates an ultimate unambiguous state of evidence *in patria* as well as our present ambiguous existence *in via*.[84]

It is to this anticipation of a putatively unambiguous state that Hick appeals in defending traditional theism against the claim that the theistic interpretation cannot, even in principle, be verified and so really has no truth-value after all. He assumes that

> . . . when we are interested in the verifiability of propositions as the criterion for their having factual meaning, the notion of prediction becomes central. If a proposition contains or entails predictions which can be verified or falsified, its character as an assertion . . . is thereby established![85]

He adds that

> . . . the theist does, and the atheist does not, expect that when history is completed it will be seen to have led to a particular end-state and to have fulfilled a specific purpose, namely that of creating "children of God."[86]

There are two reasons, I think, why one ought to find Hick's account puzzling, though not necessarily mistaken. First, Hick assumes, in effect, that only if an interpretation entails a verifiable or falsifiable prediction can it have truth-value. This assumption seems gratuitous, and we will discuss it shortly. Second, Hick spends many pages in developing, in a most interesting manner, an argument for the claim that the concept of a man surviving his death is intelligible (which I grant) and that such a person could have an utterly unambiguous experience (which I deny). It is certainly worth asking why Hick supposes appeal to eschatological verification is necessary in order to defend the thesis that the theistic interpretation has truth-value. Surely, if the sort of defense Hick envisages can be successful at all, there is an obviously easier path.[87] Were all men naturally to believe that God exists, were there no pain, had all men always freely chosen for the good, were all prayers righteously made and instantly answered, perhaps being accompanied by a voice which identified itself as stemming from a divine being and which spoke words of great profundity, etc., theism would be well nigh inescapable. Were there nothing in life for anyone but great pain, were devastating disease and warfare to rack every instant of human history at every inhabited point of the globe, were all men viciously evil and strongly inclined to demon-worship, theism could be maintained only by the heroically obstinate. Surely there are universe-descriptions which, were they true, would make theism highly plausible, though not absolutely certainly true, and others which, were they true, would make theism highly implausible, though not absolutely certainly false. The difficulty with our universe is that if the argument of the earlier chapters of this book is sound, neither the theistic interpretation nor the atheistic or any of the varieties of interpretations coming under each heading is the only plausible one. For the theist, or at least for Hick,[88] this is to be explained by the fact that God values faith and obedience given freely, not coerced by the evidence, and this account does much to make the ambiguity of the evidence compatible with a theistic reading of it. Since a total interpretation has truth value if it would not be allowable as an interpretation of some universes but would be for others, theism has truth-value without appeal to eschatological considerations, since it plainly is not an at all plausible interpretation of a universe fitting our second description. Why, then, appeal to eschatological verification?[89] There seems to be no good reason to do so unless only such verification can be unambiguous. Even then, such appeal is justified only in the sense that it would provide the strongest verification, not in the sense that it would provide the only possible verification, of the theistic interpretation.

Further, can any experience be unambiguous?

> There are, I suggest, two possible developments of our experience such that, if they occurred in conjunction with one another (whether in this life or in another life to come), they would assure us beyond rational doubt of the reality of God as conceived in the Christian faith. These are, *first*, an experience of the fulfillment of God's purpose for ourselves, as this has been disclosed in the Christian revelation, and *second*, in conjunction with the first, an experience of communion with God as he has revealed Himself in the person of Christ.[90]

Let the description of the fulfillment of God's purpose for an individual, Jones, be articulated in detail—Jones acts only from self-giving love, always resists temptation, has great peace and joy, etc. No matter how long our description becomes, and no matter how clear it is, to Jones and to others, that the description applies to Jones, is it unambiguous that God's purpose has been fulfilled in Jones? Couldn't one still quite sensibly ask, How can we be absolutely sure that this state of affairs is not merely the prologue to the dashing of all Jones' hopes and his utter degradation? How could we be unambiguously confident that Jones was not raised to such heights only to make his ultimate descent the more painful to Jones?

The question is not whether "Jones has attained God's purpose for him" can be necessarily true in the sense that its denial is contradictory, nor whether Jones would not attain complete psychological certainty about his state, nor whether such certainty might not be justified in the light of available evidence. It is simply whether Jones' state can be unambiguous in the sense that he cannot be mistaken about it in every sense in which a man who now believes that he has an experience of God might be mistaken in his belief. How will the additional claim that Jones attains the state in question after surviving his death make the state unambiguous? Yet Hick's case requires that it do so.

The addition of the second element—that Jones finds himself in communion with a man recognizably identical with Jesus of Nazareth, and with other men who have attained a like state of *agape* and peace, all of whom know themselves to have survived physical death—does not alter the case. This would indeed provide evidence for the truth of the Christian interpretation; nonetheless, the evidence would not be unambiguous. Were a skeptic permitted among the throng, he could account for all the evidence in a manner which was at least internally consistent and not flatly contradicted by the data. He might, for example, remind his cohorts of Bertrand Russell's story told in criticism of inductive inference. There was once an intelligent chicken who was firmly convinced that the future would resemble the past, so that the regularities of the latter could legitimately be anticipated in the former. His kindly master fed him well each morning; so he would continue to do so. And he did—until his master's hunger overcame his kindness. So too, the skeptic might argue, the present state of affairs is only the blissful first act of the eternal drama, which will make the second, and final, act all the more terrifying by contrast. His thesis would not be supported by the evidence, but neither would it be utterly refuted by it, since he agrees that, so far, all is well. Thus Hick has given us no reason to think that the conditions he offers as sufficient for an unambiguously theistic state of affairs would indeed be sufficient. There would still be, so to say, "logical room" for the skeptic. But if eschatological verification is not unambiguous, why appeal to eschatology for Hick's purpose at all? This is not to deny that Hick's discussion is interesting for its own sake.

Some men are fortunately wed, and have every right to their confidence in the love and fidelity of their wives. Some children are rightly confident in the good intentions and genuine love of their parents, and some parents are rightly confident of their children's filial piety. We are all happily positioned as to confidence in the existence of other minds, and solipsism is hardly a live option. Were we—now or after death—provided with evidence for the theistic, or any other, interpretation which warranted it in the way that the beliefs just listed are sometimes warranted, surely that is all that is requisite to show that the interpretation is true. And if there could be such evidence for an interpretation, or if we can describe what would count as adequate counter-evidence to an interpretation, that is enough to establish its possession of truth-value. Eschatological verification is neither necessary for that purpose, nor would it provide unambiguous proof as far as theism is concerned. We can allow, nonetheless, that Hick's suggestions do provide at least the beginning of an answer as to how one could, in principle, decide the issue between theism and atheism by appeal to possible experiences. By the same token, were all those who were theists to survive their deaths, know that they had, and all find themselves in great torment whereas they found their atheist friends had also survived and were in ecstatic bliss, the honest theist would have to take note of disturbingly disconfirming evidence to his interpretation of things. If, in an afterlife, the development of such human capacities as intelligence, compassion and sensitivity to beauty were inversely proportional to the depth of one's theistic convictions, powerful theoretical and practical support for atheism would be available. But the same holds were this true this side of the grave.[91] *Any* experience *can* be misread.

One other aspect of Hick's analysis of faith deserves mention, namely his criticism of other concepts of faith on the ground that they make propositions or statements the "objects" of faith. In one sense, of course, for all those discussed, faith as trust is faith in God. Their concern has been, however, with what such faith (trust) presupposes. Tennant put the distinction in this manner.

> Despite features in common, trust (in God) and faith are so essentially different, that it will not conduce to clearness to amalgamate them into one concept: *fiducia* toward God presupposes *fides*; *fides* involves but the *fiducia* or trustfulness that makes *any* knowledge possible.[92]

Our concern has been, and is, with *fides*, or faith that, not with trust, or faith in. This is true of Hick's volume also. Thus no implicit appeal to *fiducia* (trust) will be *apropos* on Hick's part[93] as a defense of his analysis of *fides*, in which certain events serve as the objects of faith.

So understood, revelation is not a divine promulgation of propositions, nor is faith a believing of such propositions. The theological propositions formulated on the basis of revelation have a secondary status. They do not constitute the content of God's self-revelation but are human and therefore fallible verbalizations, constructed to aid both the integration of our religious experience into our own minds and the communication of religious experience to others.[94]

In Hick's view, God reveals Himself by acting in history on man's behalf. Crucial in this regard is the sequence of events which many contemporary theologians designate *Heilsgeschichte*. The term means "history of salvation-events," referring to such matters as the call of Abraham from Ur of the Chaldees to a place unknown to him, the calling out of Israel from Egypt, the incarnation of God in the person of Jesus Christ, and Christ's resurrection from the dead. Revelation, Hick suggests, is a series of acts on the part of God—God causes events to occur in history, ultimately entering history Himself in order to "seek and to save that which is lost."

Revelation, considered as completed communication, consists in the conjunction of God's activity within our human experience, with the human recognition that the events *are* God's actions . . . . The events are always in themselves ambiguous, capable of being seen either simply as natural happenings or as happenings through which God has acted toward us.[95]

For God to act in history is for Him to reveal Himself; for men to recognize that an event in history is also a divine act makes for completed communication. The revealing act is revelatory in that, so to speak, it makes its point. Debate about whether the act alone, or only the act plus the recognition, should be called revelation would be merely verbal.

A crucial question remains about Hick's view of revelation. It is patently clear that "God called Abraham from Ur of the Chaldees" and "God raised Jesus from the dead" are not claims which are self-evidently true in the sense in which some philosophers apparently have thought "All events are caused" is, and in which most philosophers have taken "Nothing can have incompatible qualities" to be. They are not the sorts of claims which can plausibly be claimed to be "demonstrated by appeal to reason alone." Further, it is indeed such claims as these that one finds in the Judeo-Christian Scriptures, not claims at least in any explicit fashion about the necessity of a cause for every event. Hick is contending for a sort of faith neither dependent on prior statements proved by reason nor requiring that we know already what God is likely to do before we can decide what, if anything, He has done. Hick is right in stressing that his examples are claims crucial to Judeo-Christian thought. What needs equal stress is that, if we take Hick's account of revelation fully seriously, we would not know what God had done even if we could know that an event was the result of or was, *simpliciter* a divine action. For Hick, what is revealed is an act or event, whereas its significance is not clear from the event but must be formulated or interpreted (not, however, created) by us. I think that the preceding sentence faithfully captures Hick's intent when he writes that

> Faith . . . is the human recognition of ambiguous events as revelatory, and hence the experience of them as mediating the presence and activity of God.[96]

Thus for Hick, while God can act, He does not tell us what He has done, since that would require propositions, which are *ex hypothesi* not revealed. But why not? Because to reveal a proposition would coerce us and obliterate our freedom? Why so, if the act does not do this? That God revealed the significance of His action would not make the sentence expressing its significance self-evident. A matter which Hick neglects is the frequency with which God is represented in the Judeo-Christian Scriptures as speaking to men, interpreting His actions and verbally articulating His message. Thus some theologians have spoken of revelation as a divine "Tat-Wort" (deed-word) in which God acts on man's behalf and interprets His action to him.[97] Thus Hick is correct in implicitly pointing out that the propositions accepted by faith by those in the Judeo-Christian tradition are not provable by demonstration or probability argument and do not presuppose claims that are provable. But he is wrong in supposing that no propositions are involved. Indeed, if one accepts an event E as an act of God, this certainly entails that he believes "God caused E" is true. Further, if God acts but leaves the interpretation to us, of what use could this sort of "revelation" be? What rules could we use to interpret the action since *ex hypothesi* no information is ever revealed? Hick's view of revelation, while fashionable, also seems incoherent. We would be as much in the dark about God after this sort of revelation as we were before.[98]

The conception of faith as the adoption of a total interpretation has certain obvious virtues. It captures much of what is defensible in competing conceptions of faith without succumbing to the vices of those conceptions. It expresses aptly the religious viewpoint of at least the religious traditions which have historically been most closely associated with philosophical reflection. Very likely, it does so for other religious viewpoints as well. It relates both the cognitive and conative elements in religious belief which seem rather clearly to be inseparable without the obliteration of the very possibility of religious belief or life. In all these respects, Hick's view is, so it seems to me at least, quite correct. There remains, however, Hick's dubious implicit assumption that total interpretations are different in what they assert, and can be appraised rationally, just in case they entail different predictive claims which are observationally or experientially testable.

FAITH: A REVIEW

It is now necessary to review the argument of the present chapter and to attempt to consolidate it by offering an analysis of faith which includes the insights but evades the defects of the views previously considered.

First, the Locke-Aquinas tradition made faith to rest upon reason in the dual sense that the existence and nature of God were regarded as demonstrable[99] and that a proposition to be accepted by faith must first be certified by reason to have been revealed. Thus a claim to possess a revelation accompanied by a miracle is to be countenanced, since God, who is known to exist, would not permit us to be deceived about such matters and since a miracle-worker who claims to possess a revelation will be believed. Further, we can judge, to some degree, what a God possessing the properties He is known to possess would be likely to reveal, and it is reasonable to believe that He would accompany His revelations with signs and wonders. To have faith is to accept these propositional revelations as indeed of divine origin. Essentially, this expresses the Locke-Aquinas conception of the faith.

Waiving the admittedly problematic matter of false prophets,[100] several difficulties face anyone who adopts this tradition. The arguments which purport to prove that God exists are widely rejected and involve numerous assumptions that are not indubitably true.[101] Thus our putative knowledge of the existence of God, and of His nature, is far less securely founded than this tradition implies and requires. Secondly, the amount of confidence we can justifiably have as to what God will do or reveal can hardly be as profound as this tradition suggests.[102] The grace, or unmerited favor, of God in choosing the people of Israel is stressed in the Old Testament, and His unexpected graciousness is making human redemption possible through the death of Christ is frequent theme of the New Testament. The God of traditional theism is a Being whose thoughts are not our thoughts nor

His ways our ways, and He works in mysterious ways His wonders to perform. No analysis of faith operating, as does both Locke's and Aquinas', within the framework of Judeo-Christian thought can afford to neglect the mystery of God's nature, the unfathomableness of His being. While the negative test that God will reveal nothing false or immoral is no doubt acceptable, the task of identifying a revelation remains immensely problematic for Locke and Aquinas. One suspects they are able to give any plausibility to their positions only by taking for granted the claim that in the Scriptures and for Aquinas, in the tradition of the Catholic Church, we already possess a very substantial body of revealed propositions.

James' view that faith is the adoption of a hypothesis in the context of live, momentous, and forced choice does not involve resting faith on reason in the dual sense just criticized. Nonetheless, is has its own difficulties. What James seems to offer is a way of attempting to verify the belief that God exists. The essential difference between this belief and the belief, say, that bacteria sours milk is that one must at least tentatively accept the former in order to test it while this is not so with the latter. Perhaps just as we become a person's friend by being friendly to him, we can meet God only by acting as if we knew He exists (e.g., by religious exercises).[103] But if the proffered method of finding out whether God exists is viable, presumably we could run the test and settle the issue with at least some presumption of truth. Faith would be a condition of making the religious test; if the result is positive, faith ends and knowledge of God begins. If the result is negative, faith just ends. (Or, knowledge that God does not exist begins.) But all this conflicts with James' assumption that the theistic hypothesis is in fact, given all the data available to us, still live, forced, and momentous (which presupposes that there is no coercive evidence). That there is, and can be, no such evidence in the option between theism and its denial is assumed by James' analysis.

If, however, we drop the claim that faith is a precondition of empirical test, all that seems to be left in James' analysis is this: believing that God exists, or adopting the theistic hypothesis as true, has beneficial psychological consequences for some people anyway, and thus it is reasonable for just these people to accept it. But of course that would go no way toward showing that theism was true, nor that being a theist was reasonable in the light of the evidence. At most, it would show theism to be reasonable in the sense of it being prudential for some people to accept it. It is highly plausible, however, that were anyone convinced that only its good psychological consequences saves theism from being irrational or nonrational, the consequences would no longer follow. Only if one believes theism to be true is it likely to be psychologically beneficial for him to be a theist. One could defend James by making theism into a way of living which involved no claims about God, but in the light of other attempts at making this reduction[104] it hardly seems worth the effort.

One might also view James as offering a modern version of Pascal's wager. Then one construes James as saying that the prudent man will accept the truth of *God exists* because if God does exist He will look more favorably on those who graciously assent to this fact. One wonders, however, about the source of this confidence about the divine behavior. It is not justified, we may note in passing, by the Judeo-Christian tradition, where only trust in God is saving faith, not mere assent to His existence. As we have seen, "the devils believe, and tremble." What confidence can a follower of James have that he will not share their fate? But if we press James' claims in the direction of adopting a view of men and things which involves a way of life as well, we are quite close to Hick's "total interpretation" analysis.

Tennant's rejection of the claim that there is an indubitable set of statements which all rational men must honor by adopting them as their conceptual starting-point is in full accord with James' conviction that choices about such ultimate issues as the existence or non-existence of God are genuine options. Nonetheless, for Tennant they are not "passional" choices, they are to be made on rational grounds. There are, Tennant suggests, certain assumptions we must make in order for science (i.e. a system or systems of empirical knowledge) to be possible. These assumptions are verified insofar as they make possible such systems. Theology, too, has its assumptions, which do not differ fundamentally from those in science. In neither case are the assumptions indubitable, and in neither case is there any possibility of probability arguments in their favor. To have faith is to assent to these assumptions. Their truth can be tested only by the success of the systems to which they are necessary. That God exists as a fully rational being and has created an intelligible world provides a foundation for the scientist's confidence that his data are interpretable within a unified conceptual scheme. An assumption of theology is thus basic to, in the sense that it provides justification for this confidence, and it is in turn pragmatically verified by the success of the sciences. So we can postulate God's existence as well as that of the atom, and faith that scientific claims are true is paralleled by faith that religious claims are true, both being verified in the same manner.

Several defects are easily discovered in Tennant's position. Atoms are postulated to account for specifiable laboratory data; postulating God's existence does not account for any specifiable laboratory data. It is plausible that "God exists" is in crucial respects analogous to

"The future will resemble the past" or "Every event must have a cause," but not that it is closely analogous to "Atoms exist" or "There are protons, electrons, and neutrons." Again, does the interpretability of the universe presuppose an intelligent designer, as Tennant supposes when he rests science on theology? If so, proof that it does is required but not provided. Yet again, many if not most of the scientific systems we have developed are geared to describing and predicting observable data; are theological systems to be construed along the same lines? If so, it looks rather bad for them. If not, what becomes of the analogy between religious faith and scientific faith? And what now of pragmatic justification of a theological system? Thus Tennant's account is seen to be far from satisfactory.

FAITH AS TOTAL INTERPRETATION

John Hick's analysis of faith as a "total interpretation" seems far more plausible than the other views discussed in this chapter. It does not reduce religious belief to an emotive or conative attitude, though there are obviously emotive attachments and conative activities associated with the adoption, tacit or reflective, of such an interpretation. Thus it does justice to the cognitive element of religious belief. It emphasizes the difference between the claim that the Judeo-Christian God exists and the claim that bacteria cause milk to sour. The former is an axiom, so to speak, of a general conceptual scheme—a scheme which provides a way of interpreting the significance of our physical environment and our moral experience. The latter provides an explanation of an observable phenomenon via the activity of microscopically observable entities. Accounting for observable phenomena in a Wilson cloud chamber by reference to the activity of unobservable entities (atoms) is a more sophisticated example of fundamentally the same sort of explanation. It would obviously be inappropriate to construe the claim that God exists on the model of explanations of observable phenomena. The same is true for such claims as "Every event has a cause" and "The future will resemble the past" and, of course, their denials. We can see, then, the inappropriateness of Clifford's principle, which in effect regards such claims as "God exists" or "We will survive our physical deaths" as appropriately conceived on the analogy of our bacteria and atomic examples; for the latter examples, Clifford's maxim may well be correct. His evidence is plainly limited to empirical evidence, and his model the verification of lower-level scientific hypotheses. Neither the higher-level generalizations of science nor the basic tenets of a metaphysical system nor the central claims of theism fit that model. Hick makes this quite plain.

He also claims that, while perhaps neither theologian nor scientist can straightforwardly prove their respective "axioms" or basic assumptions, the latter can appeal to the relative success of his system or systems in correlating data and predicting the results of future experiments. Hick notes that traditional theism also entails that, after death, certain observations will be made. Given that the notion of surviving one's death presents no insuperable difficulties (a topic too broad to be broached here), his claim seems quite correct—though this does not entail that theism is an explanation in the sense in which theories of natural science are explanations.[105] Theism is not to be construed as a way of correlating data so as to provide for prediction and control. Hick is, of course, fully aware of this. While we have seen reasons to doubt that his use of escatological verification is necessary for attaining the end to which it was directed, to reject his claims about unambiguous experiences, and to distrust the substitution of events for propositions, it nonetheless seems clear that his analysis has much in its favor. If it is essentially correct as it stands, as seems to be the case, we need only ask whether we can add anything of value to it.

Our addition is necessarily somewhat technical. It comes in the form of the thesis that there is no need to suppose that decision procedure[106] between two total interpretations must depend on what can be predicted by proponents of the one but not the other. Hick suggests implicitly that this is the only way of deciding between such interpretations; this is to overemphasize what is only one of the ways in which decisions can be made between competing conceptual schemes, the way of crucial experiment. Crucial experiments are simply circumstances in which, on one theory, certain phenomena can be observed to occur whereas, on the other theory, these phenomena will not occur. Since either the phenomena will occur or not, one theory or other must be wrong.[107] Thus Hick's appeal to eschatological verification is an appeal to a crucial experiment that all of us must some day make. An example of a crucial experiment of a more usual nature is easily provided. According to classical physics, light should not bend as it passes near the sun during an eclipse; according to Einstein's general theory of relativity, light rays passing near the sun would be bent. On May 29, 1919 there was an eclipse, during which observations were made confirming that starlight in the gravitational field of the sun was indeed bent, disconfirming classical theory and confirming general relativity theory. Hick, in effect, extrapolates this kind of decision procedure from its context in science and applies it to a theological system.

There is, of course, nothing objectionable about this extrapolation unless it introduces an element foreign to the theological system in question. Since Hick does not propose that we carry out the experiment ourselves, but rather allows us to await its inevitable incursion into our plans, and since a doctrine of the afterlife is a part of the theological system in question, no foreign element seems to be introduced. That crucial experiments play a role in scientific testing does not entail that such experiments are relevant to establishing claims of truth value only for scientific systems.

Another sort of "test" is available, however, for systems of scientific explanation. Appeal can be made to the formal characteristics of such systems. Three formal criteria come easily to mind: consistency, coherence, and simplicity. A statement is consistent if it is not self-contradictory, and two statements are mutually consistent if they can both be true at the same time. A consistent system is simply a system comprised of mutually consistent statements. Coherence is harder to define. It presupposes consistency, but involves relevance; a coherent system is composed of mutually consistent statements which are relevant to one another, or relevant to explaining a set of phenomena, solving a problem, interpreting an event, or in some other manner. Thus a system comprized of (A) There is no highest prime number, (B) Ideas are not spatially located, and (C) Most men are over three feet tall, is not a coherent system. Simplicity is yet harder to explicate.[108] It has sometimes been regarded as only an epistemological matter. William of Occam, whose name is associated with the principle of simplicity via the term "Occam's Razor," so regarded it; for Occam, it was a principle which it is convenient for us to follow. Others, however (e.g., Leibniz) regarded it as a principle describing the way in which God had created the world. The former view of simplicity can be expressed in the methodological axiom "Assume no more entities than sufficient explanation requires," while the latter view leads to such claims as "Nature does nothing in vain." In some cases, simplicity-considerations seem indeed to be purely pragmatic. For example, efficiency of expression in a logistic system is facilitated by a larger number of formation rules than elegance permits. Simplicity (ease) of expression is incompatible with simplicity of rules (elegance). Which triumphs seems to be a matter of taste and sentiment. The present example reminds us that simplicity may refer to various things: number of entities posited, or of axioms assumed, or of rules of inference or of sentence formation permitted, or of steps of inference required to reach a conclusion, etc. What status should be assigned to considerations of simplicity (epistemological or metaphysical) is likely itself to be disputable.

That some such considerations are relevant to evaluating a system is easily illustrated. Prior to Pasteur's work, the peasants had believed that mischievous "little people" soured the milk. Pasteur discovered that bacteria were the culprits instead. Now suppose that an obstinate and perversely intelligent peasant replied to Pasteur as follows: bacteria are, in fact, tiny sheep which are at times herded into milk by the little people (who are their shepherds). Were the little people not mischievous they would not herd the sheep into the milk, in which case the milk would not sour. Hence Pasteur's discovery does not rule out the necessity of positing little people. The reply is, of course, that everything the peasant can explain, so can Pasteur, while there is nothing Pasteur cannot explain which the peasant can. In such cases, surely the simpler theory has the advantage. Nonetheless, appeals to simplicity, in any given context, must be clear as to precisely what sort of simplicity is envisioned, and will have to be shown to be legitimate and appropriate in that particular context.

These frequently-mentioned formal criteria are not the only, or perhaps even the most important, means for the evaluation of total interpretations. There are others we must discuss. What, then, are the other sorts of formal criteria which are relevant to decision procedure between conceptual schemes whether the schemes in question correlate and predict observable phenomena or not? This is the question we must now attempt to answer.

ON DECIDING BETWEEN
TOTAL INTERPRETATIONS

Suppose that I am accused of being an egotist, and deny it. Doesn't my avid denial lend some credence to the charge? Or suppose that I am accused of not being humble, and reply that I am in fact very humble indeed. Doesn't my assertion belie my humility? Such cases are not type-violations; they are not self-predicative. But they are self-stultifying, and in the following manner: asserting them reveals, or at least raises the suspicions of my auditors, that what I say is false. "Methinks the lady dost protest too much" says Hamlet to the Queen.

It is assertions which in some manner undermine themselves, arguments which if successful would defeat their own purposes or destroy their own rationale, view-points whose correctness would leave their own existence inexplicable, that interest us here. Let us call an attempt to show that an interpretation is self-refuting in some manner a "self-stultification argument." I believe it is this sort of consideration which tells compellingly against total interpretations.

An apt slogan for my contention might be "total interpretations cannot be killed; they can only commit suicide." This is simply to stress the relevance and importance of internal criticism in evaluating total interpretations. In turning from slogan to argument, I make no pretense to exhausting all possible self-stultification arguments. Indeed, I know of no way to prove that any given list is complete, though the incompleteness of any list could be shown merely by presenting a self-stultification argument which did not appear on it. More accurate statement requires that we speak of types of self-stultification arguments, and I do not pretend to have noted all the available types, much less all possible instances of each type. Perhaps offering some historical cases of what I take to be self-stultification arguments will give an inkling as to what the term means and serve to point out the importance of such arguments in traditional philosophy. Although the interpretation of historical figures is obviously intended to be correct, nothing will rest on the acceptance of my reading of them rather than another's.

I take Plato's *Theatetus* to be a negative defense of the Forms via arguing that unless one accepts the Forms one can claim no knowledge at all. At least one of its crucial theses could, I think, with slight extrapolation be put as "Either there are Forms or utter skepticism results." Thus the contention "There are no Forms" entails "There is no knowledge," since knowledge and speech in which to formulate it putatively requires a fixed object: "There is no knowledge" cannot itself be true even as a meta-statement or even expressed unless there are Forms. Essentially, this is the outline of Plato's argument. I am concerned here with its intent, not with its success or failure. It provides an example of one sort of self-stultification argument. It concerns itself with showing that, if a given position were taken seriously, true assertion would be impossible. The charge is that a philosophic position makes impossible its own truth-conditions. Plato's argument is of this sort insofar as it claims that "knowledge is of the Forms," (i.e., that true statements are such in virtue of the Forms, or that the Forms and their relations ground the truth of all statements that are true.) Hence, "There are no Forms" denies its own truth-conditions. It also falls into another classification insofar as it argues that intelligible speech, hence the possibility of assertion, whether true or false requires fixed objects of predication (the Forms). Aristotle also concerns himself with the necessary conditions of making an assertion. That the law of contradiction be true is a necessary condition of assertion-making. So consider what its denial involves. Aristotle provides an argument in Book Gamma of the *Metaphysics* to the effect that anyone who asserts that the Law of Contradiction is false must presuppose in asserting this that his terms mean what they do and not the opposite and that his statement is true and not also false, thus presupposing the law as a necessary condition of the very critique of it. This too is a self-stultification argument; to state the refutation of the Law of Contradiction would, were that possible, still be to presuppose it and not to have refuted it after all, since one could assert its denial or anything else only if it is true. Type one of self-stultification argument attempts to show that if a thesis T is true, then it is false in virtue of denying its own truth-conditions. Type two, now under discussion, endeavors to show that if a thesis T is true, it and all other theses cannot in fact be asserted.

Yet a third type argues for the claims that if a thesis T is true, no one could know that it is true. An example is provided by Immanuel Kant who, in his *Groundwork of the Metaphysics of Morals* (Section Three), tries to show that determinism makes it impossible for us to know that any thesis including itself is true. The thrust of the argument is not that determinism makes assertion impossible, or that it makes true assertion impossible, but rather that it makes it impossible for us ever to discern what assertions among those actually made are true. This entails that we cannot know that "Determinism is the correct view" is true, or that "Man is completely determined" is true; so determinism, if true, makes it impossible for us to know that determinism itself is true. Here again is a self-stultification argument; if a given view is true, then its truth-conditions cannot be discerned, so that we cannot know that it or its denial is true. Thus the second sort of self-stultification argument concerned the possibility of assertion at all, the first the possibility of true assertion, and the third, now being considered, the possibility of knowing that an assertion is true.

Choosing brevity of exposition and thus risking a reduction of plausibility proportionate to the reduction in complexity, Kant's argument can be at least characterized in this way: the phenomenal (observable) world is a world of causally ordered events; each event is what it is because of its relationships with its predecessors in the causal complex. Man is indeed a denizen of this world, but is also a member of a noumenal (nonsensory) world. "Man really finds in himself a faculty by which he distinguishes himself from everything else, even from himself as affected by objects, and that is reason."[109] This faculty is exempt from the determining influence of phenomenal events. Such events are nonrational; neither "rational" nor "irrational" are appropriately conjoined with "phenomenal event" ("appearances" in Kantian jargon). Whatever is determined by nonrational causes cannot itself be rational; thus if the functioning of the faculty of reason is determined by nonrational events, this functioning itself will be nonrational, as will its assertions. As making one assertion (*qua* phenomenal event) is neither more nor less the product of nonrational events or factors than making any other, no assertion made is more likely to be true than any other. While one may be so fortunate as to assert truly, he is so unfortunate, if his assertions are determined by nonrational factors, as not to be able to know that he asserts truly. Thus knowledge, in the sense of knowing that an assertion is true, is impossible. Hence we cannot know whether an assertion expressing determinism is true or not. If we take determinism seriously (claim that it is true) we must, to be consistent, also claim that we cannot know that it is true. To develop the argument more fully, either in terms of Kant's formulation or of the many other forms it might take, will not much further my purposes here. Suffice it, then, to note that Kant's argument is an instance of a third sort of self-stultification argument.

Other illustrations lead us to suggest a fourth type of self-stultification argument. This type concerns itself with showing that, if a given position is taken seriously, it cannot accomplish its avowed purposes. Thus the "third man" argument, in one way of reading it, argues that Plato has said that only two kinds of things exist (Forms and particulars) and that in some way appealing to the existence of Forms will help us understand why there are particulars. But how is a particular related to its Form? If by another Form, then how is that Form related to the particular? If by a particular, how is that particular related to its Form? And there are, by hypothesis, only Forms and particulars. Thus Plato fails to explain the relationship between a particular and its Form, as any answer he gives will involve a new problem to be explained, namely that of the relation of a new particular to the original Form, or a new Form to the original particular. One is offered an explanation of a phenomenon which explanation involves another phenomenon of the same sort, *ad infinitum.* The regress here is a regress of explanations, all of which are on the same level or involve the very sort of phenomenon which is purportedly being explained. Thus nothing at all is in fact explained. If we wish to explain kind K of phenomena, an adequate philosophical explanation will not include reference to a phenomenon of kind K, and if we wish to explain an instance of kind K of phenomena, an adequate philosophical explanation will not include reference to another phenomenon of the same kind. Plato's explanation is of the latter sort, and thus is inadequate.

This sort of self-stultification argument, then, argues that an explanation is inadequate because its explanation-attempts never escape reference to the very sort of phenomenon to be explained. Let's call this sort of explanation a "same-level explanation," as it offers instances of the same sort of phenomenon in its *explicans* as occur in its *explicandum.* We have seen that the argument from contingent to necessary being makes, in one of its formulations, just this accusation against the thesis that all the explanation that a contingent being requires is an infinite series of contingent beings. This kind of self-stultification argument has been directed against versions of monism as well as versions of pluralism.[110]

Berkeley's argument against any representative form of realism is another case in point. The argument endeavors to prove that any such theory leads to skepticism while pretending to escape it; that the objects purportedly represented are unknown and unknowable and for that matter could not exist unpreceived anyway. It would do an injustice to this argument to characterize it merely as showing that representative realism leads to skepticism about the objects purportedly represented. Rather, if successful, it shows that representative realism cannot do what it was constructed to do, namely permit us to claim knowledge of the external world. Its very arguments make its purpose unattainable; here is self-stultification with a vengeance.

It is, however, different in form from the "third man" argument. While Berkeley's argument accuses the representative realist of being unable to perform what he promised, it does so on different grounds. Plato's explanation never ends; the representative realist's never begins. The problem with other views, the representative realist avers, is that they make it impossible for us to know the external world. Suppose, however, that our ideas properly represent that world; then we can know what the external world is like, though we cannot be directly acquainted with it. Berkeley responds that, as we are (by hypothesis) directly acquainted with only our ideas, we can never be sure that the world is as they represent it. So the realist in question has not escaped skepticism, but rather has provided a basis for skeptical argumentation. If the realist is right, if our ideas do represent the world, then as our ideas but not the world are open to direct inspection we can be sure about our ideas but never about the world they purportedly represent. Comparison of an idea with its purported object is admitted on both sides to be impossible. This means that the external world, if it exists at all, is simply unknowable, and skepticism about it is built into representative realism.

As the realist is committed to the thesis that we know our ideas directly and the world indirectly, Berkeley is not criticising the realist from an idealist perspective, but from the realist's own. Direct versus indirect knowledge of sensible objects is not a contrast which Berkeley will, on his own grounds, admit; his use of the phrase is but reflective of the use of his opponents, whom he criticises from within their own categorical framework. If we call viewpoints intended to avoid a given position while nonetheless leading to just that position when dealt with on their own terms "self-ingestive" positions, we can note that there is an important difference between "same level" and "self-ingestive" explanations. Thus a fourth type of self-stultification argument (same level) will endeavor to show that a thesis T, in order to explain a phenomenon, posits another phenomenon of the same sort, one in need of the same kind of explanation. A fifth kind (self-ingestive) will attempt to show that a thesis T, which parades as an escape from an undesirable consequence C, in fact leads directly to C. While there may be many more sorts of self-stultification arguments, it is no part of my purpose here to try to elucidate them. Sufficient commentary has, I think, been provided to elucidate and illustrate what I mean by "self-stultification" arguments. By means of such arguments, theses crucial to conceptual systems—and hence these systems themselves— have traditionally been evaluated in a way not involving appeal to crucial tests or empirical observations. Appeal to such considerations is relevant to evaluating total interpretations. By articulating a total interpretation, developing arguments from within its framework and making distinctions required by its perspective, the conceptual commitments and the scope of a total interpretation become clear. The clearer they become, the more promising the endeavor of testing for self-stultification—of discerning its presence or absence. When self-stultification is discovered, adjustment within the system may be possible; it may not. When no self-stultification is found, its absence is not thereby demonstrated; it may be covert.

The task of evaluating total interpretations is indeed difficult. Absolute certainty may not be available. But this neither entails that the task is impossible nor that this decision procedure is question-begging or otherwise unworkable. Appeal to self-stultification arguments is, when successful, an extremely powerful critique, and seems to be peculiarly appropriate in the context of evaluating total interpretations. The existence of such decision procedures at least makes further investigation of total interpretations possible, and counters the narrow emphasis on empirical testing alone.

CONCLUSION

Although each of its chapters is hopefully sufficient unto itself, the present volume does present a sustained view of the philosophy of religion. This can be seen by summarizing its contentions. The fashionable contemporary claim that religious language is meaningless is supported by arguments quite insufficient to sustain their ambitious conclusion. Attempts to analyse religious discourse so that it involves no ontological claim, presupposes no description regarded as true of the Deity, turn out to be quite inadequate. The problem of evil, in its various formulations, does not refute traditional theism. Nor does the argument from contingency unambiguously support theism; similar comments apply to the teleological argument. Even less does the ontological argument prove its point. Religious experience provides no unequivocal evidence for religious claims. The moral argument is an articulation of morality within an already assumed theistic framework. Religious faith is an exhaustive interpretation of men and things in which they are regarded as created and providentially sustained by a Being worthy of complete devotion and obedience; this, at least, is the faith of traditional theism. Neither deductive proof from premises which are self-evident or empirically well supported, nor support via probability arguments, can vindicate this or any other total interpreetation. There are general characteristics in virtue of which exhaustive interpretations (in an older jargon, "world-views") can be compared, and criteria by which they can be appraised. The task of appraisal is detailed, arduous, and unlikely to yield results agreed upon by all men of reason. Nonetheless, it is worth the effort. Making it is an effort in apologetics (positive or negative), a task neither necessarily biased nor intellectually despicable. The present work can be viewed, if one wishes, as a prolegomena to polemics. Its purpose has been to clarify the issues and resolve some of the preliminary problems. Its thesis, in part, is that the propositions at issue cannot properly be viewed in splendid isolation. Neither proof nor disproof is nearly so straightforward a process as is often supposed, and the battlelines on religious topics have often been drawn in the wrong places. The present effort, in part, is an attempt to redraw them.

Since the issues are important, our thought about them should be as clear as possible. Hopefully, the preceding will be of some help to that end. Even that is, of course, somewhat optimistic.

FOOTNOTES ⟿ VI

1 Cf. C. J. Ducasse, *A Philosophical Scrutiny of Religion* (New York: Ronald Press, 1953), pp. 73–74.

2 *An Essay Concerning Human Understanding*, Book IV, Chapter 19, Section 1.

3 Locke's own account of faith will be discussed below.

4 See W. K. Clifford, *Lectures and Essays* (London: 1901), "The Ethics of Belief," reprinted in G. Mavrodes and S. Hackett, *Problems and Perspectives in the Philosophy of Religion.*

5 Two volumes, Dover Press, New York, 1959; Book IV, Chapter 28. All references unless otherwise indicated are to this chapter and will be cited by section number only.

6 The assumption is that seeing P to be self-evident, or finding empirical verification for P, are the only direct ways of establishing P. I use the term "empirical verification" rather than Locke's "known by sensation."

7 Sections 8 and 9. Locke doubtless has in mind such doctrines as that God exists which he holds to be demonstrably true. See *Essay*, Bk. IV, Chapter 10.

8 Section 10.

9 *Loc. cit.* Cf. . . . "to receive the truths revealed to others, which by the tradition of writings, or word of mouth, are conveyed down to them; reason . . . is that only which can induce us to accept them.

10 Section 5. Locke is especially adamant concerning this point.

11 Cf. the passages roted above under footnote 7.

12 See Section 8.

13 *Ibid.*

14 Chapter 16, Section 13, very end of chapter. But cf. his statement that intuitive knowledge provides the highest degree of certainty, Book IV, Chapter 17, Section 14.

15 *Essay*, Book IV, Chapter 19, Section 16.

16 *Essay*, Book IV, Chapter 16, Section 13.

17 *Loc. cit.*

18 From Locke's *Discourse on Miracles*, 1702. Cited in Fraser's edition of the *Essay*, p. 382, footnote 2.

19 On this point, it is worth comparing Leibniz' critique of a similar appeal to divine veracity by Descartes. See Leibniz, *Monadology and Other Philosophical Essays* (New York: Bobbs-Merrill, 1965), p. 41.

20 Cf. *Essay*, Book IV, Chapter 19.

21 We have neglected Locke's concern with "original" revelation, i.e., a case in which S believes P by faith because S believes that God has revealed P to S himself. Locke suggests that if P involves a new simple idea then S can know P to be revealed by God. But (a) what important religious belief does involve some new simple idea?, (b) would that really show that God revealed P?

22 Aquinas, *Summa Theologica*, Second Part of the Second Part, Questions 1–7. This section can conveniently be found in volume two of A. Pegis, *Basic Writings of St. Thomas Aquinas* (New York: Random House, 1945), p. 1055ff.

23 *ST*, II, II, Q 1, A 1. Pegis, *op. cit.*, p. 1056.

24 *ST*, II, II, Q 1, A 1. Pegis, *op. cit.*, p. 1057. He adds in this context that while the object of faith *qua* proposition is complex, it does not follow that the object of faith *qua* being (as what the proposition is about) is complex. So the simplicity of God is, he suggests, unaffected.

25 *ST*, II, II, Q 1, A 4; Pegis, *op. cit.*, p. 1060.

26 *Loc. cit.*

27 *ST*, II, II, Q 2, A 1; Pegis, *op. cit.*, p. 1075.

28 *ST*, II, II, Q 4, A 1; Pegis, *op. cit.*, p. 1096.

29 *ST*, II, II, Q 4, A 8; Pegis, *op. cit.*, p. 1107.

30 *Loc. cit.*; Pegis, *op. cit.*, p. 1106.

31 *ST*, II, II, Q 2, A 9; Pegis, *op. cit.*, p. 1087.

32 *ST*, II, II, Q 5, A 2; Pegis, *op. cit.*, p. 1111.

33 *Loc. cit.* Aquinas adds that demons "see many evident signs, whereby they recognize that the teaching of the church is from God, although they do not see

the things themselves that the Church teaches, for instance, that there are three Persons in God, and so forth."

34   *ST*, II, II, Q 2, A 9; Pegis, *op. cit.*, p. 1088.

35   *ST*, II, II, Q 2, A 10; Pegis, *op. cit.*, p. 1090.

36   J. Hick, *Faith and Knowledge*, Sec. ed., p. 20.

37   Hick, *op. cit.*, p. 22.

38   *ST*, I, Q 64, A 1; Pegis, *op. cit.*, Vol. I, p. 600f., esp. 602.

39   *ST*, I, Q 2, A 1; Pegis, *op. cit.*, Vol. I, p. 18ff.

40   Hick, *op. cit.*, p. 22.

41   An intellectual, not a moral, virtue. *ST*, II, II, Q 4, A 5; Pegis, *op. cit.*, p. 1101ff.

42   *ST*, II, II, Q 2, A 10; Pegis, *op. cit.*, p. 1090.

43   William James, *The Will to Believe, Human Immortality, and Other Essays on Popular Philosophy* (New York: Dover Publications, 1956), p. 1–31.

44   *Ibid.*, p. 2. All quotations will be from the essay, "The Will to Believe."

45   *Ibid.*, p. 3.

46   James describes a momentous option as "unique," "irreversible," and "significant."

47   *Op. cit.*, p. 11. I will not deal with James' claim that whether one is a sceptic or not is also merely "a passional decision;" cf. "The Will to Believe," Section III. This seems to be James' view about any "ultimate" issue.

48   James' case is stronger if one adopts his account of truth, which is open to severe criticism, but does not depend upon that account. For his view of the nature of truth, see "Pragmatism's Conception of Truth," William James, *Pragmatism* (Cleveland: World Publishing Co., 1955), Chapter Six. For criticism, see "Pragmatism and Thought," Brand Blanshard, *The Nature of Thought* (London: Allen and Unwin, 1939), Vol. One, Chapter 10.

49   James, *op. cit.*, p. 7 (parenthetic explanation mine).

50   Actually, James suggests (see p. 9, 10, 11, 14–17) that passion determines belief, so the fact that our passions cannot be commanded entails that our belief cannot even indirectly be commanded either. In what follows, however, I will not press this objection but will rather interpret James, perhaps with some license, so as not to leave his position open to this objection. Also, James does not have in mind simply conscious deliberative choices and actions. "When I say 'willing nature,' I do not mean only . . . 'deliberate volitions,'—I mean all such factors of belief as fear and hope, prejudice and passion . . ." (p. 9).

51   *Ibid.*, p. 29ff.

52   Whether this is, or would be, so generally, and whether one or another form of religious institution is beneficial to a society, are not discussed in this essay by James. Cf. on the first question, his *Varieties of Religious Experience* and our discussion in Chapter Two.

53   *Op. cit.*, p. 24.

54   *Ibid.*, p. 28.

55   *Loc. cit.*

56   *Ibid.*, p. 18.

57   "The freedom to believe can cover living options which the intellect of the individual cannot by itself resolve." (p. 29).

58   A view that James accepts. He offers "the best things are the eternal things" and "we are better off even now if we believe" this, as the basic religious beliefs. These affirmations are vague, but are also substantive.

59   F. R. Tennant, *Philosophical Theology* (London: Cambridge U. Press, 1928), Vol. I, p. 302, reprinted, 1956.

60   One might, of course, claim that whatever was beneficial was also true. (This might be a way of restating "the best things are eternal.") But that would be to have already made a choice with respect to another genuine option, and thus to raise the question of the rationality of one or another choice with regard to that option.

61   *Op. cit.,* p. 17. Cf. the quotation with which the essay ends.

62   He agrees, however, the propositions are the "objects" of faith.

63   Tennant, *op. cit.,* Vol. I, Ch. 11, Section Four, p. 297.

64   *Loc. cit.*

65   *Ibid.,* p. 298.

66   Aristotle, *Metaphysics,* Book One, opening sentence.

67   Tennant, *op. cit.,* p. 299. One could accept Tennant's account of faith without making the Aristotelian assumption.

68   *Ibid.,* p. 300.

69   Cf. *Ibid.,* p. 303. In another work, however, Tennant allows only pragmatic justification for religious claims. Essentially, this amounts to effects in the lives of believers. Scientific beliefs are also capable of only pragmatic justification. (Tennant instances "the foundations of inductive science" as an object of scientific faith.) But they are open to a higher order of probable justification. This is similar to Locke's view that to accept a statement on faith is to accept it on the basis of "third rate" evidence. Cf. *The Nature of Belief* (London: 1943), esp. p. 70ff.

70   Cf. *op. cit.,* p. 303ff.

71   *Ibid.,* p. 296. "Meaningless," in this context, signifies "rationally unintelligible."

72   The assumption being that there are such claims and that at least some of them can plausibly be regarded as religious claims.

73   Some criterion for "workable," and for degrees of "workability" would clearly be required.

74   The view, namely, that the world was created and is providentially ruled by a being not less than personal who is perfectly powerful, knowledgeable, and good.

75   *Op. cit.,* p. 332.

76   John Hick, *Faith and Knowledge,* p. 102, Hick's sense of "recognition" is admittedly technical. Cf. Hick's footnote, p. 102.

77   *Loc. cit.*

78   This assumption of Hick's will be discussed below.

79   Cf. Chapter Three.

80   *Op. cit.,* p. 97.

81   Not, of course, a conscious one.

82   Cf. Chapter One.

83   "Eschatology" means "the doctrine of last things."

84   *Op. cit.,* p. 178.

85   *Ibid.,* p. 172.

86   *Loc. cit.*

87   The present author has discussed this matter briefly in "A Reply to Professor Nielsen," *Sophia* (Melbourne, October, 1968).

88   See *op. cit.,* Chapter Six, "Faith and Freedom."

89   It would explain why Hick does if he holds that only if an interpretation can be conclusively verified does it have truth-value. But (a) there is reason to doubt that he does hold this (*op. cit.,* p. 175) (b) there is no reason to think that this is

true (c) even if it were true, it would not follow that the only way that conclusive verification is possible is by a verified prediction.

90 *Op. cit.*, p. 187. Note the admission included in the parenthesis.

91 Cf. Plantinga, *op. cit.*, p. 161.

92 Tennant, *op. cit.*, p. 301. Hick puts the difference in much the same manner; see Hick, *op. cit.*, p. 3ff.

93 Hick seems, however, to make just such an appeal. *Ibid.*, p. 29.

94 *Loc. cit.*

95 *Ibid.*, p. 28.

96 *Loc. cit.*

97 Were our purpose theological analysis, there is much here that would require more detailed treatment. I mention only those matters essential to our present topic.

98 Insofar as God's nature involves, e.g., intelligence and goodness; not, of course, as involving for example tri-unity.

99 Cf. M. D'Arcy, *The Nature of Belief* (London, 1945) for a fuller articulation of this viewpoint.

100 Cf. the magicians of Pharoah's court.

101 See Chapter Three.

102 This is true even if one rejects Kierkegaard's treatment of the near-sacrifice of Isaac.

103 This too involves a claim about what it is reasonable to expect God to do.

104 See Chapter One.

105 The concept of an "explanation" is also complex and not easy to elucidate with precision; its analysis too is beyond the scope of this work.

106 "Decision procedure" with respect to theories A and B is simply any legitimate method for deciding whether A or B is to be accepted.

107 There is, of course, the possibility that theory A entails that p will occur in circumstance C, while B entails that q will occur in C, whereas r in fact occurs in C. But there is no need to concern ourselves here with this issue; it would simply require that A or B (or both) be amended, or replaced by some other theory which can account for r.

108 Cf. the section on this topic in Foster and Martin, ed., *Probability, Confirmation and Simplicity* (New York: The Odyssey Press, 1966).

109 Cf. *Groundwork*, p. 119.

110 Unless one could appeal to the thesis that effects must resemble their causes in all respects important for the representative realist's claim—a topic we need not deal with here. Berkeley's argument occurs in *Principles of Human Knowledge*, Sec. 18–20.

BIBLIOGRAPHY ⌒ VI

Buber, M., *Two Types of Faith*. New York: Harper Bros., 1961.

Carnell, E. J., *Christian Commitment*. New York: Macmillan, 1957.

Farmer, H. H., *Towards Belief in God*. London: SCM Press, 1942.

Frank, E., *Philosophical Understanding and Religious Truth*. London: Oxford U. Press, 1945.

Heaney, J., ed.,   *Faith, Reason and the Gospels.* Westminster, Md.: Newman Press, 1961.

Heschel, A.,   *God in Search of Man.* New York: Meridian Books, 1959.

Machen, J. G.,   *What Is Faith?* Grand Rapids: Eerdmann's, 1946.

Oman, J.,   *Grace and Personality.* London: Fontana Books, 1960.

Tillich, P.,   *The Dynamics of Faith.* New York: Harper Bros., 1957.

Index